Emerging Standards
of
International
Trade and Investment

Emerging Standards
of
International
Trade and Investment

Multinational Codes
and Corporate Conduct

Edited by
Seymour J. Rubin
and
Gary Clyde Hufbauer

Rowman & Allanheld
Publishers

ROWMAN & ALLANHELD

Published in the United States of America in 1984
by Rowman & Allanheld
(A division of Littlefield, Adams & Company)
81 Adams Drive, Totowa, New Jersey 07512

Copyright © 1983 by The American Society of International Law

Library of Congress Cataloging in Publication Data
Main entry under title:

Emerging standards of international trade and
  investment.

  1. International economic relations—Addresses,
essays, lectures. 2. International Business enter-
prises—Addresses, essays, lectures. I. Rubin,
Seymour J.
K3823.E45 1983   341.7'5   83-13859
ISBN 0-86598-133-7

83 84 85/10 9 8 7 6 5 4 3 2 1

Printed in the United States of America

Contents

Prologue

The essays that follow reflect the emergency, in recent years, of a number of codes, or guidelines, or standards of conduct, affecting international economic relations. They have been drafted in various forums—global or regional, or among nations having common interests. Some reflect more in the way of conflict, or possible conflict avoidance, than coordination or cooperation. All are part of an effort to deal with the international economic problems of the world in an era which can loosely be characterized as the post-Bretton Woods period.

It has been thought that there are common to all of these several efforts certain issues of interpretation and of implementation. The volume has thus concentrated on those issues. The individual authors have each been asked to address the substantive aspects of the international agreements—or proposed agreements—about which they wrote, in the context of issues of interpretation and implementation.

The individual chapters have thus addressed themselves to a common set of problems. But each of the authors has been free to adhere to a pattern, or to deviate, as he saw fit. Drafts of the papers have been circulated to a panel, whose members are listed below. After review, authors have revised their papers, and in some cases again discussed the papers and again revised. What has emerged has thus benefited from a group analysis, but each chapter remains the responsibility of the individual author or authors.

Organizations with which the authors are affiliated do not take responsibility for the views expressed. Nor does the American Society of International Law, which sponsored this work, and which as a society does not take positions on matters of public policy.

The American Society of International Law is grateful to the panelists who took part in this collegial effort, and especially to those listed in the Table of Contents as authors. It is also deeply grateful to the Ford Foundation, which made possible the work of the panel, and this resulting volume, by a generous grant.

The members of the panel were:

John H. Jackson, Chairman
University of Michigan Law School, Ann Arbor, Michigan

Gary C. Hufbauer, Rapporteur
Institute for International Economics, Washington, D.C.

Hans W. Baade
University of Texas School of Law, Austin, Texas

Robert C. Cassidy
Kaye, Scholer, Fierman, Hays & Handler, Washington, D.C.

Lloyd N. Cutler
Wilmer, Cutler & Pickering, Washington, D.C.

Joel Davidow
Mudge, Rose, Guthrie & Alexander, Washington, D.C.

Arghyrious A. Fatouros
Aristotelian University of Thessaloniki, Greece

Isaiah Frank
School of Advanced International Studies
Johns Hopkins University, Washington, D.C.

David G. Gill
Exxon Corprtion, New York, New York

John Lawrence Hargrove
American Society of International Law, Washington, D.C.

Robert E. Herzstein
Arnold & Porter, Washington, D.C.

Monroe Leigh
Steptoe & Johnson, Washington, D.C.

Philippe Lévy
Ambassador of Switzerland
Federal Office of External Economic Affaairs, Berne, Switzerland

John L. Moore, Jr.
Surrey & Morse, Washington, D.C.

Seymour J. Rubin
American Society of International Law, Washington, D.C.

Daniel Tarullo
Harvard Law School, Cambridge, Massachusetts

Detlev F. Vagts
Harvard Law School, Cambridge, Massachusetts

Donald Wallace, Jr.
Georgetown University Law Center, Washington, D.C.

Introduction

JOHN H. JACKSON

It is common today to talk of the growing interdependence of the world, yet there seems no other way to adequately express what is happening in international economic relations. Whether it is the effect of United States interest rates on housing starts and therefore on the market for jute from Calcutta, or the effect oil prices and oil marketing structure have on Mexican unemployment and Mexican emigration to the United States, or the impact of capital flows (influenced by interest and inflation rates) on the employment of workers in Michigan, the world has shrunk. Every nation finds that its actions and policies are circumscribed by the interdependent world environment. Dependence of every nation on exports and imports is rising as a percentage of its total economic activity, and each nation's security, in a troubled and dangerous world, is affected by decisions taken elsewhere on the globe.

How did this increasing interdependence come about? Perhaps the technological innovations of the post-World War II era would have, at least in the absence of armed conflict, created these conditions. The time and cost of transport and communications have fallen so that these barriers to greater trade and capital flows and service exchanges have diminished. We watch local wars in our living rooms. Businessmen order goods or shift huge sums of money across oceans, literally in seconds. Information systems are changing the character of markets, and also affecting business techniques such as the control of inventories, the use of borrowed money, the response to changing interest rates, and the adoption of new technology.

But these scientific developments could not have had the influence they have had, if governments resisted them, as we can observe in the case of those governments that do resist them. We must recognize that

John H. Jackson is Professor of Law at the University of Michigan Law School, Ann Arbor.

the international institutions established by governments after World War II have made their contribution. If some world organizations have failed to perform in the manner contemplated, they have nevertheless contributed symbiotically to the general trend of the world economic environment made possible by the scientific innovations.

By the late 1960's, the liberalization of trade and financial flows promoted by the postwar system—sometimes broadly called the Bretton Woods system—(including GATT, the IMF, OECD, and related organizations) had progressed far enough for the world to experience an unprecedented surge of trade and to benefit from such liberalization. But at the same time, new problems were emerging. The receding waters of tariff and other overt protection inevitably uncovers the rocks and shoals of a variety of other barriers. Creating free trade requires attention to a group of interrelated activities such as the flow of capital, the flow of labor, the flow of technology and services, and these in turn revolutionize the methods by which governments have traditionally controlled such matters as fiscal and monetary policy, taxation, environment regulation, product standards, and liability for product defects. The propensity for government summit meetings is obviously not *un*related to these world economic trends of interdependence. Likewise, the attempts by governments to pursue coordination through international organizations is similarly related.

The basic problem is, that despite all the talk about sovereignty, independence, and equality of nations, these concepts are fictions if used to describe today's real world. What is the sovereignty of the government of a country whose trade is so dependent on a neighbor that the government cannot freely set its own interest rate or tax structure? What is the so-called independence of a government whose national economy depends almost entirely on one export commodity? What is the equality of nations when one has hundreds of millions of inhabitants while another has less than a million, when one has an economy measured in trillions of dollars while another has a total economic product less than that of many private corporations operating from a base in another country?

Some would say it is best that sovereignty is no longer so complete, that governments have not shown themselves particularly fit to exercise the powers and responsibilities which sovereignty implies, and that therefore the cold reality of the international economic environment is a welcome restraint on misconceived and misapplied governmental policies. Yet regardless of one's sympathy for such a viewpoint, it is impossible to ignore the frustration which governments face today, be they good governments or bad governments; be they despotic governments, or democratic; be they rational, or irrational. Even the rational benevolent democratic government (both large and small) finds it difficult to carry out its mandate on behalf of its citizens. Cleaning up the environment is hard when smoke drifts from your neighbor and the ocean becomes oil covered. Providing citizen-desired full employment is difficult when economic downturns starting in other countries spread to your own. Establishing even your democratically voted tax system becomes difficult if that system is perceived as less advantageous to investors who can take their money to other nations which are willing to bid for their favors.

Two centuries ago, sovereignty might have enabled a government to carry out a national goal even democratically arrived at, for example, to exalt a particular religion, or to give extraordinary rewards to persons of artistic or musical talent. In today's world of mobile resources and mobile people, what government can keep the doctors at home, when another nation pays much more? What government can tax to promote equality or greater government services, when other locations bid for talent? Without judging the validity or correctness of the policies themselves, it is easy to see how a government can be frustrated.

Indeed, interdependence has some potential large prices attached, even though it has brought and should continue to bring great benefits. Two such prices can be mentioned: the price of uniformity, and the price of the growing remoteness of government decision-making. As to the first, interdependence based on a set of international rules under the Bretton Wood system, imposes serious pressures on a government to "harmonize" many of its policies with other governments. Governments realize, for example, the self-defeating nature of competitive export finance programs or competitive currency devaluation. Thus a rational approach is to coordinate, to harmonize. The price is less diversity, and less freedom to go in your own direction.

The same pressures are leading to greater internationalization of government decisions. Governments, not without reason, have been very slow to entrust international institutions with much concrete decision-making power. Yet we have the elaborate Tokyo Round of Multilateral Trade Negotiations in the context of GATT that has brought to the international scene new legal obligations on certain governments concerning even their own governmental purchasing procedures, concerning their methods of establishing safety and other standards of products, and concerning their use of tax or regulatory measures which may affect the competitive nature of their exports. A key question for the future is one which we can call essentially the "federalism" question; i.e. how can the necessary advantages of coordination and harmonized decision-making be obtained in the world, while at the same time reserving for the smallest possible unit of government, the decision-making authority that it needs to be responsive to its own constituents.

In the search for an appropriate policy or mix of policies with which to try to alleviate some of this frustration, and to effectively manage this new world interdependence, sovereign nations have been taking a variety of approaches, some of which are proving inconsistent with approaches of other nations and inconsistent with broader objectives for an appropriate evolution of a technique of managing interdependences.

The stark reality which must be faced is that nations disagree fundamentally about how to organize their internal economies, and how to synchronize their internal economies with world markets. These differences involve primarily different degrees of governmental involvement in the economy, but also basic structural differences in economies, such as normal debt-equity ratios for enterprises, or the degree of job security for workers.

These differences can cause great stress when they create distorted conditions of competition between imports and domestic products. These conditions lead to allegations of "unfair trade," or "predatory monetary policy," and create numerous economic disputes among nations, which we see reported daily on the front pages of our newspapers.

The variety of approaches being tried for international coordination and discipline, include two divergent methodologies. In some cases a more rigorous or "legalistic" approach has seemed appropriate. The large question is always whether or not new international rules can be successfully implemented or enforced. In other cases, a "softer" approach is being utilized. One such softer approach is the development of so-called "voluntary" codes of conduct. On close examination, however, officials and scholars are realizing that the word "voluntary" may not fully describe the potential impact of such codes. One significant and highly interesting jurisprudential question is which approach—more rigorous norms with enforcement mechanisms, or "softer" approaches described as "voluntary"—will in fact be more effective in establishing the appropriate balance of international discipline with the need and desire for adequate diversity in the world.

In this volume, the American Society of International Law reports on a two-year research program that was designed to probe some of these and similar questions. By commissioning individual authors who are expert in their subjects, asking them to address some common themes, and bringing them together with other perceptive commentators, the Society encourages a systematic but comparative examination of some very perplexing questions. Not one of the participants believes that this research effort has achieved a "break-through" which will resolve these questions for all time, but we all have profited by the free interchange of views on some extremely difficult conceptual problems, and we hope that the reader will also benefit by a report of these.

ONE

A Preface to the Codes

SEYMOUR J. RUBIN

In the years since World War II, there have been two major periods of making international economic accords. In the first, the principal results were the Bretton Woods agreements and organizations—the Articles of Agreement of the International Monetary Fund, the International Bank for Reconstruction and Development, and the General Agreement on Tariffs and Trade. The accords of that period have long provided the basis for much of world trade and investment activity. But in recent years the Bretton Woods system, as many have pointed out, has shown signs of excessive wear, and major efforts are being made, with doubtful success, to reconstitute it.

The second period, to which a beginning date cannot be assigned with precision, overlaps the first period. The second period represents an effort to constitute a system in some respects parallel, in some respects supportive of, but in many respects contradictory to the main tenets of, the Bretton Woods system. Roughly speaking, one can say that this second period began in the early 1960's, perhaps with the formation of the United Nations Conference on Trade and Development in 1963, and has continued with accelerated force, especially during the decade of the 1970's. Without attempting precision in nomenclature, one can, again rather generally, characterize this as the period of the "New International Economic Order," even though that term, as used in many UN documents, is acceptable to many nations only if it is put in lower case, and if the article "a" is substituted for "the" when reference is made to any "new international order."

The differences between the Bretton Woods System and the "new international economic order" are substantial. Nevertheless there are a

Seymour J. Rubin is Professor of Law, American University; Executive Vice President, American Society of International Law; and United States Representative, United Nations Commission on Transnational Corporations, 1974 to present.

good many similarities. In both cases, the impetus toward negotiation arose out of a perception that changed circumstances necessitated a new set of rules to govern the way in which trade and investment flowed across national boundaries. In both situations, nations perceived that the existing rules or standards which regulate, directly or indirectly, the international flow of trade in goods, services, investment capital and technology were unsatisfactory, and that the consequent organizational structure was deficient. In both cases, new standards of conduct were put forward, together with institutional arrangements for their administration. In both cases, the growing interdependence of nations, and of their economic systems, has been acknowledged. Even a good deal of the rhetoric is similar. The "beggar thy neighbor" policies of the protectionism of the 1930s, of the United States Smoot-Hawley tariffs and British "imperial preference" were rejected in the negotiations leading to the abortive International Trade Organization and the surprisingly successful General Agreement on Tariffs and Trade. Similarly, some degree of responsibility for fashioning national economic policies in light of the needs of other nations has been reflected in numerous recent declarations and agreements and conferences, from the founding of the UN Conference on Trade and Development (UNCTAD) to the findings and recommendations of the Brandt Commission to the 1981 Cancun Summit declarations. The basic premises—that the world is not only "a dangerous place" but also one which requires rules or standards of international economic order—are not different. But there is nonetheless much that is different in the circumstances of the two periods.

From the perspective of the 1980's, the international economic order of the years after World War II to the mid 1960's seems deceptively simple. The basic issue was one of reconstruction, in the wake of both the Great Depression and a devastating world war. What was important was to reconstitute the pre-war economies, but to do so in a manner that would prevent future disasters rooted in excessively self-centered and nationalistic policies. The Bretton Woods system thus sought policies of mutually beneficial cooperation—in the trade field via GATT (and the abortive ITO); in the area of international monetary policy via the International Monetary Fund; in the area of reconstruction (with a nod toward development) in the International Bank for Reconstruction and Development. Though differences existed, it seemed possible to arrive at generally acceptable principles and procedures. With the exception of the increasingly evident conflicts between market economies and those of the "Socialist" states (sometimes referred to as the "Sino-Soviet bloc"), there was basic agreement between the important national actors on the world scene. Some disagreements of course were recognized, even in the terms of the agreements being negotiated. The GATT, for example, never dealt effectively with such issues as agricultural policy, or with the rules by which regional preferences might be granted an exception to the fundamental most-favored-nation principle. And some residual doctrinal differences were reflected in the drafting of the Articles of Agreement of the IMF. But the main actors were few, more or less agreed on broad policy, and able to put together the institutional framework.

Relationships with the less developed nations were noted, but scarcely thought to pose central questions. The World Bank (as it subsequently came to be known) of course had "development" in its title; but the first task was that of reconstruction. Loans, on a somewhat concessional basis, but always to "sound" development projects, and based to a large extent on capital raised from the private market, could be the chief vehicle for improving the economic situation of less advantaged countries. This sort of provision of capital to deserving countries could be supplemented by bilateral programs of technical assistance, like that announced by President Truman in his Point Four program, or perhaps by the moderate provision of funds under the aegis of the then fledgling United Nations. As time went on, and as the task of reconstruction seemed largely accomplished, more attention could be given to development, via institutions like the World Bank's International Development Association, designed to provide a "soft loan" window for the developing nations. A few other efforts were also mounted: the United States, after years of opposing the concept, finally acceded to establishment of the Inter-American Development Bank. Progress, it was thought, would benefit both developed and less developed nations, and have its institutional reflection. Improvements would come, as Walt Rostow put it, through almost inevitable and eminently satisfactory stages of economic growth, until self-sustained economic development was achieved.

In this somewhat unrealistic euphoria, the major powers hardly had in mind what subsequently became known as the "North-South dialogue." Development would come through the rebuilding of the world of the major industrial nations, with some special aid and concessions to the less developed. Though the developing nations were not regarded as being—and inevitably remaining—the hewers of wood and drawers of water, attitudes toward them tended to vary between a species of indifference, tempered by acknowledgment of the importance of access to raw materials (itself affected by the assumption that current arrangements, one way or another, would endure) and an attitude composed in roughly equal parts of obligation and comfortable benevolence. Commodity agreements aside (and these were opposed by many industrialized nations as being both ineffective and distortive), there was little in the area of international economic agreement which directly addressed the problems, real or fancied, of developing (or as they were then less politely denominated, undeveloped or less developed) nations. Private foreign investment, and its concomitants, transfer of technology, the

proper conduct of transnational enterprises, and the like, were dealt
with by proposals to guarantee the security of investment, in such documents as Articles 11 and 12 of the abortive 1948 ITO Charter and the
OECD's 1967 Draft Convention for the Protection of Private Foreign Investment. In these cases, the underlying thesis was that private foreign
investment was beneficial to the host nation; that a general standard of
good conduct ought to be accepted by the investor, both in fairness and
in the context of enlightened self-interest; but that a guaranty of security
and of fair treatment, especially in the case of nationalization, was the
best way to increase the flow of investment and its consequent develop-
mental benefits.

Certainly, analysis more extensive than this would qualify many of
these generalities. Even in what now seems to have been an age of inno-
cence, there were those who called attention to issues which have since
come to occupy center stage. By the end of 1948, such countries as India,
Pakistan, and Israel had come onto the world scene. Other colonial de-
pendencies were emerging into independence. Nations which had for
long been politically independent, like those of Latin America, or of
Southeast Asia, were showing signs of previously unknown independence of policy. And attention was being given to the possibility that previously plentiful natural resources would become scarce, a possibility
that enhanced the importance and the negotiating strength of the
developing nations. But these were, at the time, but fledgling developments. And responses tended to be in the vein of the Alliance for Progress, an effort compounded of enlightened self-interest and faith in the
efficacy of American tutelage. It was not acknowledged in the philosophic underpinnings of these programs that the benefits to be brought
by the Alliance for Progress and similar efforts were in the nature of an
entitlement, owed to the developing nations. Though the notion was not
publicly articulated, there was little real doubt as to the rightfulness—
indeed, perhaps the inevitability—of the preeminence of the industrialized nations.

These unstated major premises shaped the form and content of central international economic and political understandings. In a sense,
great power supremacy was as much assumed in matters of international
economic intercourse as it was in arrangements for permanent
representation on the Security Council of the United Nations. The
Bretton Woods arrangements were thus negotiated and put in place;
lesser powers were expected to, and did, fall in line. Not unnaturally, the
content of those arrangements acknowledged the positions of the developing countries as a matter of courtesy, perhaps of enlightened self-
interest, but hardly as a matter of right.

From the mid-1960's onward, tendencies which had earlier been all
but imperceptible began to accelerate until, by the late 1970's the picture

had entirely changed. A number of factors were responsible for this transformation.

There was, in the first place, a virtual explosion of decolonialization and emergence of new, independent (and restive) nations. In 1963, when UNCTAD came into existence, there was already a "Group of 77"; that Group, though retaining the same title, is by the 1980's an assemblage of some 110 nations. Some of these are nations which, though they have enjoyed at least a nominal political independence for many years, were for the first time asserting an independent will; and they found in the G-77 a means for asserting that will. The "Non-Aligned" movement emerged. The United Nations and its various bodies, like the Economic and Social Council and the General Assembly, served as admirable arenas not only for declamations and in some cases denunciations but also for the passage of resolutions which, for all their non-enforceable character, nevertheless had an impact.

New institutions were born, from the UNCTAD itself to the United Nations Commission on International Trade Law (UNCITRAL) to the United Nations Industrial Development Commission (UNIDO) to the United Nations Commission on Transnational Corporations (UNTNC). In each of these, dominance—or at least voting power—was in the hands not of the former power elite, but of the developing nations, with the Socialist states as their willing allies and ofttimes instigators. In each of these, it was assumed by the majority, as a basis for discussion, that the "old" economic order had been constructed by the western industrialized nations largely for their own benefit and largely at the expense of the developing nations. Though the quality and the attitudes of the secretariats of these institutions varied, the principle of "equitable geographic representation" tended to concentrate both leadership and personnel among the nationals of developing countries. All these circumstances gave impetus to the initiatives and force to the views of the developing nations.

It was not only in the United Nations and its directly subsidiary bodies that these initiatives and views found expression. The quadrennial assemblages of UNCTAD focused on the asserted inequity and need for readjusting the world economic system, in matters as basic as trade, investment, commodity agreements and a "common fund", and in concomitant international arrangements such as those of the 1910 Paris Patent Convention. Regional organizations like the Andean Common Market enacted rules designed to strengthen their external position vis-à-vis the industrialized North. Organizations like the GATT became forums for advocacy of "equity" as opposed to "equality": "special and differentiated treatment" for developing countries replaced "most-favored-nation" treatment as a central theme. An outpouring of books, periodicals, articles, from the pens of scholars and research institutes, in developed as well as developing nations, provided an intellectual apologia for these initiatives.

The volume of literature on the phenomenon of transnational corporations (TNC) quickly rose to extraordinary proportions. An early and seminal volume was J. J. Servan-Schreiber's *Le Defi Americain* (1968), but its popularity did not prevent a substantial misreading of its message. The book basically suggests that the initiative, ingenuity and management skills of American entrepreneurs had enabled them to establish dominant positions in European industry; and that the indicated response should be emulation. (To say this, in 1982, is to evoke a strong feeling of nostalgia for the day when the United States was regarded not as a laggard but as the exemplar of innovation and enterprise.) Nonetheless, the message taken from Servan-Schreiber seemed to be that the difficulties of transnational economic activity exceeded its benefits. What caught the attention of the new majorities in international institutions were the problems supposedly associated with private foreign investment and the TNCs. Whether these problems were couched in theories of "dependencia" or of the "global reach" of TNCs, or in the more moderate terms of "sovereignty at bay," they had the immediate consequence of frequent calls for a new international economic order, which in turn were transformed into meetings on global or regional bases, the common theme of which was the need for some sort of new international regulatory apparatus.

Additional to the stimulus of ferment was the observable fact that the old arrangements—the Bretton Woods system—were no longer working very well, even for the industrialized nations. The GATT had always been acknowledged to be an imperfect instrument—a web of exceptions held together by tolerance of violations, as was suggested by its ingenious first Director General. Nevertheless, it did its job well for many years. But those years, despite evident difficulties, were a period of expanding trade. In the rising tide of world commerce, occasional contretemps could be accommodated—the problems of the Common Agricultural Policy of the European Economic Community, the Canadian-American automotive agreement, the preferences and reverse preferences of the Yaounde Agreement, even the Nixon tariff surcharge of August 1971—all these could somehow be dealt with.

By the mid 1970's, the situation had changed. The strains imposed by the sudden fourfold upward surge of oil prices, the accelerating decline of the most-favored-nation principle, a wave of protectionism in investment as well as trade, coupled with a world recession and the rise of new competitors on the world market, combined to underline the inadequacies of the Bretton Woods system. Competition for markets among the industrial nations increased, as did charges and countercharges of unfair conduct. The need for new sources of finance, and for new export markets became urgent, especially among the non-oil developing nations. At the same time, levels of unemployment rose, in developed as well as developing nations. Calls for "industrial policy"—that is, measures designed to protect the domestic economy—were as frequently heard in international conferences as calls for a "liberal trade policy." Another phrase, curiously enough originating with the reputedly logical French, "organized free trade," was floated and quickly withdrawn. Its implication, that open markets could be dangerous to the health of the domestic economy, nevertheless survived. Meanwhile, the Tokyo Round of Multilateral Trade Negotiations (the MTN) produced some reduction of tariff and nontariff trade barriers, but it also arguably legitimated violation of the most-favored-nation commitment of Article I of the GATT—the so-called "cornerstone" of the GATT.

This recital perhaps paints too bleak a picture of underlying problems, though the proliferation of devices such as "voluntary" restraint agreements and "orderly marketing arrangements," as well as evident strains on the world banking system, might argue the contrary. The economic circumstances of the 1970's—in which a whole new set of rules, regulations, standards, and codes for the conduct of international trade and investment were to be structured—were very different from those of the years immediately following the end of World War II. There was a whole new and much larger cast of characters on the stage, with backgrounds, motives, objectives and perceptions much different from that which had earlier prevailed. If one can make a somewhat dangerous generalization, one might say that the principal actors of the earlier period were moderately united in their view of how the world worked, and more or less agreed as to the substance and the procedures of a desirable world economic order. In contrast, the world of the 1970's and 1980's contains not only a larger but also a more divergent cast, part of which contests the premises and objectives of the other, and holds the other to blame for many of its ills.

Of course disputes are not confined to the developing-developed country relationship, or even to the contest between market and socialist philosophies. The differences among the market economy, industrialized nations, are themselves sufficient to cause apprehension whether a reconstitution of the Bretton Woods system is a possible or adequate response to present problems.

In western industrialized nations, unemployment in the second half of 1982 exceeded 28.5 million workers. Only in Japan, because of strong export performance and policies which have led both to growth and to comfortable labor-management relations, in the main, has unemployment risen little; the rate was predicted to be no more than 3 per cent for

1982, and in fact was only 2.6 per cent for the latest month reported by *The Economist* for May 7, 1983. In the United States, by way of contrast, the same report showed an unemployment figure of 9.0 per cent for March of 1982 and, despite the beginning of an apparent recovery in industry as well as in stock market values, 10.3 per cent for the same period a year later. In Britain, the latest figures available (for March of 1983) showed an unemployment rate of 13 per cent. The figures were in double digits in Australia, Canada, Holland, and Italy, with the Federal Republic of Germany and France not far behind in this dismal situation. In these circumstances, the tide of protectionism rises, the line between "fair" and "unfair" trade practices blurs, and companies on both sides of the Atlantic and the Pacific blame each other for their difficulties. But the objective remains, at least formally agreed, of reducing trade barriers, and of fashioning a world trading system based on comparative advantage. If there are obvious and frequent falls from grace, the market economies continue to profess the good old time dogma.

Between the industrialized West on the one side and the developing world on the other—terms which oversimplify the vast diversity among the members of such groupings—the situation is different. Despite their expressed concern for the growth of the developing nations, the actions of the industrialized West reflect a persistent concern about transfers of jobs and production. It is now estimated that by 1990 the industrial nations which were the core of the original GATT membership will account for less than half of total world production. The 1960 figure was two-thirds. The reaction to such estimates is less pleasure at the growth in developing nations which they imply than pain in anticipation of the consequences in industrialized nations. The newly industrialized countries (NIC's)—the Mexicos, Indias and Brazils—meanwhile continue their natural drive for a larger share of world output. In times that are difficult for all, and in which all nations have to cope with unemployment, it is but natural that the language of understanding, sympathy and support sometimes conflicts with the harsh realities of national policies. For example, the recent Multifiber Agreement, entered into by the members of the EEC and the United States, sets stringent limits on the growth of textile imports—one of the natural areas for a developing nation—with special limitations on Hong Kong, Taiwan, and South Korea.

The search, in these circumstances, for standards and rules which could be applied to world trade and investment, for the mutual benefit of all, is thus a difficult one. It is additionally complicated by the premise of many of the proposals which have emerged, mainly in United Nations forums, that (1) a vast shift in resources must take place from North to South, from the industrialized to the developing nations, and (2) that this proposed transfer of resources is a matter of obligation on the one side and of right on the other. The undertone of many current economic discussions is that of reparation, not of mutual interest and benefit.

As Oscar Schachter has pointed out in *Sharing the World's Resources* (1977), "broad and generalized demands of poor countries for preferences and grants are often advanced as entitlements owed to them because of past exploitation, oligopolistic restraints or other allegedly illegitimate practices of the industrialized societies." The consequent concept of "permanent sovereignty over natural resources" was forcefully expressed in a 1974 General Assembly resolution asserting that states and peoples which have been subjected to "foreign occupation, alien and colonial domination" have rights to "restitution." The concept of rectification of past wrongs could well be extended; but it has mainly been advanced, as Schachter points out, "as a right of disadvantaged countries with . . . the implication of a double standard in its application to developed and developing states." That asserted right is the basis in large part of such efforts as the proposals in UNCTAD for a code with respect to transfer of technology and a revision of existing international agreements in patent protection, and in the United Nations Economic and Social Council for a code relating to transnational corporations. That the industrialized nations have sympathized with some of these objectives—as evidenced by the OECD Guidelines for Multinational Enterprise, for example, and the inclusion of a restrictive business practices chapter in the draft ITO Charter—in no way detracts from the fact that these initiatives originated with developing nations, closely associated with the notion of a new international economic order.

The thesis of "permanent sovereignty" is inextricably associated with the demands of the developing countries. Yet it might conceivably be espoused by the industrialized nations, as a shield against such demands. The term "permanent sovereignty" is generally linked with "natural" (that is, subsoil) resources, but it can as well be applied to other types of resources. Resources may be derived from the fact that millions of years ago verdant and tropical forests grew in one or another area of the world, and were subsequently transformed into oil or coal. Climatic conditions are similarly responsible for the grain producing capacities of the United States, Canada, or Argentina, as for the difficulties encountered by the "New Lands" efforts of the Soviet Union. Other resources derive from human effort and ingenuity. Concepts of permanent sovereignty, though sanctified in many a General Assembly resolution, would not seem to give a better entitlement to the resources bestowed by the Lord than those created, presumably with His help, by man. Unlikely though it is that this argument will be put forward in another round of the

North-South debate, it has some relevance to the considerable and evident reluctance to consent, in the name of equity, to an externally-mandated and massive transfer of the resources produced by man, whether these be goods or technology, to the developing nations.

In these circumstances, to work out mutually acceptable norms of resource-sharing—or to arrive at an acceptable definition of new international economic order—presents difficulties that were not faced by the drafters of the GATT or of the IMF, and which are quite different than the compromise of claims as to fair or unfair trade as between, say, Japan and the United States. The phrase "transfer of resources" itself suggests that the benefits are more on the side of those who receive than of those who transfer; and unrequited generosity has seldom motivated the actions of nations. Even the lavish praise given by Churchill to the United States' Marshall Plan did not obscure the basis of "enlightened self-interest"—often stated by the proponents of the Marshall Plan—which made possible its enactment.

The observable consequence, despite a great deal of stated consensus, is that international economic agreements on matters of principle are more difficult to achieve now than they were previously. The stress on "matters of principle" is important. There are many instances of industrial and developing nations coming together on the terms of a specific transaction, a transfer of technology and the terms for payment, but there are few examples of agreed general principles that would regulate the on-going relationship between the parties to cover *all* transfers of technology, capital, or skills. Many individual capital-exporting, industrial nations have been able to arrive at bilateral investment protection agreements with developing nations; but few have been party, on either side, to broad multilateral agreements that would establish general principles in those same subject areas. To the industrial nations, the key words and phrases are "fair treatment," "efficiency," "equality," "reciprocity" and the like. To the developing nations, the key phrases are "equity," "special and differentiated treatment," "full sovereignty over natural resources," and "respect for host-country laws, regulations and practices." The industrial nations emphasize that an investment must make economic sense, and that only in that way can the interests of both parties be advanced; the developing nations suggest that the enterprise must fit into the economic, social and possibly cultural patterns of the host nation. The two points of view are not irreconcilable; but they give different emphasis to different criteria.

An additional difficulty arises in the context of a multilateral rather than a bilateral agreement. Nations which share a generally agreed point of view do not always agree on details, including important details. One nation may prefer one form of words, another may prefer a different form. The concerns of all industrial or developed nations are not identical; neither are those of the many developing nations, which range from the large to the tiny, from the "newly industrialized" to the "least developed", and from the oil-rich to the resource-poor. The consequence is that the multilateral arrangement tends to be cast in terms of least common denominators so far as concessions are concerned, and most elevated standards so far as demands are concerned.

The resultant problems are evident. They are amply illustrated in the individual chapters of this volume, which deal with a variety of international economic agreements or proposed agreements, which have occupied the international agenda in recent years.

TWO

Company Law Harmonization in the European Community

DETLEV F. VAGTS

1. Introduction

In considering the problems of interpreting international economic
agreements it seems logical to investigate, by way of analogy, the process
of harmonizing company law within the European Community.[1] The
states of the Community have sought, with impressive success, to implement a treaty clause that, tersely and without detail, sets forth the objective of harmonizing the members' company laws. The lessons from that
progress ought to illuminate the path to be trodden by states setting out
to develop common international rules for their economic activity.

On the other hand, there are reasons to question the appositeness for
our purposes of a study of the European Community's harmonization
directives. One asks, is European law really "international" or is it rather
a variety of federal law?[2] The Community comprises a group of closely
related states, an inner circle of the OECD as it were. They have been
willing to commit themselves to a surprising degree of coordination at a
supra-state level. That statement may seem oblivious to the periodically
reemerging strains of Gaullism, Thatcherism and other forms of
nationalism, to the intractability of conspicuous problems such as the status of agriculture, the treatment of the budget, and so forth. But viewed
from the other perspective, what is surprising is that there is a budget,
that it goes in part to pay civil servants belonging to the whole community, and that a continous flow of decisions is ground out by these institutions.[3]

Detlev F. Vagts is Professor of Law, Harvard Law School.

Another question: are we dealing in fact with guidelines? One notes that EC directives, once approved by the Council, are in fact binding. They are more than "soft" law in that proceedings can be taken against a state that ignores them. Moreover, according to the Court of Justice, directives begin to have self-executing effect after remaining unimplemented by a state. Finally, do we learn much about the process of interpretation? In a sense the guidelines "interpret" the treaty clauses. On the other hand one finds that the task of interpreting the directives themselves has not loomed large. There have been, in some cases, very substantial delays in processing them through the draft state but they emerge in so detailed and specific a form that there has been as yet little room for fierce struggles over their meaning.

It is thus with a sense that both contrast and comparison must be kept in mind that we set out on this venture.

2. The Context of the Directives

When the EC was established by the Treaty of Rome in 1957,[4] it envisioned a common market not only in trade in goods but also in labor and investment. Each of these categories of free movement would be complementary and allow productive activity to take place where it could most naturally and efficiently go forward. Within the original Six the abolition of straightforward trade barriers was supposed to be achieved in three stages, being completed in 1969. That target was met somewhat in advance, as was the target with respect to the three new states that in 1973 joined the Community.[5] Nevertheless, indirect measures of protectionism continued to be troubling; a struggle has been conducted by the Commission of the European Community and the Court of Justice, against national rules that disadvantage foreign imports. The American lawyer will recognize a general resemblance between those cases and the learning accumulated over the years in the U.S. Supreme Court decisions interpreting the Commerce Clause.[6]

Indirect barriers predominate against the right of establishment, i.e., the right to move direct investment across borders, although some states—France in particular——maintain direct barriers to foreign investment.[7] These barriers are principally disciplined by Article 54, which is part of a chapter on "Right of Establishment." That chapter is, in turn, part of Title III on the "Free Movement of Persons, Services and Capital." Article 54 provides that the Council of Ministers and the commission are to "draw up a general programme for the abolition of existing restrictions of freedom of establishment." As a subsidiary goal those institutions in particular are to act

> by coordinating to the necessary extent the safeguards which, for the protection of the interests of members and others, are required by Member

States of companies or firms . . . with a view to making such safeguards equivalent throughout the Community.

That goal is to be pursued by issuing directives. The issuing authority is the Council.[8] In that body each state is represented by a minister. The ministers act by majority in most cases, but when a "qualified majority" is required, they cast weighted votes. The Council acts upon a proposal by the Commission,[9] the body that supervises the Brussels-based administrative-bureaucratic functioning of the Community. It is to consult with the Economic and Social Committee and the Assembly, now elected by the people of the member states.[10]

The process in question is one of several which are found in the complex and subtle structure of the Treaty of Rome. Some of the treaty's provisions are self-executing and may bind both states and individuals without more ado. In other cases Community organs may issue regulations that have similar direct binding effect —for example, the famous antitrust Regulation 17.[11] Those organs may also issue decisions that bind those to whom they are directed.[12] Directives, however, are described as "binding," "as to the result to be achieved," upon each member state but as leaving the form and means of enforcing them to the national authorities.[13]

The directives with which we are concerned are contained in one of several groups of provisions aimed at achieving "approximation" of national laws.[14] The philosophy underlying all of these provisions is that, while rules that exclude or discriminate against outsiders are the primary target of the Community-building operation, there is a second layer of obstacles. These are national rules that are simply different. They may not have any anti-foreign intention, but merely because they are different and strange they make it harder for a foreigner to function across a border. Since there is some inertial hindrance in any case to entering a region where a different language is spoken and where employers, clients and customers have different habits and expectations, anything that can be done to even out the legal differences will help promote ease of intercourse.

For the American corporate lawyer, it is interesting that company law was put on the list of topics that specially called for coordination.[15] The United States has fifty separate corporation law systems, and attempts to diminish the discrepancies between them by such means as the Model Business Corporation Act have proven much less successful than the Uniform Commercial Code or the Uniform Partnership Act.[16] Also it has separate state blue sky laws governing the sale of securities, laws which federal legislation explicitly safeguards from preemption. Only in 1982 did the Supreme Court, despite that provision, hold a state law —one governing tender offers—unconstitutional in the face of an explicit federal scheme.[17] It is presumably the degree of federal control through the Securities and Exchange Commission and the laws it administers—and perhaps the tendency of multistate corporations to incorporate in Delaware—which keeps the amount of anarchy in American corporation law from reaching an unacceptable level.[18]

Within Europe the differences between company law systems were not vast, although it would probably be fair to say that they were about as far apart as the American poles, California and Delaware. The range was in fact widened by the inclusion of Great Britain's non-civil law system in 1973.[19] Most of the states had separate laws and titles for close and public corporations. Some had a two-tier management system[20] and others only a single board; some assigned rather central roles to auditors and others were quite relaxed about the accounting process. States differed about the availability of company defences as to unauthorized conduct and about the consequences of defects in the process of incorporating. Beyond all of these differences lay the gap between Germany with its board-level co-determination system and all of the other Community members.

Aside from company law the areas specified in the Treaty of Rome as worthy of harmonization are the following:

1. customs rules
2. legislation on aliens based on public order, health and security
3. legislation as to access to self-employed activities
4. exchange controls on capital movement
5. indirect taxes
6. commercial policy
7. export subsidies
8. social legislation.

Some of these areas have seen more activity than the accomplishments made under Article 54. As of 1978 one could count 100 directives designed to eliminate technical trade barriers, with a general guess that it might take as many as 300 to finish the job. Of the 100, no fewer than 41 concerned motor vehicles.[21]

Additionally, Article 100 calls for "approximation" of national rules that "directly affect the establishment or functioning of the Common Market." It thus constitutes a "general welfare" clause of wide potential.[22] However, Article 100 requires unanimity in the Council of Ministers whereas a "qualified majority" is all that is now required under the more specific authorization of Article 54. There has been some controversy over the appropriateness of resort to Article 100 in environmental quality and consumer safety matters. Article 235 provides a further back up: If the treaty has not provided the necessary power to attain one of the objectives of the Community, the council may "take the appropriate measures."[23] Article 220 provides that member states shall enter into negotiations with each other for various purposes. These include, most relevantly, the mutual recognition of companies and the possibility of transborder mergers. Two major company law initiatives have relied upon those powers. One, the convention relative to the Mutual Recognition of Companies and Legal Persons, was signed in 1968 but has not yet been ratified.[24] The other, the statute of the European company, or *societas europaea*, has had a long history from the original draft by Professor Sanders to the present.[25] Under that proposal firms could be created for Europe-wide operations under a Community charter, thus bypassing the regime of harmonized state laws altogether. To succeed it would have to solve all at once all the questions of harmonization, including co-determination, which the directives take up one at a time.

3. The Company Law Directives

The history and present status of company law harmonization directives is probably best seen at a glance in Table 2.1. One notices first of all the deliberate pace of the process. The commission took until 1964 to produce the first draft of the First Directive and until 1966 for a second. The council issued the First Directive in 1968.[26] Then the draft directives started to pile up. The Commission produced four drafts in 1970–72. The extension of the Community in 1973 to include Denmark, Ireland, and the United Kingdom caused a pause, and only in the later 1970's—two decades after signature—do the final products begin to stream forth. The Fifth Directive, the one with the most serious political problems, particularly in connection with the hotly disputed issue of co-determination, has been lingering in the workshop since 1972.[27] A new group of directives, largely in the area that would in the United States be classified as securities regulation (a federal subject) rather than corporation law (a state subject) was prepared in 1976-82 and has been half enacted.[28] This history hints that there is more to the process than the simple steps of the Commission preparing a proposal and the Council acting on it.

What goes into that process has been most fully and lucidly explored by Professor Eric Stein in his 1971 volume and most particularly in his meticulous case study of the First Directive.[29] He notes, first of all, that in the 1960s there was considerable ferment in national corporation law thinking that culminated in a new German *Aktiengesetz* in 1965[30] and a new French *loi des sociétés* of 1966.[31] The prior German law on public corporations dated to 1937 and was infected with Nazism in some of its language though not significantly so in its ideas. The law on closed corporations (*Gesellschaften mit beschrankter Haftung*) had not been heavily

Table 2.1 Table of Company Law Directives

NUMBERED DIRECTIVES

Number	Subject	Date of commission draft	Date of council directives
1	Guarantees for protection of Associates and Third Parties	(1st) Feb. 19, 1964 (2nd) Oct. 3, 1966	March 9, 1968
2	Guarantee for Stockholders	April 24, 1970	Dec. 13, 1976
3	Mergers	June 14, 1970	Oct. 9, 1978
4	Coordination of Annual Accounting Requirements	Nov. 16, 1972	July 25, 1978
5	Structure of Public Companies	Oct. 19, 1972	
6	Prospectus Requirements*	Jan. 13, 1981	
7	Group Accounts	May 4, 1976 Amended: Dec. 14, 1978	
8	Approval of Persons Responsible for Statutory Audits	April 24, 1978 Dec. 5, 1979	

Table 2.1 *(Continued)*

UNNUMBERED DIRECTIVES

Subject	Date of commission draft	Date of council directives
Coordinating the Conditions for Admission of Securities to Listing	March 10, 1976	March 5, 1979
Coordinating Requirements of Listing Particulars for Admission of Securities*	Dec. 13, 1972	March 17, 1980
Information to be Published on Regular Basis by Companies with Shares Admitted to Listing	Feb. 1, 1979 Aug. 16, 1980	Feb. 15, 1982

*Because the number "6" was never officially placed on a directive, confusion arose. Both the CCH Common Market Report and the Encyclopedia of Community Law apply the term "6" to the directive on listing of securities of March 17, 1980. Both Lutter (see note 33) and Nobes (see note 40) apply it to the prospectus requirements directive proposed on January 13, 1981, replacing one proposed in (1972) J. C. E. Cl313/61.

amended since its enactment in 1892 and resisted serious amendment until 1980. The French *loi des sociétés* still bore the date of 1867 though it had been tinkered with fairly often. Less conspicuous revision took place in the other four of the original six states. The Netherlands, for example, fell into line with the other states in adopting a separate form and name for the privately held or close corporation. The effect of these developments, which continued while the first draft of the First Directive was in process, was ambiguous. On the one hand they tended to make the states more aware of problems common to all modern systems of company law and thereby led to a certain narrowing of differences. On the other hand, there was a tendency for national lawyers and legislators to entrench themselves wearily behind their own latest reform achievements and to resist further improvements.

The first part of the process takes place inside the Commission. There was a problem, first of all, of internal allocation of functions.[32] The competence for the freedom-of-establishment chapter (including Article 54(3)(g)) was assigned to the Directorate General for the Internal Market, called D.G. III. Approximation on the other hand was given to the Directorate General for Competition (D.G. IV). Was the integration of company law properly more an establishment issue or more a harmonization issue? Differences of national origin, of bureaucratic "turf," of comparative workloads and others contributed to the interest of the struggle. The contest had the potential of affecting substance. If changes in company law had to be justified as directly easing freedom of establishment there would be less Community activity than under a roving mandate to harmonize. Finally matters came to a head in the reorganization of 1967 that accompanied the consolidation of the institutions of the European Economic Community with those of the Coal and Steel Community and the Atomic Energy Authority. The winner was a newly shaped Directorate for the Internal Market and Industrial Affairs. However, from 1961-62 to 1967 there were working groups within each of the directorates. The members of the working groups were selected by the national ministries of justice and were typically lawyers on the ministries' staff or, in some cases, law professors.

From the ranks of the working groups, discussion and controversy spread into the public domain;, that is, to the rather elitist and specialized body of persons aware of the importance of these issues. At no time did these issues attract a genuinely wide public. The banking, legal, and industrial associations of the Community established bodies to keep in touch with developments. Later the labor unions began to watch out for their somewhat divergent interests. Indeed, the unions became heavily involved as company law directives crossed the border into labor law and tackled co-determination. The unions became involved in this almost as much as they were involved in community exercises that were classified as labor or "social" matters, such as the Vredeling proposal on restructuring business operations. The legal journals began to publish quantities of articles debating both the general theory of harmonization and the details of the legislation. Gradually that literature became more comparative and cosmopolitan and less parochial.[33]

4. The Individual Directives

The First Council Directive deals with "safeguards" as the term is used in Article 54, i.e., with protections for outsiders who deal with companies.[34] Companies governed by the directive include both publicly traded companies and limited liability companies as well as limited partnerships with transferable shares. First, it provides for disclosure of basic data about the legal status of the company, its capital accounts and the authority of its officers. That disclosure is to be made both by deposit in a commercial register and by publication in an official bulletin. Second, it lays down some rules about the liability of firms for acts committed by agents or officers of the company in excess of their authority. In particular it required actual knowledge or direct notice—not by mere publication—before a third party could be ruled unable to hold the firm to its commitment. Finally, it limits the variety of cases in which a company can be found null and void for defects in its execution. It requires a judicial decree to establish nullity and provides for the safeguarding of the company's obligations in the ensuing liquidation. The member states were given eighteen months to carry out the directive (a timetable that was not met).

The Second Directive turned to safeguards for investors.[35] It prescribed the information to be made available in the statutes (roughly comparable to both articles of incorporation and bylaws). It laid down rules to be applied to dividends and other distributions. It prescribed a minimum initial capitalization figure and safeguards for valuing any non-cash assets exchanged for stock. Capital increases and decreases are to be regulated in prescribed ways.

The Third Directive concerned mergers.[36] The general topic of merger has been a heavily charged issue in Community debates. On the one hand, worries about excessive industrial concentrations fueled by the American example and American theory led some to wish to discourage acquisitions by enterprises with substantial market shares.[37] On the other hand, there were eloquent proponents of the idea that mergers should be encouraged in Europe since the scale of American enterprises was so much larger than the European.[38] The theory, associated with Servan-Schreiber,[39] that Europe needed to defend itself against the U.S.-based giants had appeal to many. In particular there was a sense that artificial obstacles to mergers between a corporation of state X and a corporation of state Y should be reduced; if anything, mergers between two state X corporations were the more likely to cause local monopolies. In a gross sense, German writers and public officials tended to be more concerned about monopoly and their French counterparts about the problems of being under-scale. Interestingly, the Third Directive deals only with the problems of mergers between two companies of one member state. The problems inherent in merging two corporations belonging to the separate legal systems of X and Y are put off into the future.

The Fourth Directive deals with the coordination of financial statements.[40] Here the contrast between the generalities of, for example, the UN Code on Transnational Corporations, or even the OECD Guidelines, and the specifics of pronouncements under Article 54(g)(3) comes out most vividly.[41] While in general terms the directive demands a "true and fair" view of the company's financial position, it goes on to make that requirement very concrete. As to both balance sheet and income statement a choice is provided between layouts—two for the balance sheet and four for the income statement. Within each layout a substantial number of specific headings and individual accounts are prescribed. The methods of deriving the figures (values) to be set alongside each account are prescribed—with some room for national variations or management choices. On balance, one would describe the regime set up by the Fourth Directive as rather more detailed and specific than the rules which, within the United States, constitute the generally accepted accounting principles that circumscribe the choices permitted to corporate managers and their auditors.[42]

The three (unnumbered) directives of 1979, 1980, 1982 coordinating the admission of securities to official stock exchange listing follow the pattern set in the Fourth Directive in that they prescribe in considerable detail the data to be provided by applicant companies both at the initial admission to listing and periodically thereafter.[43] However, they also lay down substantive conditions for admission—the size of the company, how long it has done business, the negotiability and distribution of the securities, and so on.

The proposed Seventh Directive on Group Accounts and a possible Ninth Directive that has been described as near to the proposal stage deal with the concept of groups of companies.[44] By that phrase, which is largely of German origin (the term *Konzern* is the German version), is understood a set of interrelated companies bound together by links of control and ownership.[45] American accounting is very familiar with group accounts in that the consolidation of the financial statements of affiliated firms has long been required accounting practice; in this regard, European practice is just catching up. On the substantive side there is a major difference of approach. We in the United States tend to view corporations as separate entities, even though interrelated, and then try to make them behave as if they were functioning at arm's length. The German approach tends to regard the units as basically one *Konzern* and then gives shareholders and creditors of one part claims against the whole. It remains to be seen how far this approach will find acceptance in the legal thinking of other European states.

A word is in order about the proposed Fifth Council Directive despite the fact that it has never received approval.[46] That lack of success reflects some of the most deep-seated controversies within the Community. The draft does provide for a mandatory two-tier structure of company organization; that is, for a supervisory organ and a management organ. In this it adheres to the German model, on which one body is responsible for normal business operations and another body selects, dismisses and supervises the active managers. This step by itself has reverberations in other states which did not have the German system, even in a state such as France which made the two-tier system optional in 1966. But those reverberations are fairly limited and technical. The critical issue is that of workers' participation in the supervisory body, i.e., the German institution of board-level co-determination.[47] The "whereas" clause proposed by the Commission notes the differences in the laws of the member states, and affirms that they must be eliminated, but leaves it to member states "to choose between a number of equivalent arrangements." What is "equivalent" is a deeply political issue, one that—unlike most harmonization issues—reaches audiences outside the world of corporation technicians and arouses strong feelings among union leaders and their constituencies. Co-determination is seen as co-option in some quarters and opinion about it is divided in both labor and management groups. Disappointment over the failure to go further in the direction of generalizing co-determination throughout the Community has led to stagnation here—as it has in the case of the *societas europea*.[48]

5. After Promulgation

Given the explicit differentiation in the Treaty of Rome between regulations and directives, the Court of Justice might have differentiated more sharply the manner in which questions of their meaning and effectiveness are to be tested. One might, for example, have concluded that the only way in which a nation's failure to comply with a directive could be challenged would be by a proceeding brought by the Commission under Article 169 if it "considers that a Member State has failed to fulfill an obligation under" the Treaty of Rome (or by a similar action by a member state under Article 170).[49] Instead, the Court has entertained a series of referrals under Article 177 coming from national courts that seek an answer to questions about the meaning of directives which have arisen in cases over which they have jurisdiction.[50]

There have been a number of directive cases before the Court, including one concerning the First Company Law Directive which is discussed below. A central case is *Van Duyn*[51] in which the Court gave direct effect to a commission directive on freedom of movement of persons so as to render ineffective a British action aimed at barring proselytizers for Scientology. The Court was unwilling to let a state impose a national law that had not been changed due to a default by the member state on its Community obligation. Naturally, the Court will not consider the interpretation of a national statute which is not mandated by the directive; to do so would be to impair the flexibility of the state in an area beyond that which the Commission felt ready to include in its mandate. It can still be regarded as unsettled whether a directive not yet embodied into national law can be given effect in a controversy between two private entities in which the defaulting government is not a party.[52]

Only one case[53] has really dealt with issues of carrying out one of the company law directives. Friedrich Haaga GmbH is a limited liability company based in Stuttgart, Germany. It was ordered on August 11, 1971, by the official in charge of the Commercial Register, to indicate the powers of the managers and, in particular, to make it clear that a sole manager would have sole representative authority. In that action the Register relied upon a West German statute of August 15, 1969,[54] which was intended to put into effect the First Directive and added to §8 of the Limited Liability Company Law a subsection (3): "The application must indicate what power of representation the managers have," and to §10(l) a sentence "In addition, it must be indicated what power of representation the managers have." Under the law, unchanged in this respect, powers were to be exercised jointly if there were several managers and individually if there was only one. Friederich Haaga, Junior, was the sole manager of the firm as the Register disclosed. Friederich Haaga resisted the demand of the registry. One can feel the irritation of Herr Haaga at this imposition. It was totally clear to anybody who knew the German law that he had the right to represent the company and he was being asked to spell out the obvious. He resisted, thus joining the ranks of EEC litigators, who put principle above the actual stake—like Flaminio Costa and his 1925 lire electric bill.[55] However, Haaga lost all the way up through the German courts. The German Supreme Court, acting under Article 177 of the Rome Treaty, asked the Court of Justice for an interpretation of the First Directive. The Commission presented its view, agreeing with Haaga that the additional statement was superfluous. However, Advocate General Mayra and the Court disagreed. They assumed that the

German law should be construed in parallel with the EC directive. That directive, the court concluded, sought to iron out variations between the member states' laws as to the authority of managers to represent the firm. There had been a sharp difference between the German rule, which made the firm responsible, almost without exceptions, for what its top management did, and the French rule which carefully limited liability for unauthorized actions.[56] The directive sought to minimize this gap substantively, but also to achieve a situation in which foreigners could quickly and accurately learn from the Commercial Register the scope of the power of the person they were dealing with. Hence, this should be spelled out so as to minimize the need for research in national laws. And so Herr Haaga had to add the sentence to his registration.

6. Conclusion

The experience of the European Community with the company law guidelines stands as an example of what can be done, given very favorable circumstances, to harmonize divergent national laws and practices. Given a small group of states closely related geographically and economically, given a body of law largely technical and arbitrary in character, and given a generally popularly supported move toward integration, very significant changes can be made. Nevertheless, two issues which divided the states in a basically political way—interstate mergers and co-determination—brought two projects of the Commission to a standstill. Thus the lessons of the company law exercise for truly multilateral work involving countries of sharply different cultures and economics tend, on balance, to cast their weight in the direction of modesty of scope and intensity.

Notes

1. The European Economic Community (now often referred to simply as the European Community) was created by the Treaty of Rome ("the Treaty") in 1957. In this article the translations used appear in a 1973 volume entitled "Treaties Establishing the European Communities" published by the Office for Official Publications of the European Communities. The original text has been altered by the Treaty Establishing a Single Council and a Single Commission of the European Communities (eff. July 1, 1967) and by the Acts (of 1973 and 1981) Concerning the Conditions of Accession and the Adjustments to the Treaties.

Official actions of the Community's organs are reported in its Official Journal, hereafter cited as "[1979] O.J.E.C. L100/21." Prior to 1973 it was not published in English but a special English version of important earlier documents was later published.

2. See, e.g., Stein, Treaty Based Federalism, A.D. 1979, 127 U.Pa. L. Rev. 897 (1979).

3. The literature on the EC is enormous. To pursue issues more deeply one could consult the bibliography in the CCH Common Market Law Reporter (vol. 3, heading "Books and Periodicals"), or in the Common Market Law Review (under "Survey of Litera-

ture"). In the notes to this article, I have given preference to works in English. One introduction to the field is E. Stein, P. Hay & M. Walbroeck, European Community Law and Institutions in Perspective (1976).

4. See note 1.

5. See Treaty arts. 8, 13–14. 1973 Act of Accession art. 32.

6. The Supreme Court reviewed the theory of the Commerce Clause cases most recently in *Edgar* v. *MITE Corp.*, 102 Sup. Ct. 2629 (1982). For comparisons, see E. Stein, P. Hay & M. Walbroeck, *op. cit.* note 3, 420–426.

7. See Torem and Craig, Control of Foreign Investment in France, 66 Mich. L. Rev. 669 (1968); Torem and Craig, Developments in the Control of Foreign Investment in France, 70 Mich. L. Rev. 285 (1971); C. Wallace, Legal Control Techniques of Industrialized Host States (in press).

8. See Treaty arts. 145-54.

9. Treaty arts. 155-63.

10. On the Assembly, see Treaty arts. 137-54. Provision for direct election of delegates, as contemplated by art. 138 (3), was made in Council Decision No. 76/787, 1976 O.J.E.C. L 278/1. On the Economic and Social Committee see arts. 193-98.

11. (1959–62) O.J.E.C. 87 (special English ed.) As to direct effect, see art. 189 and discussion in E. Stein, P. Hay, M. Waelbroeck, *op. cit.* note 3 at Ch. 2 (1976).

12. Treaty art. 189(4).

13. Treaty art. 189.

14. On the general topic of approximation see Harmonization in the E.E.C. (C. Twitchett ed. 1981); W. Schmeder, Die Rechtsangleichung als Integrationsmittel der europaischen Gemeinschaft (1978). Schwartz, Voies d'uniformitisation du droit dans la Communauté européen, 105 J. du droit int. 751 (1978). In general, this article uses the term "harmonization" in preference to synonyms such as "approximation."

15. Thus Schmitthoff writes:

First, unless the national company laws in the Community are identical in all essential aspects, a movement of companies to the state with the laxest company law will take place in the Community. If it may be said without giving offense to our friends in the U.S.A., the Community cannot tolerate the establishment of a Delaware in its territory. This would lead to a distortion of the common market by artificial legal technicalities.

The Future of the European Company Law Scene in the Harmonization of European Company Law 3, 9 (Schmitthoff ed. 1973).
I have noted the problems of dealing with fugitive corporations when (l) there is no federal securities law and (2) no restrictive rule on foreign corporations' entry. Book Review, 18 Am. J. Comp. L. 863 (1970), reviewing G. Grassman, System des Internationalen Gesellschaftsrechts (1970). As to the problems of combining conflicts rules with free corporate access see further, H.G. Koppensteiner, Internationalen Unternehmen im deutschen Gesellschaftsrecht 92-188 (1971).

16. The status and influence of the Model Act can be traced in the Model Business Corporation Act Annotated (1971) (published by the American Bar Foundation) which claimed adoption "substantially in whole by 20 states and in large part by 10 additional states" (p xiii). The Uniform Commercial Code has been adopted in all states (though only in part in Louisiana) and the Uniform Partnership Act in 49.

17. *Edgar* v. *Mite Corp.*, 102 Sup. Ct. 2629 (1982).

18. The need for a greater element of federalization in U.S. corporation law continues to be debated. *Santa Fe Indus., Inc.* v. *Green*, 430 U.S. 462 (1977), discussing Cary, Federalism and Corporate Law: Reflections Upon Delaware, 83 Yale L.J. 663 (1974). Compare Drexler, Federalism and Corporate Law, A Misguided Missile, 3 Sec. Reg. L.J. 374 (1976); Hazen, Corporate Chartering and the Securities Markets, 1978 Wisc. L. Rev. 391.

19. For a contemporaneous reaction see Dalton, Proposals for the Unification of Corporation Law within the European Economic Community: Effect on the British Company, 7 N.Y.U.J. Int'l L & Pol. 59 (1974).

20. For a study of the relative advantages of the one- and two-tier systems see Vagts, Reforming the Modern Corporation: Perspectives from the German, 80 Harv. L. Rev. 23 (1966); A. Conard, Corporations in Perspective 368-69 (1976).

21. Harmonization in the E.E.C. 21 (C. Twitchett ed. 1981).

22. Treaty, art. 100.

23. Close, Harmonization of Laws: Use or Abuse of the Powers under the EEC Treaty? 3 Eur. L. Rev. 461 (1978).

24. For a translation of the Convention see 2 CCH Common Mkt. Rptr. ¶6255.

25. The draft convention on the *societas europaea* appears in English in Bull. E.C. No. 4/75 (Suppl.) 1975. See B. Goldman, Droit Commercial Européen 728 (3d ed. 1975); Vagts & Waelde, The Societas Europaea, 29 Bus. Law. 823 (1974).

26. 1968 O.J.C.E. L65/8; See generally E. Stein, Harmonization of European Company Laws: National Reform and Transnational Coordination ch. 6 (1971).

27. Bull. E.C. No. 10/72 (Suppl.) (1972).

28. (6th) Directive (proposed), 1980 O.J.E.C. C3 55/39. 7th Directive (proposed), 1976 O.J.E.C. C12l/2, as amended, 1979 O.J.E.C. C14/2, 8th Directive (proposed), 1978 O.J.E.C. Cl12/6, as amended, 1979 O.J.E.C. C317/6. The directives actually enacted appear in note 43.

29. E. Stein, Harmonization of European Company Laws: National Reform and Transnational Coordination (1971).

30. The Aktiengesetz, 1965 I B.G.Bl. 1089, has been translated by R. Mueller and G. Galbraith. For commentary see E. Ercklentz, Modern German Corporation Law (1979).

31. Loi 66-537, J.O. July 26, 1966, An English translation was prepared by Commerce Clearing House in 1971. For commentary, see Rawlings, The French Company Law, 30 Bus. Law. 1251 (1975).

32. See Stein, *op. cit.,* note 29, at U.S.

33. P. Meinhardt, Company Law in Europe (1975), R. Pennington, Companies in the Common Market (2d ed., 1970), S.N. Frommel and J.H. Thompson, Company Law in Europe (1975). For comprehensive recent reviews of European company law see, e.g., M. Lutter, Europaisches Gesellschaftsrecht (1979); European Company Law Texts (C. Schmitthoff ed. 1974); The Harmonization of European Company Law (C. Schmitthoff ed. 1973).

34. See note 25.

35. Directive No. 77/91, 1977 O.J.E.C. L26/l; Morse, The Second Directive: Raising and Maintenance of Capital, 2 Eur. L. Rev. 126 (1977).

36. Directive 78/855, [1978] O.J.E.C. L 295/36.

37. See, e.g. Lang, Regulating Multinational Corporate Concentration—The European Economic Community 144 (Mich Yearbook of Int'l Leg. Studies II, 1981); L. Phlips, Effects of Industrial Concentration—A Cross-Section Analysis for the Common Market (1971).

38. E. Stein, *op. cit.,* note 29, at 82–85.

39. J. J. Servan-Schreiber, Le Defi Americain (1967).

40. Directive 78/660, [1978] O.J.E.C. L 222/11; Nobes, Harmonization of Company Law Relating to the Published Accounts of Companies, 5 Eur. L. Rev. 38 (1980).

41. See the chapters in this volume by A.A. Fatouros and Philippe Lévy.

42. See Vagts, Disclosure and the Multinational Enterprise: The Costs of Illumination in Legal Problems of Codes of Conduct for Multinational Enterprises 315 (Horn ed. 1980).

43. Directive 79/279, 1979 O.J.E.C. L66/21, as amended by Directive 82/148, 1982 O.J.E.C. L62/22. Directive 80/390, 1980 O.J.E.C. L00/l, as amended by Directive 82/148, 1982 O.J.E.C. L62/22. Directive 82/12l, 1982 O.J.E.C. L48/26.

44. See Derom, EEC Approach to Groups of Companies, 16 Va. J. Int'l L. 565 (1976); Groups of Companies in European Laws (K. Hopt ed. 1982).

45. Motomura, Protecting Outside Shareholders in a Corporate Subsidiary, 1980 Wisc. L. Rev. 61.

46. Lang, The Fifth EEC Directive on the Harmonization of Company Law, 12 Common Mkt. L. Rev. 155, 345 (1975).

47. For an early comparative look at co-determination see Vagts, Reforming the Modern Corporation: Perspectives from the German, 80 Harv. L. Rev. 23 (1966), and a more

recent one, Summers, Worker Participation in the U.S. and West Germany, 28 Am. J. Comp. L. 367 (1980).

48. See note 25 *supra.*

49. G. Bebr, Development of Judicial Control of the European Communities (1981).

50. *Ibid.*

51. *Van Duyn* v. *Home Office*, 1974-8 E.C.R. 1337; CCH ¶8283 (1974).

52. Easson, Can Directives Impose Obligations on Individuals?, 4 Eur. L. Rev. 67 (1979).

53. *In re Firma Friedrich Haaga GmbH.* 1974-7 E.C.R. 1201; CCH ¶8289 (1974).

54. Law implementing the First Council Directive on the coordination of Company Law, 1969 I B.G.Bl. 1146. The German law on limited liability companies (GmbH Gesetz) has recently been amended rather thoroughly. 1980 I B.G.Bl. 836. Ercklentz, The GmbH Law Amendments of 1980, 15 Int'l Law. 645 (1981).

55. *Costa* v. *E.N.E.L.* 1964 E.C.R. 585, CCH ¶8023.

56. See sources cited note 26 *supra.*

THREE

Toward an International Code on Illicit Payments

LLOYD N. CUTLER

DANIEL M. DRORY

During the 1970's, the United States labored strenuously for a binding international agreement to halt illicit payments to foreign public officials. These efforts succeeded in eliciting pious condemnations of bribery. No one openly favors corrupt payments to public officials. Yet today an international antibribery code remains an elusive prospect. Seven years after the U.S. initiated negotiations in this area, the movement to achieve a binding multilateral code against bribery is at a standstill.

Faced with this apparent failure, we need to reassess our goals and prospects. Why is an international antibribery code desirable? Should we and the other industrial nations simply regard payments to officials as a cost of doing business in certain foreign markets? Or are we right in believing that such payments corrupt not only the recipients but also our own advocacy of free markets? If this is our belief, is it practicable to continue seeking a binding international agreement banning these payments? If not, what other course is open to stop this practice?

1. Roots in Watergate

The origins of the efforts to secure an international antibribery code can be found in the Watergate investigations. In connection with the investigations of domestic political contributions, U.S. corporations were shown to have channelled large sums to the Nixon presidential campaign committee through secret corporate funds paid out by means of agents. This led the Securities and Exchange Commission (SEC) to raise

Lloyd N. Cutler is a member of the District of Columbia Bar, and Partner, Wilmer, Cutler, & Pickering; A.B., J.D., Yale.

Daniel M. Drory is a member of the District of Columbia Bar, and Associate, Wilmer, Cutler & Pickering; A.B., Yale; J.D., Stanford.

the question whether corporations had used agents to effect other con-
cealed payments. The SEC initiated its own investigations in 1974, and
in 1975 it established a program to encourage voluntary self-
investigation and disclosure.

Under the SEC's voluntary program, outside directors, auditors and
counsel inquired into their corporations' use of agents in foreign transactions. They discovered that millions of dollars had been paid to mid-
dlemen for transmission to foreign government officials, political parties
and purchasing agents for state enterprises, and that corporate records
had been falsified to conceal these acts. The SEC's own investigations
turned up other instances of questionable foreign payments.[1]

The disclosures—while involving only a small minority of U.S. corporations and excluding many notable multinationals—scandalized the
Congress. By 1977, more than four hundred corporations (including
about 20 per cent of the Fortune 500) had admitted questionable payments totaling over $300 million, including substantial sums for trans-
mission to government officials, politicians and political parties abroad.
The corporations included major firms engaged in oil and gas production, aerospace, chemicals, and communications equipment.[2]

By the time the dust had settled, a party leader had been discredited
in Japan (by revelations of payments by Lockheed), Prince Bernhard
had resigned from public office in the Netherlands (in connection with
similar allegations), and other governments had been shaken or severely
embarrassed. The disclosures "cast a shadow" over international business[3] and threatened to upset U.S. relations with its closest allies.

2. The Forms of "Illicit Payments"

Payoffs to public officials took several forms. Perhaps the most common
was the so-called "facilitating payment," or "grease" payment. This was
the $100 or $1,000 payment to the customs official who threatened to
delay a shipment if he was not rewarded for his efforts; the payment to
the government clerk who would have held up a visa application unless
paid off. These payments are a nuisance and disturbing fact of life in
many countries where public officials are poorly paid and accustomed to
private compensation for their efforts.

Another common form of questionable payment was the benefit
conferred on a public official, or political party, in order to create good
will. Its purpose was not to influence any particular government decision. It was intended to create a favorable atmosphere to the long-run
benefit of the paying corporation.

A third form, and our major concern, was bribery, i.e., the payment
to an official—or to a self-proclaimed intermediary—in order to influ-

ence a specific official decision. Bribes took the form of direct cash payments to officials or their relatives, indirect payments through commissions paid to sales agents or consultants, political contributions, and the like. Some were initiated by the business firm; some were akin to extortion, initiated by the foreign official or by an intermediary who may or may not have shared his commission with the official who supposedly sought the bribe. The payments involved millions of dollars, and they were intended to be hidden, because otherwise they could not have been lawfully made or retained.

3. International Initiatives

Early on in the congressional investigation of foreign payments, it became clear that foreign bribery was essentially an international problem. U.S. corporations were attracted to this view because they were competing with firms of other nations for contracts with the country whose officials were accepting or seeking bribes, and because of the widespread belief that their competitors were offering such payments.

Congress urged the Executive to attack the problem on an international front. In 1975, the Senate resolved by a 93–0 vote that, whereas the practice of bribery, kickbacks and other payments had been revealed to be widespread, and whereas U.S. corporations were coerced to participate in them in order to compete abroad, the U.S. should immediately initiate international negotiations

> with the intent of developing an appropriate code of conduct and specific trading obligations among governments, together with suitable procedures for the settlement of disputes, which would result in elimination of such practices [as bribery, indirect payments, kickbacks and unethical political contributions] on an international, multilateral basis, including suitable sanctions to cope with problems posed by nonparticipating nations, such codes and written obligations to become part of the international system of rules and obligations within the framework of the General Agreement on Tariffs and Trade, and other appropriate international trade agreements. . . .[4]

A series of international resolutions began in 1975. On December 15, 1975, the United Nations General Assembly adopted by consensus Resolution 3514 (XXX), which condemned "all corrupt practices, including bribery, by transnational and other corporations, their intermediaries and others involved, in violation of the laws and regulations of the host countries. . . ." The resolution called on governments to gather information on such practices, cooperate with other governments, and take "all necessary measures which they deem appropriate . . . to prevent such corrupt practices. . . ." It also requested the U.N. Economic and Social Council (ESOSOC) to study the problem of corrupt payments as part of its program on the regulation of transnational corporations.[5]

At a meeting of the U.N. Commission on Transnational Corporations in March 1976, the U.S. proposed the negotiation of a treaty to control corrupt practices.[6] Specifically, the U.S. urged that ECOSOC establish a working group to prepare, as a priority matter, an international agreement to limit corrupt payments. The agreement was to be based on the following principles: (i) the agreement would apply to transactions with governments; (ii) the agreement would apply equally to the payer and recipient of corrupt payments; (iii) host governments would agree to provide clear guidelines on the use of agents and establish criminal penalties for corrupt practices within their territories; (iv) governments would cooperate and exchange information on corrupt payments; and (v) governments would agree to uniform legislation for disclosure of gifts, payments and political contributions.[7] ECOSOC established an Ad Hoc Intergovernmental Working Group in August 1976 to consider the problem,[8] and sessions began in November 1976.[9]

The Organization for Economic Cooperation and Development (OECD) also addressed the issue of corrupt payments. Following a U.S. initiative, the OECD included language in its Guidelines for Multinational Enterprises condemning the illicit payment of foreign officials.[10] Specifically, the Guidelines provided among its "General Policies" that multinationals should

> (7) not render—and they should not be solicited or expected to render —any bribe or other improper benefit, direct or indirect, to any public servant or holder of public office;
> (8) unless legally permissible, not make contributions to candidates for public office or to political parties or other political organisations. . . .[11]

The United States "strongly endorse[d]" the OECD's Guidelines and stated that "strong collective measures" were needed to eliminate corrupt payments.[12] However, the Guidelines were principles for voluntary adoption by multinationals. They did not require OECD member countries to pass implementing legislation and imposed no criminal sanctions, or disclosure requirements, on the corporations themselves.

Another resolution was the official statement of the Organization of American States (OAS) in 1975. The OAS "condemn[ed] in the most emphatic terms" corrupt payments by multinationals and urged member states to clarify their laws on such payments.[13]

An important private-sector initiative was the International Chamber of Commerce (ICC) proposal aimed at reducing foreign bribery and extortion. Noting that much bribery results from extortion and that local laws against corruption varied widely in their effectiveness, the ICC rec-

ommended that (i) local antibribery laws be strengthened and strictly enforced, (ii) governments require enterprises to disclose, upon specific request, payments made to agents in transactions with any government,
and (iii) an international agreement be concluded to ensure that effective measures are taken against bribery and extortion. The ICC also proposed voluntary rules of conduct for international business.[14]

4. Unilateral Action

By December 1977, there was still no immediate prospect of a binding
international agreement on corrupt payments. The U.S. Congress decided to act unilaterally to outlaw bribery by U.S. corporations of officials abroad. The result was the Foreign Corrupt Practices Act of 1977
(FCPA), signed into law by President Carter on December 20, 1977.[15]

The FCPA prohibits all SEC-regulated issuers—and other U.S. "domestic concerns"—from "corruptly" offering, giving or authorizing payment of anything of value to a "foreign official," or foreign political
party, for the purpose of influencing an official act or decision, in order
to obtain a business advantage.[16]

The FCPA also contains an accounting provision. This requires issuers (i) to "make and keep books, records, and accounts, which, in reasonable detail, accurately and fairly reflect the transactions and dispositions
of the assets of the issuer"; and (ii) to "devise and maintain a system of
internal accounting controls sufficient to provide reasonable assurances"
that transactions are properly executed and recorded.[17]

The FCPA was only one of several legislative actions taken by the
United States against questionable foreign payments. The Tax Reform
Act of 1976 eliminated deductions for bribes paid by controlled foreign
corporations to foreign officials.[18] The International Security Assistance and Arms Export Control Act of 1976 regulates the payment of
agents' fees in connection with foreign military sales, and also requires
reports on payments made to secure foreign sales of defense items.[19]

5. Failure in the U.N.

The U.S. continued to negotiate for an agreement at the U.N. After
more than seventy formal and informal meetings, the negotiators obtained a draft agreement in the Working Group and submitted a draft to
ECOSOC in 1978.[20] In July 1978, ECOSOC established a preparatory
committee to complete a final draft with a view toward holding a diplomatic conference on an antibribery agreement.[21] The preparatory
committee worked on the draft in 1979. A draft International Agreement on Illicit Payments (Draft U.N. Agreement) was transmitted to
ECOSOC in May 1979.[22]

The Draft U.N. Agreement provided that contracting states would adopt criminal penalties against "[t]he offering, promising or giving of any payment, gift or other advantage" to a public official, domestic or foreign, as "undue consideration for performing or refraining from the performance of his duties in connexion with an international commercial transaction."[23]

The Draft Agreement also provided that contracting states would ensure that enterprises within their territories would maintain "accurate records of payments made by them to an intermediary, or received by them as an intermediary, in connexion with an international commercial transaction."[24] In addition, the contracting states would report to the U.N. Secretary-General every two years on their efforts to implement the agreement.[25]

The Draft U.N. Agreement has never been ratified by the U.N. General Assembly. For three years, the U.S. attempted to convene a diplomatic conference to conclude an international agreement on corrupt payments. These efforts were unsuccessful.[26] In mid-1981, a former State Department official described U.S. attempts at securing an international agreement as "vigorous but futile."[27] As of July 1982, there are no active proposals for an international code on corrupt payments.

6. Why Have We Failed?

Why are we still without a binding international agreement to control illicit payments? One reason is that U.S. efforts were concentrated on the U.N. There, the developing countries insisted on linking the bribery problem to the question of a comprehensive code for multinationals,[29] to a ban on payment of taxes and royalties to "an illegal minority regime in southern Africa,"[30] and to other complex issues regarding the conduct of multinationals.[31] In other words, a relatively narrow issue was tied to the resolution of much broader questions unlikely to be settled by international agreement in the near future.

However, there is a more fundamental reason for our failure. Quite simply, our allies have not been interested in achieving a binding international agreement to stop bribery of officials in third countries. While our principal trading partners have endorsed high-level policy statements against corrupt payments—for example, at the Venice Economic Summit conference in June 1980, our allies in Europe, Canada and Japan publicly reaffirmed their opposition to bribery of foreign officials[32]—even our closest allies appear to regard these payments as a necessity, and as a cost of doing valuable business in certain markets around the world. A former State Department official who was involved in the U.N. negotiations put it this way:

[O]ur major trading partners have resisted U.S. efforts to establish international controls over bribery and extortion involving foreign officials. Some of our closest allies have told us privately that payments are necessary in certain foreign markets and their economies are not strong enough to risk the loss of business in those markets by curtailing payments by their companies.[33]

In short, nothing has really changed since the following appeared in the French business magazine, *Le Nouvel Economiste*:

It has become dangerous to do business with certain American multinational corporations especially to the extent that "sensitive" matters are involved. The American press and Congress—which are often kept well informed by Soviet diplomats—seem intent upon revealing bit by bit the basis of certain transactions. Inasmuch as the "contracts of the century" are increasing in number and are (nearly) always accompanied by substantial gratuities, the risks of such disclosure are far from negligible. . . . Thus, the somewhat cynical observation of one French industrialist: "the label 'made in France' offers an added guarantee."[34]

Virtually every country outlaws bribery of domestic public officials. However, many countries tolerate the bribery of foreign officials by their own nationals, and some appear to encourage it. At least one major industrial nation (West Germany) grants a tax deduction for these payments. The United States is virtually alone in prohibiting its own nationals from bribing foreign officials.[35] Thus, it is not surprising that the U.S. has stood practically alone in pressing for rapid, effective measures by other states to end the practice.[36]

7. A Continuing Problem

Neither the passage of seven years nor foreign resistance to an international code has altered the fact that foreign bribery is a critical problem for government and business.

Foreign bribery interferes with the operations of other governments. Bribes disrupt the procedures by which foreign states determine public needs and award government contracts on the basis of merit. It cannot be argued that some nations embrace corruption as an accepted procedure; domestic bribery is illegal in every country, and there is no nation in which the disclosure of a bribe to a high-ranking government official is not a major scandal.

Foreign bribery poses a serious danger to the conduct of our own foreign policy. In paying bribes or making foreign political contributions, international corporations may be conducting an independent foreign policy, for example by trying to advance the power of one domestic political group over another. Thus, bribery exposes a corporation's home state (the "country of origin") to foreign policy risks not of its creation or under its control. It may also produce a backlash against the country of origin and international business generally.

Foreign bribery distorts the competitive marketplace, and corrupts our advocacy of free market principles to developing nations. If we want to win general acceptance of the basic principles of the free market, we cannot ourselves engage in practices that override price, quality and service as the major criteria for making public contract awards.

Foreign bribery is damaging to the reputation of international business. It is safe to say that a very small percentage of international business transactions involves actual foreign bribery. Yet the revelations of the past few years have created a public image of international business as corrupt.

Foreign bribery is wasteful and inefficient. It is not possible to say definitely how much has been paid in bribes to foreign officials. But the figure must run into tens and perhaps hundreds of millions of dollars just in the past ten years. Even more important, bribery results in contract awards to less efficient suppliers at higher prices and lower quality.

And foreign bribery continues. In November 1981, the Justice Department advised Congress that it had under investigation 54 cases of possible foreign bribery by U.S. corporations, five of which involved possible bribery of foreign heads of state.[37] Without any domestic legislation to limit these activities, foreign-based firms also continue to make corrupt foreign payments.

Bribery of foreign officials thus remains an international problem of the first order. It is essential, no less than it was six years ago, that effective measures be taken to limit this practice.

Moreover, it is essential that these be international measures. Unilateral action by the U.S. is an incomplete solution. No one country has a monopoly on foreign bribery. Indeed, bribery often springs from competition between firms of different nationalities. To the extent that extortion is a problem, it is not confined to one nation. It is necessary to have international measures that match the international dimensions of this problem.

As we have learned through the FCPA, unilateral action raises a host of its own problems. One is that unilateral action—in particular, our criminalization of bribery committed abroad by persons subject to the jurisdiction of the United States—may violate the principles of international comity. These principles hold that a state must limit the exercise of its jurisdiction over foreign conduct where another state has substantially greater interest in regulating that conduct.[38] There can be no doubt that the state where the bribery occurs has primary interest in the case; *its* political process has been disrupted by the bribery, *its* legal process has been called into question, and *its* officials will be exposed by an prosecution. Under principles of international comity, it may be inappropriate for another state to extend its jurisdiction over such cases, unless the state primarily affected requests the other state to do so. It would certainly be inappropriate of the state primarily affected objects to another state's exercise of jurisdiction.[39]

Unilateral action also gives rise to problems of investigation and enforcement. Even where international agreements exist for the exchange of information, it is unrealistic to expect authorities abroad to be forthcoming with evidence of embarrassing payments made to their own officials. The crucial witnesses to the bribery may not be amenable to the jurisdiction of either the prosecuting country or the country whose officials were involved. Absent a complete record, it is not possible or acceptable to prosecute a case of alleged foreign bribery.

In addition, unilateral action may disadvantage firms based in the acting state, while foreign firms remain free to use bribes as a means of obtaining valuable foreign contracts. Under the FCPA, it is probable that U.S. business has lost opportunities to foreign competitors who were not forbidden by their own governments to make corrupt payments abroad. At the very least, U.S. business has incurred costs in complying with the FCPA's accounting requirements to which foreign competitors are not subject.[40]

8. Basic Approaches

There are two basic approaches to controlling bribery through an international agreement. The first approach is criminalization. The second is disclosure.[41]

(A) CRIMINALIZATION. The criminalization approach involves two elements. Nations would be required to clarify, and strictly enforce, laws against bribery of their own officials. They would also be required to enact laws to prohibit bribery of foreign officials. The U.N. Draft Agreement contained both requirements.

There is nothing controversial about the first element. As noted, virtually every country in the world already forbids domestic bribery. The problem—and indeed a major reason why we have a foreign payments question at all—is that some nations are unwilling or unable to enforce their existing statutes. There is no reason to believe that these laws will be enforced more effectively under an international agreement than they are enforced now.

The second element raises many of the problems of unilateral action to criminalize foreign bribery. Absent a broad international agreement including the developing nations, there are serious problems of international comity, enforcement and proof.

The main difficulty with the criminalization approach is that the prospects of achieving a broad international agreement are all but nonexistent. Even assuming that our principal trading partners would be willing to sign a binding agreement for criminalization, the cooperation of the developing nations would still be needed in order for the agreement to be effective. Our U.N. experience shows that this cooperation is unlikely over the near term.

In November 1981, the U.S. Senate approved a bill to amend the criminalization provisions of our own FCPA.[42] Under the Business Accounting and Foreign Trade Simplification Act (S. 708), it would still have been unlawful for a domestic concern to make a corrupt payment to a foreign official for the purpose of influencing an official decision, in order to obtain a business advantage. However, a U.S. concern would have become criminally liable for corrupt payments by a third party (*i.e.*, an agent) only where the U.S concern had "direct[ed] or authorize[d]" the payment (as opposed to the current FCPA, which punishes a U.S. concern having a "reason to know" that a bribe would be paid).[43] Moreover, the bill expressly excluded from criminalization: (i) "facilitating" payments; (ii) payments or gifts which are lawful in the foreign official's country; (iii) payments or gifts which are a "courtesy," a "token of regard," or the like; (iv) expenditures associated with selling or purchasing goods or services; and (v) "ordinary expenditures" associated with the performance of a contract for a foreign government.[44]

(B) DISCLOSURE. This approach involves the public reporting of foreign payments. The underlying idea is, as Justice Brandeis said, that sunlight is the best disinfectant. This was the approach advocated in 1976 by President Ford's Task Force on Questionable Corporate Payments Abroad.[45] It was rejected in the final version of the FCPA, which embraced a criminalization approach.

The disclosure approach has advantages. It is relatively simple to enforce, and it is more achievable than criminalization. In order to be an effective deterrent, a disclosure approach need be agreed only with the major industrial nations, where most of the headquarters of the firms which engage in international bribery are based. Such an agreement could be attempted either through agreement of the twenty-four OECD nations or, if this fails, through a series of bilateral agreements with those major trading partners who can be persuaded to do so.

9. A Proposal

Disclosure, rather than international criminalization, is the most practical approach for putting a stop to bribery of foreign officials. The question is how to ensure that disclosure is both reasonable (taking into account legitimate business needs) and effective.

A simple and practicable solution may be to require disclosure of all payments above a certain amount (say $50,000 per year) to agents or officials, by name and amount, in connection with all transactions with foreign governments and state-owned enterprises. In addition, all contributions to foreign political parties above a set minimum (say $1,000) should be disclosed.

The simplicity of these requirements makes them relatively easy to enforce. No questions about intent, or reasonable knowledge that a bribe would be paid to a foreign official, will arise. The minimum thresholds would eliminate any need to report the relatively innocuous "grease" payments. These disclosures could be made annually and with a significant time delay after the year-end, in order to protect a corporation's legitimate interest in the secrecy of on-going negotiations. If a particular firm failed to disclose, its international competitors who do disclose could be relied on to inform against the laggard, and at the request of these competitors, their governments could make appropriate representations to the laggard's home state.

If it were known in advance that embarrassing payments would have to be disclosed, most such payments would not be solicited or made. In this modest way, we might achieve an international regime to ensure that foreign bribery is finally halted. The need for such a regime continues. Despite the distressing absence of any international consensus to act against foreign bribery, the United States should persist in its efforts to build one.

Notes

1. *See* Cutler, *Watergate, International Style*, 1976 For. Pol'y 160, 160–63; Herlihy & Levine, *Corporate Crisis: The Overseas Payment Problem*, 8 Law & Pol'y Int'l Bus. 547, 577–94 (1976). The history of the SEC's voluntary disclosure program is summarized in Securities and Exchange Commission, Written Statement submitted to the Subcommittee on Telecommunications, Consumer Protection and Finance of the House Committee on Energy and Commerce with Respect to the Commission's Administration and Enforcement of the Foreign Corrupt Practices Act of 1977 (Nov. 18, 1981) at 5–9. For a sample of the payments disclosed, see Securities and Exchange Commission, *Report on Questionable and Illegal Corporate Payments and Practices*, Exhibit A (submitted to the Senate Comm. on Banking, Housing and Urban Affairs) (Comm. Print 1976).

2. House Comm. on Interstate and Foreign Commerce, *Unlawful Corporate Payments Act of 1977*, H.R. Rep. No. 640, 95th Cong., lst Sess. 4 (1977) (hereinafter cited as H.R. Rep. No. 640).

3. H.R. Rep. No. 640, *supra* note 2, at 5.

4. RSP–S. Res. 265, 94th Cong., lst Sess., 121 Cong. Rec. 36,108 (1975). "It is not enough to restrict [U.S.] companies without making any effort to end the basic problem internationally. . . . What we face is not our problem alone. It is an international one and

we must find an international solution." 121 Cong. Rec. 30,306 (1975) (remarks of Sen. Ribicoff). *See also* Statement of President Gerald Ford (dated Aug. 3, 1976), *re- printed in Foreign Payments Disclosure: Hearings on H.R. 15481, S. 3664, H.R. 13870 and H.R 13953 Before the Subcomm. on Consumer Protection and Finance of the House Comm. on Interstate and For. Commerce*, 94th Cong., 2d Sess. 38 (1976) ("[T]he questionable payments problem is an international problem which cannot be corrected by the United States acting alone").

5. U.N. Doc. A/RES/3514(XXX) (adopted Dec. 15, 1975), *reprinted in* 15 Int'l Legal Mat. 180 (1976).

6. *See* Slade, *Foreign Corrupt Payments: Enforcing A Multilateral Agreement*, 22 Harv. Int'l L.J. 117, 127-29 (1981) (hereinafter cited as *Foreign Corrupt Payments*).

7. Annex VI (Paper Submitted by the Delegation of the United States of America) to Report of the Commission on Transnational Corporations, *reprinted in* 15 Int'l Legal Mat. 779, 810 (1976).

It is primarily the responsibility of each State to set forth clear rules relevant to [corrupt practices] within their territories. . . . However, the dimensions of the problem are such that unilateral action needs to be supplemented by multilateral cooperation. . . . The most effective method of achieving such international cooperation is through an international agreement dealing with corrupt practices.

Ibid. at 809–10.

8. U.N. Doc. E/RES/2041(LXI) (adopted Aug. ll, 1976), *reprinted* in 16 Int'l Legal Mat. 1222 (1977).

9. See U.N. Economic and Social Council, Corrupt Practices, Particularly Illicit Payments in International Commercial Transactions: Concepts and Issues Related to the Formulation of an International Agreement, U.N. Doc. E/AC.64/3 (1977) at 4.

10. Organization for Economic Cooperation and Development, Guidelines for Multinational Enterprises (1976) (Annex to OECD Declaration on International Investment and Multinational Enterprises), reprinted in 15 Int'l Legal Mat. 969 (1976) (hereinafter cited as OECD Guidelines).

11. OECD Guidelines, *supra* note 10, at 972.

12. 75 State Dep't Bull. 73, 76 (July 1976) (statement by Sec'y of State Kissinger).

13. Resolution CP/RES. 154 (167/75), reprinted in 14 Int'l Legal Mat. 1326 (1975).

14. Report adopted by the 131st Session of the Council of the ICC (Nov. 29, 1977), reprinted i 17 Int'l Legal Mat. 417 (1977).

15. Pub. L. No. 95-213, 91 Stat. 1494 (codified at 15 U.S.C. §§ 78a note, 78m, 78dd-l, 78dd-2, 78ff (Supp. IV 1980)).

16. Sections 103, 104, 15 U.S.C. §§ 78dd-l, 78dd-2 (Supp. IV 1980). The FCPA defines a "foreign official" as "any officer or employee of a foreign government or any department, agency or intermediary thereof, or any person acting in an official capacity for or on behalf of such government or department, agency, or instrumentality." It expressly excludes any government employee whose duties are "essentially ministerial or clerical."

17. Section 102, 15 U.S.C. § 78m(b)(2) (Supp. IV 1980).

18. 26 U.S.C. § 964 (1976).

19. 22 U.S.C. §§ 2394a, 2776, 2779 (1976 8 Supp. IV 1980).

20. U.N. Economic and Social Council, Report of the Ad Hoc Intergovernmental Working Group on the Problem of Corrupt Practices on Its Fourth, Fifth and Resumed Fifth Sessions, U.N. Doc. E/1978/l15 (1978). See U.N Economic and Social Council, Report of the Ad Hoc Intergovermental Working Group on the Problem of Corrupt Practices on Its First, Second, Third and Resumed Third Sessions, U.N. Doc. E/1977/6006(1977); *Corrupt Practices in International Commercial Transactions*, 73 Am. Soc'y Int'l L. Proc. 36, 45–46 (1979) (remarks of F. Willis) (hereinafter cited as *Corrupt Practices*).

21. U.N. Doc. E/1978/71.

22. U.N. Economic and Social Council, Report of the Committee on an International Agreement on Illicit Payments on Its First and Second Sessions, U.N. Doc. E/1979/104 (1979) (hereinafter cited as Draft U.N. Agreement). For article-by-article discussions of the Draft U.N. Agreement, see *Foreign Corrupt Payments*, *supra* note 6, at 130–41; Note, *A Comparison of the Foreign Corrupt Practices Act and the Draft International Agreement on Illicit Payments*, 13 Vand. J. Transn. L. 795, 803–12 (1980).

23. Art. l.l(a), 2(a). The Draft Agreement provided that sanctions shall be applicable to both natural and legal persons. Where the law of a contracting state did not recognize criminal liability of legal persons, the state would have been required to take "appropriate measures . . . with the objective of comparable deterrent effects." Art. 1.2.

24. Art. 6.

25. Art. 9. Other provisions included agreement among contracting states to provide mutual assistance in investigation of foreign payments. Art. 10.

26. See *Business Accounting and Foreign Trade Simplification Act: Hearings on S. 708 Before the Subcomm. on Securities and the Subcomm. on Internat. Finance and Monetary Policy of the Senate Comm. on Banking, Housing, and Urban Affairs*, 97th Cong., lst Sess. 270 (1981) (hereinafter cited as *Hearings on S. 708*) (remarks of M. Feldman).

27. *Ibid.* at 254 (remarks of M. Feldman).

28. As of March 1983, two alternative proposals for a paragraph on corrupt payments still appear in the draft U.N. Code on Transnational Corporations (TNC Code). One proposal is the following:

> Transnational corporations shall refrain, in their transactions, from the offering, promising or giving of any payment, gift or other advantage to or for the benefit of a public official as consideration for performing or refraining from the performance of his duties in connexion with those transactions.

> Transnational corporations shall maintain accurate records of payments made by them, in connexion with their transactions, to any public official or intermediary. They shall make available these records to the competent authorities of the countries in which they operate, upon request, for investigations and proceedings concerning those payments.

The other proposal is as follows:

> For the purposes of this Code, the principles set out in the International Agreement on Illicit Payments adopted by the United Nations should apply in the area of abstention from corrupt practices.

TNC Code, ¶ 20 (bracketed), U.N. Doc. E/C.10/1982/6. Whether, with the failure of the Draft U.N. Agreement, any language on illicit payments will appear in the final TNC Code remains to be seen.

29. Hearings on S. 708 at 270. *See also Corrupt Practices, supra* note 20, at 48 (remarks of F. Willis).

30. *See* Draft U.N. Agreement, *supra* note 22, Art. 7 (bracketed).

31. *See* U.N. Doc. E/1979/104 at ¶ 57 (delegation "speaking on behalf of the Group of 77" stating that the Draft U.N. Agreement should not enter into force "until the code of conduct on transnational corporations . . . [has] come into force").

32. *See* 80 Dep't State Bull. 11 (Aug. 1980).

33. *Hearings on S. 708, supra* note 26, at 254–55 (remarks of M. Feldman).

34. Quoted *in* Cutler, *Watergate International Style*, 1976 For. Policy 160,166.

35. See *Foreign Corrupt Payments, supra* note 6, at 119 n.15, 122–23. On Swedish legislation affecting certain foreign payments, see Bogdan, *International Trade and the New Swedish Provisions on Corruption*, 27 Amer. J. Comp. L. 665 (1979).

36.

> [E]xperience has demonstrated that some of our measures have overshot the mark, that the United States should not seek to impose its values on other countries at the expense of all other U.S. interests in those countries; and, most clearly, that the international community is not yet prepared to join with the United States in a meaningful international response to [the] problem [of foreign bribery].

Hearings on S. 708, supra note 26, at 254 (remarks of M. Feldman).

37. *Foreign Corrupt Practices Act—Oversight: Hearings Before the Subcomm. on Telecommunications, Consumer Protection, and Finance*, 97th Cong., lst & 2d Sess. 185–215 (1982); N.Y. Times, Nov. 19, 1981, §D, at l, col. 3. See also "Oil Firm, Officer Charged by U.S. In Pemex Probe," Wall St. J., Sept. 20, 1982, at 4, col. l (U.S. investigation of illicit payments in Mexico); "In Nigeria, Payoffs Are A Way of Life," Wall St. J., July 12, 1982, at 23, col. 2.

38. See Restatement (Second) of Foreign Relations Law of the United States §40 (1965); Association of the Bar of the City of New York, Report on Questionable Foreign Payments By Corporations: The Problem and Approaches to a Solution, *reprinted in Unlawful Corporate Payments Act of 1977: Hearings on H.R. 3815 and H.R. 1602 Before the Subcomm. on Consumer Protection and Finance of the House Comm. on Interstate and Foreign Commerce*, 95th Cong., lst Sess. 59, 74–76 (1976) (hereinafter cited as N.Y.C. Bar Report).

39. A state may have a technical basis for exercising jurisdiction over foreign bribery, even where the conduct occurs wholly outside its borders. Under international law, a state may prosecute its citizens for conduct abroad that violates its laws. See, e.g., J. Brierly, *The Law of Nations* 299 (1963). Moreover, international law permits a state to punish behavior outside its boundaries that has a direct and substantial effect on its own interests. See Restatement (Second) of Foreign Relations Law of the United States §18 (1965).

40. See, e.g., *Foreign Corrupt Payments, supra* note 6, at 118. One recent example of the FCPA's effects is the Enserch-Davy case before the U.K. Monopolies Commission. Enserch Corp. (a U.S. corporation) proposed to acquire Davy Corp. Ltd. (a U.K. contractor for process plant projects). In recommending disallowance of the merger, the Monopolies Commission noted that Enserch, owing to the FCPA, had a policy against use of any agent who is a "government employee in a position relevant to the contract." The Commission believed that "[t]he application of this policy [to Davy, as a subsidiary of Enserch,] might well affect Davy's business prospects in certain countries, particularly as European and Japanese competitors will not be subject to the same legal constraints." U.K. Monopolies and Mergers Commission, Enserch Corporation and Davy Corporation Limited —A Report on the Proposed Merger 66 (1981).

41. See generally N.Y.C. Bar Report, *supra* note 36, at 67–82.

42. See Cong. Rec. S13,983 (daily ed. Nov. 23, 1981). S. 708 failed to pass the House during the 97th Congress. Substantially the same amendments were reintroduced in the Senate in February 1983. Cong. Rec. S981 (daily ed. Feb. 3, 1983).

43. S. 708, 97th Cong., 1st Sess., §5 (1981) (hereinafter cited as S. 708). See Cong. Rec. S13,984 (daily ed. Nov. 23, 1981). Compare FCPA §§ 103–104, 15 U.S.C. §§78dd-l, 78dd-2 (Supp. IV 1980).

44. S. 708, §5, Cong. Rec. S13,984 (daily ed. Nov. 23, 1981). S. 708 also would have revised the accounting provisions of the FCPA in several respects. For example, S. 708 provided that no criminal liability could be imposed for failure to comply with the FCPA's accounting requirements. S. 708, §4, Cong. Rec. S13,984 (daily ed. Nov. 23, 1981). In addition, S. 708 reaffirmed the Senate's belief that

> a solution to the problem of corrupt payments . . . demands an international approach; accordingly, appropriate international agreements should be initiated and sought by the United States agencies responsible for trade agreements and by the President.

S. 708, §2, Cong. Rec. S13,984 (daily ed. Nov. 23, 1981). S. 708 would have required the President to report to Congress on the progress of negotiations toward an international agreement against corrupt foreign payments. S. 708, §9, Cong. Rec. S13,985 (daily ed. Nov. 23, 1981).

45. See Letter from Elliot Richardson (then Secretary of Commerce and Task Force Chairman) to Senator W. Proxmire (June ll, 1976), reprinted in *Prohibiting Bribes To Foreign Officials: Hearing on S. 3133, S. 3379 and S. 3418 Before the Senate Comm. on Banking, Housing and Urban Affairs*, 94th Cong., 2d Sess. 39, 61–66 (1976).

FOUR

The OECD Declaration on International Investment and Multinational Enterprises

PHILIPPE LÉVY

The system of law lingers behind society in its progress and delays to translate newly formed social relations into enforceable rights and obligations until (in many cases) long after they have been fully formed.

John P. David

1. Background

Private foreign direct investment has been, until recently, the stepchild of intergovernmental economic cooperation. Since the abortive attempt of the Havana Charter in 1948, which contained a chapter on international investment, only isolated and limited efforts have been made to establish international rules on governmental policies with respect to foreign investment.

Soon after the Second World War, the countries of Western Europe created an organization to deal with almost every field of international economic activity—the Organization for European Economic Cooperation, which became in 1960 the Organization for Economic Cooperation and Development (OECD) and today has twenty-four member states including the United States. At its creation, this organization was limited, in the field of direct investment, to the liberalization of entry. All member states of the organization (with the notable exception of Canada) have adhered to the Code of Liberalization of Capital Move-

Philippe Lévy is Ambassador, Federal Office for Foreign Economic Affairs of Switzerland. My colleagues Dr. H. Gattiker, A. Matteucci, and H.-U. Mazenauer made many valuable suggestions on this chapter. I am thankful for their time and efforts.

ments adopted by the OECD Council on December 12, 1961. The Code is a *legally binding* commitment to liberalize, *inter alia*, the entry of direct investment; it covers, however, only transactions and transfers between residents and non-residents and not the activities of the investor after the establishment of operations.[1] Although a specific committee of the organization regularly discusses problems connected with the code, and although some minor further liberalizing steps were taken, international investment was simply not in the forefront of OECD activities throughout the 1960's with the notable exception of a draft Convention on the Protection of Foreign Property (1967).

The growing concern of some governments with the phenomenon of multinational enterprises constituted the starting point, after 1970, for renewed international efforts to regulate direct investment activities. The Executive Committee in Special Session (ECSS) of the OECD, consisting of high officials responsible for foreign economic affairs, began consideration of multinational enterprise issues early in 1973. In so doing, it followed the recommendations addressed to the OECD by the "Rey Group," a body of twelve high-ranking persons that had been asked to analyze trade and related problems in a longer-term perspective.[2]

Two opposite tendencies quickly emerged within both the Rey Group and the ECSS. While some favored an instrument regulating, to the extent possible, the activities of multinational enterprises in a binding way, others wanted to seize the opportunity and further the liberalization and protection of foreign direct investment. In fact, the two subjects constitute two sides of the same coin: the first deals with the behavior of foreign investors, the other with their treatment by governments. Hence, OECD governments agreed from the outset that a new international instrument would cover both.

After lengthy negotiations, the governments of OECD member countries adopted, on 21st June, 1976, the *Declaration on International Investment and Multinational Enterprises*.[3] At the same time, the OECD Council took three Decisions relating to it.

The Declaration consists of a preamble and five substantive parts:

   I. Guidelines for Multinational Enterprises;
  II. National Treatment;
 III. International Investment Incentives and Disincentives;
 IV. Consultation Procedures;
  V. Review.

The three decisions of the council relate to inter governmental consultation in fields I, II, and III.[4]

The Committee on International Investment and Multinational Enterprises (CIME) was formed to carry out the tasks assigned by the Declaration (namely Consultations and Reviews) and by the three Decisions (Resolution of the Council of 28th November 1979). The CIME has two main subsidiary bodies: a Working Group on the Guidelines and a Working Group on International Investment Policies.

Before describing the substance of the Declaration and the way it is interpreted and implemented, it is necessary to discuss briefly its legal character.

The Declaration is couched in the form of a declaration by the governments of OECD member countries. According to the OECD Convention, the Council acts in the form of Decisions and Recommendations.

Decisions of the organization are, except as otherwise provided, binding on all the members (OECD Convention, Art. 5a). But they are binding on any member only after it has complied "with the requirements of its own constitutional procedures" (Art. 6.3).[5] Decisions are normally taken by the Council by mutual agreement of all the members (Art. 6.1). A member may, however, abstain from voting on a decision; such abstention does not invalidate the decision, which is then applicable to the other members but not to the abstaining member (Art. 6.2, for example, Canada did not adhere to the OECD Code of Liberalization of Capital Movements).

According to Article 5(b) of the convention, the OECD may make *Recommendations*—RSP—to members. They "shall be submitted to the members for consideration in order that they may, if they consider it opportune, provide for their implementation" (Rules of Procedure of the Organization, Rule 19b). Thus, although members are to give consideration to a recommendation, they are not bound to implement it. The procedure for the adoption of recommendations is identical to the one for decisions.

As the OECD Convention does not contain any provision on "*Declarations*," the Declaration of 21st June, 1976 is not an "Act of the Organization." Like other OECD Declarations (of which a small number have been adopted since 1961), it has not been made by the Council, but rather by the individual member governments acting in concert. Its legal character is thus determined by its wording and form, which give the measure of the extent to which the subscribing governments are expected to live up to such a declaration or to ensure that other addressees within their jurisdiction comply with them.

The first element of the Declaration of 21st June the "Guidelines for Multinational Enterprises" is embodied in a "joint recommendation" addressed by the governments of OECD member countries to multinational enterprises "operating in their territories." There were good reasons for this formation: binding rules would have to take the form of a Decision by the council, which would then be either self-executing or would have to be incorporated into the national law of each subscribing country. In the light of the complexity and variety of the subjects covered by the Guidelines, this was deemed to be neither feasible nor desirable.

As a political consequence, those parts of the 1976 Declaration which could have taken the form of a legally binding instrument (following thereby the example of the OECD Codes of Liberalization), namely those dealing with governmental policies and activities, took the same legal form as the Guidelines. Although not a Recommendation of the Council, parts II and III of the Declaration nevertheless constitute a significant moral obligation with a novel legal character. Some of the difficulties encountered since 1976 in the interpretation and implementation of the provisions on "National Treatment" and "International Investment Incentives and Disincentives" are due to their unusual legal nature.[6]

Some lawyers have raised the question whether the Guidelines might not, in the course of time and after having been widely applied, pass into the general corpus of customary international law. By virtue of the Guidelines, multinational companies would then become—in this respect at least—subjects of international law. Persons, whether physical or legal, are traditionally not subjects of international law. Nevertheless, the 1976 Declaration, having been adopted by twenty-four governments, including the most important home and host countries for foreign investment, carries considerable political clout and might eventually acquire a normative character for enterprises. Sten Niklasson, the Chairman of the former Intergovernmental Working Group on a Code of Conduct of the U.N. Commission on Transnational Corporations, has expressed the view that "although traditionally only states are subject to international law, the part of the [U.N.] code regarding the activities of TNCs can be seen as a pioneer effort to set international standards directly applicable to TNCs, wherever they operate. This might become an embryo to a new part of international law, to which internationally operating enterprises are subject."[7]

At this stage, however, OECD governments are far from endorsing the Niklasson approach. In their first report on the Declaration, they have expressed the common view that the role of the Guidelines "is to introduce, where relevant, supplementary standards of behavior of a non-legal character, in particular with respect to the international scope of operation of these enterprises."[8]

2. Guidelines for Multinational Enterprises

In drafting rules of behavior for multinational enterprises in 1974/1976, OECD governments faced two major difficulties. For one, they were entering unknown territory: No other intergovernmental body had yet attempted to establish such rules. Furthermore, they held widely diverging views as to the role of foreign investment in a national economy. Hammered out in lengthy negotiations, the Guidelines reflect these difficulties. Large parts are couched in very general terms.

The Guidelines consist of: (i) eleven introductory paragraphs that explain the role of multinational enterprises in the economic life, the objectives of OECD activities in this field, the legal nature of the Guidelines and their addressees; (ii) a brief preamble; and (iii) seven substantive chapters: General Policies; Disclosure of Information; Competition; Financing; Taxation; Employment and Industrial Relations; and Science and Technology.

It was partly because of the innovative nature and the broad terms of the Guidelines that a review of the entire Declaration "within three years" was decided upon in 1976. A widely felt need to redraft the Guidelines or add extensive clarifications could not be ruled out. In fact, OECD governments concluded in 1979 that the further promotion of the Guidelines "would be best served by providing enterprises with a stable framework" (Review Report, para. 7) and made only one change to the Guidelines so as to cover an issue that had simply been forgotten in the drafting process.[9]

Nevertheless, as the 1979 Review Report states "experience at the national and international levels has revealed the existence of areas of uncertainty as to the meaning of certain provisions of the Guidelines which is due in part to the general wording utilized. After considering these areas of uncertainty, the Committee [CIME] has decided it would be useful to seek to develop explanatory comments in response to some of the questions which have been raised" (Review Report, para. 26).

Most of the explanatory comments originated with the Trade Union Advisory Committee to OECD (TUAC), which since 1977 has presented some twenty-five "cases," mainly as "illustrations" of problems created by the activities of foreign controlled enterprises, and has asked for clarification of the precise scope and intent of some of the provisions of the Guidelines. In a few instances, Governments have requested "an exchange of views on matters related to the Guidelines and the experience gained in their application."[10]

The Business and Industry Advisory Committee to OECD (BIAC) requested elaboration of definitions of the various elements contained in the chapter on Disclosure of Information. A special group of accounting experts of OECD governments has undertaken this task, the results of which have been published ("Clarification of the Accounting Terms in the OECD Guidelines," OECD, 1983).

The interpretation procedure based on "illustrative cases" broadly speaking works in the following manner: "Cases" are usually submitted either during the formal consultations which are held annually at the

level of CIME or during informal consultations which take place annually between the Working Group on the Guidelines and BIAC and
TUAC. The Working Group does not delve into the facts of actual cases
that may underlie the illustrative case, since the CIME is not allowed "to
reach conclusions on the conduct of individual enterprises" (Decision,
para. 4). Instead, the Working Group analyzes the problems raised as an
indication of possible difficulties of interpreting the Guidelines. Usually,
the result of this exercise takes the form of a note, which after approval
by CIME, is handed over to the two Advisory Committees, which may
later present further comments, in writing or orally. These "clarifications" are later published in the periodical reports. The first report was
the "Review of the 1976 Declaration and Decisions" published in 1979;
the second report is the "Mid-Term Report" made public in mid-1982.
While these contributions by CIME do not modify the Guidelines, they
explain their meaning and provide guidance for their application.
Agreed to by the twenty-four member states, they undoubtedly carry a
considerable weight.

The Guidelines chapter on Employment and Industrial Relations has
so far received the most attention from CIME and its Working Group.
This is not surprising in view of the very active involvement of trade unions, the growing industrial adjustment difficulties encountered by
OECD nations, and the large differences between the approaches of
individual OECD governments in the social policy field.

After 1977, a question arose as to the relationship between the OECD
Guidelines and the ILO Tripartite Declaration of Principles. Pointing to
differences in both geographical scope and material coverage, the 1979
OECD Review Report stated:

> "Wherever [the ILO] principles refer to the behavior expected from enter-
> prises, they parallel the OECD Guidelines and do not conflict with them.
> They can, therefore, be of use in relation to the OECD Guidelines to the
> extent they are of a greater degree of elaboration. It must, however, be
> borne in mind that the responsibilities for the follow-up procedures of the
> OECD Guidelines and of the ILO Declaration are institutionally sepa-
> rate."[11]

At the end of 1980, a similar question arose with respect to the Set of
Multilateral Agreed Equitable Principles and Rules for the Control of
Restrictive Business Practices adopted by the United Nations General
Assembly. The next ordinary Review Report, to be issued in 1984, might
clarify the relationship between the Guidelines and the Restrictive Busi-
ness Practices Code.

Neither the lengthy debates within CIME and its Working Group
(with or without BIAC and TUAC) nor the occasionally vague character
of "clarifications" should lead to the conclusion that the addressees of

the Guidelines, namely the multinational enterprises and, in some circumstances, domestic enterprises,[12] deliberately ignore the Guidelines or encounter major difficulties in their application. This is not so. To my knowledge, only one enterprise has informed the authorities of its home country that it refuses to accept and apply the Guidelines. It is my feeling that the overwhelming majority of enterprises with important international activities in the OECD area act in general accordance with the Guidelines. A notable exception to this statement (at least outside the United States) is the chapter on Disclosure of Information. But it must be added that progress in disclosure can be measured rather easily by just reading annual reports of companies.

A great deal of promotional activity has been undertaken, especially since 1979, by governments, BIAC,[13] TUAC and national economic associations to make the Guidelines known and to persuade enterprises to express their support. Only a comparatively small number of enterprises, however, has complied so far with the recommendation contained in the 1979 Report that enterprises concerned state publicly their acceptance of the Guidelines, preferably in their annual reports. The reasons for the somehow unexpected reluctance of many multinational enterprises, in particular those in the service sector and the smaller or medium size firms, are diverse. Some of the provisions of the Guidelines are not fully applicable to particular sectors (e.g., banks, insurance companies); top managers of smaller or medium size companies feel that their firm does not belong in the category of multinational enterprises; many corporate lawyers just feel uncomfortable with this unusual "legal animal." Some firms point to a lack of precision in the Guidelines, even though this feature should constitute an advantage for the companies, for it affords a certain leeway in interpretation. Many firms share a nagging fear that a public expression of support would give the Guidelines a binding character as applied to their enterprise, even though this interpretation has no basis in the Guidelines themselves or in the reports and publications which have been authorized by the OECD Council.

Finally, attention must be drawn to two further elements in the Decision of the Council on intergovernmental consultation procedures concerning the Guidelines. The first is paragraph 5 which offers member countries the opportunity to request that consultations be held in the Committee "on any problem arising from the fact that multinational enterprises are made subject to conflicting requirements." This procedure is different from the one dealt with in paragraph 1 which provides for an exchange of views "on matters related to the Guidelines and the experience gained in their application as well as for clarifications of the Guidelines." So far there has been no formal recourse to paragraph 5. Despite the pipeline sanctions, antitrust blocking statutes, and other well-publicized conflicts, the absence of recourse to paragraph 5 would seem to contradict the conventional view that multinational enterprises face a barrage of conflicting requirements imposed by two or more governments. Such problems are, however, frequently discussed bilaterally.

The second element relates to paragraph 3 which gives an individual enterprise, if it so wishes, "the opportunity to express its views either orally or in writing on issues concerning the Guidelines involving its interests." It is known that some enterprises mentioned in the "illustrative cases" presented by governments or by TUAC considered using this opportunity. In practice, only one or two corporations have expressed themselves in writing. Their letters were circulated among the members of the Working Group on the Guidelines and were used as a contribution to the clarification work.

3. National Treatment

OECD Governments encountered unexpected difficulties in the application and interpretation of the "National Treatment" part of the 1976 Declaration and the relevant Decision. The national treatment provisions were established for the protection of business firms, but business showed itself hesitant to use them. BIAC submitted its first substantial paper on the subject five years after the launching of the Declaration. [14] This delay was rather unexpected. Unlike rules of behavior for enterprises, national treatment is not a new topic of international economic cooperation. For example, most bilateral investment protection agreements between OECD countries and developing countries contain a national treatment article.[15]

The most relevant provision of the Declaration reads as follows: "Member countries should, consistent with their needs to maintain public order, to protect their essential security interests and to fulfill commitments relating to international peace and security, accord to enterprises operating in their territories and owned or controlled directly or indirectly by nationals of another Member country (hereinafter referred to as 'Foreign Controlled Enterprises') treatment under their laws, regulations and administrative practices, consistent with international law and no less favorable than that accorded in like situations to domestic enterprises (hereinafter referred to as 'National Treatment')."

Three features are worth noting:

   (a) Reasons for exceptions to the rule are contained in the Declaration itself (public order, essential security interests, commitments relating to international peace and security);

(b) Exceptions other than those mentioned under (a) are to be notified (Decision of the Council on National Treatment, para. 1 and 2);

(c) International law is referred to as a separate rule, additional to "National Treatment." [16]

The question of what was meant by "National Treatment" was of immediate importance since member governments were legally bound to notify the organization, within sixty days after 21st June 1976, of all existing measures constituting exceptions to it, "including measures restricting new investment by 'Foreign-Controlled Enterprises' already established in their territory." The Working Group on International Investment Policies "reviewed" the notifications and undertook a first comprehensive overview on the different categories of exceptions. The notifications, together with a summary in the form of synoptic tables, were published by the OECD in 1978.[17] The publication stresses its interim character "as there were remaining gaps in the information available to the Organization, unsettled issues as to whether certain measures are within the scope of the national treatment instrument, and differences in the degree of specificity of the notifications of the various Member countries."[18]

This first analysis already contains some indication of the difficulties involved when interpreting "National Treatment" in the sense of the 1976 Declaration. Not surprisingly the area of "administrative practices" was discovered to be of particular importance, but an area where transparency is inherently difficult. The 1978 publication expresses the view: "It is believed that discrimination through seemingly arbitrary decisions or prolonged delays is often more burdensome to the foreign-controlled enterprises than restrictive laws or regulations which are known and predictable" (para. 7). This opinion was shared by BIAC in its 1980 submission (para. 42).

Since 1978, the Working Group has made considerable progress in increasing the transparency of policies and practices relevant to "National Treatment" and in clarifying the coverage of the instrument. Internal reports were produced on: Government aids and subsidies; measures related to the maintenance of public order and essential security interests; fiscal measures; Government purchasing and public contracts; investment by established enterprises; and access to local financing.[19]

In reviewing the work program for the period leading to the 1984 Review, the CIME instructed the Working Group in December 1981 to make further efforts towards transparency and clarification, to assess the relative importance of the different categories of exceptions to "National Treatment," to define ways and means to extend the application of "National Treatment," and to update the 1978 publication. The CIME underlined—and this is of particular importance—that the ultimate objective of the instrument is to extend the actual application of "National Treatment" in OECD member countries.

One problem discussed at length in the 1979 Review Report and treated anew afterwards in the Working Group is the relationship between the "National Treatment" instrument and the Code of Liberalization of Capital Movements. According to the 1979 Report, these are "complementary instruments with respect to the treatment of international investment" (para. 90). They are complementary aspects of OECD's generally liberal approach toward international investment. The two instruments cover two distinct aspects of investment activities: the Code refers to transactions and transfers between residents and non-residents, including transactions preliminary to establishing a new enterprise, whereas the "National Treatment" chapter of the 1976 Declaration deals with the treatment of a foreign-controlled enterprise *after* establishment. The 1976 Declaration underlines the difference by specifying that it "does not deal with the right of Member countries to regulate the entry of foreign investment or the conditions of establishment of foreign enterprises" (Part II, para. 4). Recently, the OECD Committee on Capital Movements and Invisible Transactions devoted considerable time to the question of the application of the Code of Liberalization of Capital Movements to inward direct investment.

It was not before 1981 that member governments made use of paragraph 6 of the Decision of the Council on National Treatment. This provision says that the CIME "shall act as a forum for consultations, at the request of a Member country, in respect of any matter related to this instrument and its implementation, including exceptions to 'National Treatment' and their application." In 1981, a number of governments requested consultations on the new National Energy Plan of Canada.[20] These consultations appear to have had a very limited impact.

When the Decision of the Council was revised in 1979 a further paragraph was added in order to provide specifically for exchanges of views with BIAC and TUAC. Periodic use of this provision has since been made and it has helped to overcome the reluctance of business circles to use the "National Treatment" instrument in pursuit of their own interests.

4. International Investment Incentives and Disincentives

Just as with the Guidelines for multinational enterprises, OECD governments entered unknown territory with Part III of the 1976 Declaration dealing with international investment incentives and disincentives. The negotiations on the three relevant paragraphs were difficult; their significance is somehow vague. They read as follows:

1. that they recognize the need to strengthen their co-operation in the field of international direct investment;
2. that they thus recognize the need to give due weight to the interests of Member countries affected by specific laws, regulations and administrative practices in this field (hereinafter called measures) providing official incentives and disincentives to international direct investment;
3. that Member countries will endeavor to make such measures as transparent as possible, so that their importance and purpose can be ascertained and that information on them can be readily available."

The relevant Decision of the Council establishes a consultation mechanism open to a member country:

which considers that its interests may be adversely affected by the impact on its flow of international direct investments of measures taken by another Member country specifically designed to provide incentives or disincentives for international direct investment. Having full regard to the national economic objectives of the measure and without prejudice to policies designed to redress regional imbalances, the purpose of the consultations will be to examine the possibility of reducing such effects to a minimum.

At first, OECD governments were rather reluctant to approach the subject of incentives and disincentives. As stated in the 1979 Review Report, no major effort was undertaken in the first three years of its existence nor did a member country avail itself of the consultation mechanism.

The Review Report, however, expressed the urgent need for more transparency. Consequently, the CIME instructed the Working Group on International Investment Policies in November 1979 to undertake a medium-term work program of an analytical nature concentrating on those types of investment incentives and disincentives measures which appeared to be most relevant to the international investment process. A fairly extensive Survey Report constitutes the result of this work. It was published by OECD in 1982.[21]

The 1976 Declaration does not define an "incentive" or a "disincentive." Hence, the Working Group had first to solve the rather difficult issue of definition. For the purpose of the survey, the following definition was chosen: "An incentive (or disincentive) will be understood as any Government measure designed to influence an investment decision by increasing (or reducing) the profit accruing to it." The Survey Report adds that this definition includes measures which may lead a potential investor to modify a project even if these measures do not influence directly the profitability of the project as long as they affect the risk involved.

The Survey Report found a wide variety of instruments used by member countries. The report classifies them as fiscal, financial and non-financial incentives. In addition, distinctions were made between automatic and discretionary measures, between measures applying to all enterprises and applying only to certain enterprises, between temporary and permanent measures, and between measures of immediate impact and those which become effective only in the course of operations.

The Working Group on International Investment Policies went further than just compiling and classifying notifications. It also carried out a study on the effects of investment incentives and disincentives on the international investment process. The task was not easy given the diversity of situations in which enterprises find themselves and the range of motivations affecting investment decisions at the international level. The study observes that the vast majority of incentive programs are not specifically aimed at attracting foreign investment but rather apply to foreign and domestic investors alike. The study comes to the conclusion that there is a growing risk of increased competition in the use of investment incentives by Governments at all levels. Therefore, stress is laid on the need for closer cooperation in this area to avoid harmful effects on other countries. "Investment incentives, and in particular tax incentives offered by the country concerned, seem to influence investment decisions through their effect on the relative price variables or cash flow variables." Compared to expected market growth, investment incentives have a rather limited direct impact. On the other hand, they can affect the timing of the investment expenditure without exerting a lasting impact on the level of capital stock. Finally, they have an influence on the geographical distribution of investments, specifically in a regional context.

As far as disincentives are concerned, including preconditions or "performance requirements," the Working Group concluded that they may influence international investment decisions even in circumstances where incentives play a minor role. This view was shared by BIAC: "Business persons respond more strongly to disincentives than incentives, for while the latter may be temporary, the former may signal serious, long term obstacles to investment."

In this field, BIAC's contribution, based as it was on practical experience, was particularly valuable. An amendment was introduced in 1979 in the Decision of the Council on international investment incentives and disincentives inviting BIAC and TUAC periodically to express views on matters relating to international investment incentives and disincentives (para. 3 of the Revised Decision). Taking advantage of this new opportunity, BIAC in 1981 submitted to the CIME the study "Relationship of Incentives and Disincentives to International Investment Decisions."

Work on investment incentives and disincentives will be pursued. The CIME has told the Working Group to give high priority both to the issue of further efforts towards increased transparency and exchange of information and to the issue of trade-related incentives and disincentives (including those in developing countries). Further work is also needed to identify characteristics of firms that make their decisions concerning the location of international investment relatively more sensitive to investment incentives and disincentives.

Just as in the field of "National Treatment," there is common ground between the incentives/disincentives part of the 1976 Declaration and the Code of Liberalization of Capital Movements. The CIME excluded from its Survey Report those disincentives that result from restrictions on inward direct investment, including preconditions or "performance requirements" linked to authorization for inward direct investment. These matters pertain to the Code and hence come under the surveillance of the Committee on Capital Movements and Invisible Transactions. The same assignment of roles also applies to disincentives resulting from restrictions on outward direct investment, including preconditions or "performance requirements" linked to the authorization for outward investment. Some overlapping may also exist with GATT and notably with its Code on Subsidies and Countervailing Measures. The forthcoming OECD work on trade-related aspects of investment incentives and disincentives may throw more light on these jurisdictional matters.

5. Conclusions

As Marina von N. Whitman has pointed out, governments are creators of market imperfections and thus a factor in determining patterns of direct international investment.[22]

The interdependence of nations, in particular within the OECD area, is growing. It is therefore not surprising that some additional rules of "recommended behavior" for governments are felt necessary in order to avoid undue harm to the interests of other countries. It is no coincidence that this happened at a time of low investment, reflecting weak economic growth in the OECD area, persistent excess capacity in many sectors, and growing unemployment. Simultaneously, a need was felt to give more certainty and assurance to foreign direct investors regarding their behavior, their rights and their duties. These concerns led to the establishment of the 1976 OECD Declaration on International Investment and Multinational Enterprises, as well as to work undertaken in other forum, like the United Nations and the Development Committee of the World Bank and the IMF.

Six years after the launching, it might not be premature to compare the practical results achieved with the goals of the 1976 Declaration as expressed in its preamble, which reads:

— that international investment has assumed increased importance in the world economy and has considerably contributed to the development of their countries;

— that multinational enterprises play an important role in this investment process;

— that co-operation by Member countries can improve the foreign investment climate, encourage the positive contribution which multinational enterprises can make to economic and social progress, and minimize and resolve difficulties which may arise from their various operations;

— that, while continuing endeavours within the OECD may lead to further international arrangements and agreements in this field, it seems appropriate at this stage to intensify their co-operation and consultation on issues relating to international investment and multinational enterprises through interrelated instruments each of which deals with a different aspect of the matter and together constitute a framework within which the OECD will consider these issues.

The following conclusions might be drawn from the comparison between aspirations and events:

1. Domestic investment growth has decelerated in the OECD area during the period under consideration, but international direct investment has remained more buoyant. [23]

2. Multinational enterprises may well play an even more important role in the economies of OECD countries, and their number may have increased and more smaller and medium-sized enterprises have acquired multinational status.

3. While explicit commitment to the Guidelines remains somewhat limited, an increasing number of multinational enterprises have taken note of the Guidelines as an indication of what behavior governments recommend to them. The firms seem to appreciate these rules of conduct as a contribution to more stability and security and therefore to an improved foreign investment climate.

4. Acting as a "reflected image," work undertaken under the two parts of the Declaration addressed to governments has had a similar effect by improving the clarity of governmental policies and practices for foreign investors and putting governments under international scrutiny in the field of investment policies.

Some observers feel (or felt before 1976) that voluntary international instruments are a recipe for inaction. To the contrary: A large amount of work was carried out by governments at home and within the OECD; new work programs were agreed upon; private organizations undertook efforts at the national and international levels. As a result, both governments and enterprises today are under pressure to act in a way which takes due account of the interests of the other economic partners, namely governments, competitors, labor and the public in general.

There is still no "GATT for Investment." There is no more assurance about its possible creation today than at the time when the idea was launched.[24] For quite some time, "hard law" in this important economic field will be almost nonexistent. The work undertaken within OECD, as well as in other forums, does however lead to some sort of internationally agreed standards of a "soft law" type. Their value should not be underestimated, as they influence both the conduct of international investors and their treatment by governments. These internationally agreed rules of conduct and treatment inevitably have a harmonizing effect on laws, regulations and practices of governments, although the process may be slower than hoped. Those who expected that national laws would be progressively amended in order to incorporate some or all of the provisions of the OECD Guidelines may have to wait many years. There are indications, however, that, when drafting or amending legislation in the fields covered by the OECD Declaration, OECD governments and the European Communities at least examine the possibility of taking its provisions into account.

The relationship between the 1976 Declaration and international law is subtle. Wishful thinking should not obscure the issues. The Declaration has been approved by twenty-four governments representing not only the most important countries of origin but also of destination of international direct investment. It is applied there. It can thus be considered as a common definition of the way these governments want foreign investors to be treated and to behave. This expression of will has a spreading effect. But it is quite clear that this is a slow ongoing evolutionary process. Further efforts will be needed to ensure the fullest possible application of the principles underlying the OECD Declaration of 1976.

Notes

1. For further details *see* OECD, *Controls and Impediments Affecting Inward Direct Investment in OECD Member Countries*, Paris 1982.

2. OECD, *Policy Perspectives for International Trade and Economic Relations*, Paris 1972, para. 194–201.

3. Revised edition published in 1979 by the Organization for Economic Cooperation and Development, Paris.

4. On 13th June, 1979, an addition was introduced in the Guidelines and the three Decisions were revised.

5. According to Rudolf L. Bindschedler, this provision was introduced because of the United States, but has only been used once. *See* Bindschedler, "Rechtsakte der internationalen Organisationen," in *Berner Festgabe zum Schweizerischen Juristentag 1979*, Berne 1979, pp. 371–372.

6. The OECD Guidelines on the Protection of Privacy and Transborder Flows of Personal Data were issued as a normal Recommendation of the Council on 23rd September, 1980.

7. Statement made on 2nd September, 1981, in Geneva at the 7th session of the Commission. The phrase "Transnational corporations" is UN terminology for multinational enterprises.

8. OECD, *International Investment and Multinational Enterprise: Review of the 1976 Declaration and Decisions*, Paris 1979, para. 38. (hereafter *Review Report*).

9. This issue had already been included in para. 57 of the Tripartite Declaration of Principles concerning Multinational Enterprises and Social Policy adopted by the Governing Body of the International Labour Office on 16th November, 1977. It deals with the transfer of employees from the enterprises' component entities in other countries in order to influence unfairly negotiations with representatives of employees or to hinder the exercise of a right to organize.

10. Decision of the Council on intergovernmental consultation procedures on the Guidelines for multinational enterprises, adopted on 13th June, 1979, para. 1.

11. *Review Report*, para. 30.

12. According to para. 9 of the introduction to the Guidelines.

13. BIAC, *A Report for Business on the OECD Guidelines for Multinational Enterprises*, (Paris 1980). The 1982 Mid-Term Report contains some information on promotional activities.

14. BIAC Committee on International Investment and Multinational Enterprises, National Treatment: A Major International Investment Issue of the 1980s. Paris 1982.

15. See, for example: Agreement between Switzerland and Malaysia concerning the promotion and reciprocal protection of investments of lst March 1978, Art. 3.2: "Each Contracting Party shall in particular ensure fair and equitable treatment within its territory to the investment of the nationals or companies of the other Contracting Party; *this treatment shall be no less favorable to that granted by the Party to its own nationals or companies* or to the treatment granted to nationals or companies of the most favored nation". (Emphasis supplied)

16. On "National Treatment" under general international law, see: Heinrich Gattiker, "Behandlung und Rolle von Auslandsinvestitionen im modernen Völkerrecht: Eine Standortbestimmung," in *Schweizerisches Jahrbuch für internationales Recht*, Zürich 1981, p. 25.

17. OECD, National Treatment for Foreign-Controlled Enterprises Established in OECD Countries, Paris 1978.

18. *Ibid.*, para. 5.

19. *See* "Mid-Term Report," Chapter II.

20. For further details see "Mid-Term Report," para. 41.

21. OECD, *Investment Incentives and Disincentives and the International Investment Process*, Paris.

22. Marina von N. Whitman, *International Trade and Investment: Two Perspectives. Essays in International Finance, No. 145*, Princeton University, July 1981, p. 6.

23. For more details, see OECD, *International Investment and Multinational Enterprises, Recent International Direct Investment Trends*, Paris 1981.

24. P.M. Goldberg and Ch. P. Kindleberger, "Toward a GATT for Investment: A Proposal for Supervision of the International Corporation," 2 *Law and Policy in International Business*, 295, 1970. See, for a differing view, S. Rubin, "Multinational Enterprise and National Sovereignty: A Skeptic's Analysis", 3 *Law and Policy in International Business* 1, at 36 *et. seq.*, 1971.

FIVE

The MTN Subsidies Code: Agreement Without Consensus

DANIEL K. TARULLO

1. Introduction

Given the basic differences among nations over the use of subsidies to productive enterprises, it is only a slight exaggeration to say that the real accomplishment of those who negotiated the Subsidies Code[1] is simply that they reached agreement at all. The Code, one of ten concluded in 1979 under the auspices of the General Agreement on Tariffs and Trade (GATT)[2] during the "Tokyo Round" of Multilateral Trade Negotiations, elaborates upon the rather broad guidelines of the General Agreement pertaining to the use of both governmental subsidies and offsetting or "countervailing" measures. Objections to subsidies, particularly subsidies directly tied to export performance, are based both on free-market principles of opposition to any measures that distort relative costs, and on a notion of the "unfair" advantage held by the subsidized producer over its putatively efficient but unsubsidized competitors. National measures to negate the effect of subsidies usually take the form of special "countervailing duties" on imported merchandise whose production or export was subsidized in the exporting nation. Such national regulation has frequently been considered arbitrary or over-zealous, in effect a nontariff barrier in itself. For this reason both the GATT and the Subsidies Code establish standards and procedures for the imposition of countervailing measures.

Daniel K. Tarullo is Assistant Professor, Harvard Law School; and former Special Assistant to the Under Secretary of Commerce for International Trade.

A detailed analysis of the wisdom—economic and otherwise—of the various forms of subsidization and national measures to combat them is beyond the scope of this chapter. The literature on this subject is extensive and growing.[3] However, an awareness of the reasons for disagreement over the propriety of governmental subsidies is essential to an understanding of the Code and its prospects for successful implementation.

In one important respect, the absence of international consensus on the use of subsidies is nothing less than a reflection of varying views on the proper role of government in economic affairs. Representatives of most less-developed countries (LDCs) assert, for example, that governmental subsidies are proper and necessary vehicles for development. Subsidies may be used to nurture an infant industry until it can compete internationally, and thereby significantly contribute to a nation's development. Export subsidies may be used to compensate for the frequently overvalued currencies of many LDCs; often very little would be exported at all without the subsidies. The industrialized countries, on the other hand, generally renounce export subsidies as unnecessary and provocative instruments of trade expansion. Yet the governments of the industrialized world have themselves deviated from unreconstructed free-market principles to grant a range of subsidies for redistributive or other social reasons. The generally accepted notion that the twentieth century welfare state has a direct responsibility for the employment of its people has led, particularly in some Western European nations, to subsidization of industries that are chronically threatened by international competition but are also large employers. The U.S. Government's guarantee of loans to the Chrysler Corporation might suggest that an industrial state will not permit a large company to go out of business. This protection of private capital—and, to a lesser extent, jobs—represents a stunning deviation from the gospel of capitalism. Such patterns of subsidization coalesce vocal and politically powerful constituencies for their retention. When the subsidized industries export, there are often cries of protest from the importing nation's industries, which may also be relatively vulnerable to foreign competition.

Many subsidies are rationalized not as socially imperative deviations from principles of economic efficiency, but as correctives for distortions from other sources.[4] An export subsidy to compensate for an overvalued currency is one example. Another is a situation where the social benefits of an enterprise are thought to outweigh the expected benefits to the parties engaging in that enterprise. For example, the technical expertise gained by workers in a specific enterprise may spread more or less without cost to other parts of the nation's economy. Under such circumstances, it can be argued, subsidies to the enterprise make perfect economic sense. A related concept is that, where governments do intervene to support domestic production, subsidies are frequently preferable, on efficiency grounds, to tariffs or quotas.[5] Application of these principles to specific subsidy programs can be subject to considerable dispute and can appear, to competing producers in other nations, as *post hoc* rationalizations that simply mask efforts to gain competitive advantage.

A final area of conflict over the use of subsidies has developed quite recently as Japan and some Western European countries have used subsidies as part of a general industrial policy. Particularly in Japan, subsidies are granted not to troubled industries that happen to be large employers but to promising high technology industries.[6] The subsidies and other protective measures may be removed once a particular industry is internationally competitive. Some argue that these subsidies complement or accelerate the market forces that will eventually lead to expansion of these industries. Yet, competitors in other nations feel disadvantaged. Charges of "unfairness" are levelled, and calls for protection from these illicit competitive practices may follow.

There is both breadth and depth to the conceptual disagreements just recounted, both among and within countries.[7] These disagreements have sharpened in the decades since the GATT was established, as most governments—including that of the United States—have intervened more actively in their national economies. As new forms of subsidies are used, competing industries and their government representatives in countries with relatively fewer subsidy programs urge countermeasures. The threat of countermeasures, not to mention their actual imposition, disrupts trade, creating new sources of conflict. The conflict is inflamed by an almost moral indignation on the part of each side at the position of the other.

Under these circumstances there was no chance for an international subsidies code based upon a consensus on the proper role and limitations of subsidies. The basis for agreement had to be, and was, a desire to reduce trade frictions that the conflicting national practices had created: to agree where possible to prohibit specific types of subsidies, to blunt the harsher countermeasures of the United States in particular, and to develop a more effective forum for discussion and resolution of inevitable disputes. The aim, in short, was to dull the edges of the underlying conceptual conflict. Even so, the negotiations were difficult and almost abandoned.

As finally drafted, the Subsidies Code embodies elements of conflicting positions on the use of subsidies. Barely three years after the Code was signed, unresolved issues have emerged from the Code's ambiguities as concrete trade disputes. Recourse to the rules of the Code in such circumstances is fruitless. What remains to be answered is whether even a highly competent effort to work out problems on an *ad hoc* basis will be enough to contain conflicts related to the use of subsidies.

2. Subsidies Regulation Before the Tokyo Round

The Tokyo Round negotiations on a subsidies code were significantly circumscribed by pre-existing international rules. This circumstance affected the negotiations and final product in both favorable and unfavorable ways. The GATT rules on subsidies and countervailing measures, while relatively sparse in themselves, carried nearly three decades of practice and the experience of several efforts at elaboration. To a large extent, the negotiators could build upon and refine a scheme already in place.

By the same token, the negotiators were locked into an approach to subsidies problems that had been formulated when the problems themselves were both different and less troubling. There was no chance that a wholly new approach would be accepted, even had one been proposed. As the previous section demonstrated, *any* approach will encounter the fundamental absence of consensus; yet one cannot but wonder whether a fresh start would now have a better chance for success.

(a) Development of the Pre-Code Rules[8]

The "Proposals for Consideration by an International Conference on Trade and Employment,"[9] published by the U.S. Department of State in 1945, contained the basic ideas for international subsidy rules that have since prevailed: (1) prohibition of "export subsidies" on manufactured products; (2) special and ambiguous rules for export subsidies on non-manufactured ("primary") products; and (3) guidelines for the legitimacy of "domestic" subsidies based upon eventual trade effects rather than on the nature of the subsidy itself. This amalgam is better understood in the context of stated U.S. interests at the time. First, the U.S. interest in preserving the legitimacy of its price support and export subsidy programs for agricultural products—particularly wheat and cotton—accounts for the differential treatment accorded primary products.[10] This incidental derogation from free market principles was criticized by some at the time[11] and afterwards[12] as undermining the U.S. position in arguing for other rules more consistent with market ideals. And, we shall see, the United States would eventually find itself arguing for *stronger* restraints on primary product subsidies.

The second explanatory factor is simply that "domestic" subsidies were not, and would not for two decades become, of great concern. Indeed, programs of general (i.e., non-export performance-based) aid to industry would not become the subject of a U.S. countervailing duty order until 1973 and, through the late 1960's, would not be the subject of GATT consultations. Thus, the inattention to problems raised by domestic subsidy programs is not surprising.

The international conference proposed in the State Department publication ended in 1948 with the "Havana Charter for an International Trade Organization."[13] The provisions of the charter dealing with subsidies followed the concepts laid down in the U.S. proposals.[14] A member state was required to notify the Organization of the nature and effects of any subsidy "which operates directly or indirectly to maintain or increase exports of any product from, or to reduce, or prevent an increase in, imports of any product into, its territory." Member states were also obliged to discuss the possibility of limiting any subsidization that caused another member to consider its interests seriously prejudiced. Following the U.S. suggestion, the charter prohibited export subsidies, defined as any subsidy resulting "in the sale of such product for export at a price lower than the comparable price charged for the like product to buyers in the domestic market." Articles 27 and 28 of the Charter conferred special treatment on primary product subsidies both more explicitly and more elaborately than had the U.S. proposals. A domestic price stabilization scheme for primary commodities which sometimes resulted in export prices lower than domestic prices was not to be considered a prohibited subsidy so long as the system (1) did *or might* also result in higher export prices, and (2) did not "stimulate exports unduly or otherwise seriously prejudice the interests of other Members." Further, *any* export subsidy on a primary product could be exempted from the general prohibitions if the granting member felt that its interests would otherwise be "seriously prejudiced." Unilateral suspension of the general prohibition on export subsidies was thus permitted, limited only by a vague obligation to cooperate in efforts to reach an international commodity agreement for the particular product and by the ambiguous requirement that the member not apply the subsidy "in such a way as to have the effect of maintaining or acquiring for that Member more than an equitable share of world trade in that commodity." Disagreements over what constituted an "equitable share" were to be decided by the Organization in accordance with the Charter's list of factors to be considered.

The Havana Charter, of course, never took effect.[15] Thus the only multilateral rules on subsidies were the notification and consultation requirements mentioned above, which were included in Article XVI of the 1947 General Agreement on Tariffs and Trade (GATT), originally intended only as an interim arrangement until the Havana Charter took effect. The following decade was spent devising a means to implement the rules of the Havana Charter, rather than developing or modifying the concepts behind these rules. This effort was eventually, though only partly, successful.

In 1955, the Contracting Parties to the GATT finally adopted provisions on export subsidies similar to those proposed in the Havana Charter. Paragraphs 2 to 5 and the interpretive notes were added to Article XVI of the GATT at that time. The principal obligations were contained in paragraphs 3 and 4. While the Havana Charter had prohibited all export subsidies and then made an exception for primary commodities freely available, the amended Article XVI made no pretense of a general prohibition where primary products were involved. The new paragraph 3 urged contracting parties to "seek to avoid the use of subsidies on the export of primary products." Then, acknowledging that export subsidies on primary products would be used, the drafters of these paragraphs resurrected the ambiguous formula of the Havana Charter. If a party did use an export subsidy for a primary product,

> such subsidy shall not be applied in a manner which results in that contracting party having more than an equitable share of world export trade in that product, account being taken of the share of the contracting parties in such trade in the product during a previous representative period, and any special factors which may have affected or may be affecting such trade in the product.

An interpretive note repeats the Havana Charter's exclusion of certain price stabilization schemes from the definition of "export subsidy."[16]

Paragraph 4 forbids parties from granting "either directly or indirectly any form of subsidy on the export of any product other than a primary product which subsidy results in the sale of such product for export at a price lower than the comparable price charged for the like product to buyers in the domestic market." Thus the "dual-pricing" standard of the 1945 U.S. proposals and the Havana Charter was also revived in the 1955 amendments, though it was now applicable only to non-primary products. However, the obligation not to use export subsidies did not actually take effect until late 1962 and, even then, was accepted only by seventeen industrialized countries.[17] During the seven-year interval between adoption of the language and effectiveness of the obligation, various GATT countries simply refrained from adding or increasing subsidies beyond 1955 levels through a series of "standstill" agreements.[18]

Thus stood the GATT rules on subsidies until the Tokyo Round. All GATT parties were bound to the notice and consultation requirements. Most (and, by 1969, all) parties further agreed not to grant export subsidies on primary products if the subsidies would gain for a state more than an "equitable share" of world export trade in that product. Finally, seventeen industrialized countries agreed not to grant any form of subsidy on non-primary products if the result was a lower price for export than for domestic sales. The refusal of other countries—particularly less-developed countries—to assume this obligation may be traced back to the Havana Charter negotiations, when LDC's and others dependent on primary-product exports objected to the more lenient treatment proposed for primary product subsidies.[19] Indeed, the United States and other industrial countries appear to have written the rules in their own favor by disallowing manufactured product export subsidies (likely to be granted by LDCs), but permitting some export subsidies on primary products (in which LDCs are more likely to be competitive without subsidies) and also permitting domestic subsidies (which, in the 1940's and 1950's, most importantly included farm programs).

This pattern of rules is based not so much on regulating the kinds of subsidy programs maintained by governments as on limiting demonstrable adverse effects of a government's subsidies on other nation's trade. A 1960 GATT working party on Article XVI:4 did adopt a "non-exhaustive" list of eight practices "which are considered as forms of export subsidies by a number of contracting parties."[20] Yet the Article XVI:4 requirement of a lower price for export than for home consumption prevented even this somewhat informal list from serving as a standard for proscribed practices. The rules for export subsidies on primary products and domestic subsidies are based to an even greater extent on tests of "effects" rather than "conduct." The "more than an equitable share of world export trade" standard applies to primary products.

As to domestic subsidies, there are no clearly applicable rules whatever, beyond the notice and consultation requirements of Article XVI:1, which apply to any subsidy "which operates directly *or indirectly* to increase exports."[21] Here, too, a GATT working party had tried to introduce some further discipline, in a 1955 report on trade barriers:

> So far as domestic subsidies are concerned, it was agreed that a contracting party which has negotiated a [tariff] concession under Article 11 may be assumed, for the purpose of Article XXIII [relating to "nullification or impairment" of a party's GATT benefits for which countermeasures may be authorized], to have a reasonable expectation, failing evidence to the contrary, that the value of the concession will not be nullified or impaired by the contracting party which granted the concession by the subsequent introduction or increase of a domestic subsidy on the product concerned.[22]

By the Kennedy Round of tariff reductions in the mid-1960's, almost all tariffs had been reduced at least once. Thus, on its face, this understanding might seem to limit most domestic subsidies. In practice, though, the statement seems to have had little effect, perhaps because of the problems associated with dispute settlement under Article XXIII of the

GATT. Of course, even if the statement was generally and actively accepted, it too would be a standard based on the effect of subsidies (i.e., adverse effects on parties) rather than on a prohibition of certain practices.

The heavy emphasis of Article XVI on adverse effects of subsidies on other parties suggests that the scheme for subsidies regulation would inevitably take the form of *ad hoc* discussions as problems arose. Discussions could be held in accordance with Article XVI or under the formal dispute settlement procedures of GATT. The admittedly ambiguous approach of Article XVI might have functioned better had GATT provided either prompt, respected determinations of adverse effects in specific cases or a process for proscribing altogether certain kinds of subsidies. However, the GATT of the 1960's and 1970's fulfilled neither the quasi-adjudicatory nor the quasi-legislative roles to the satisfaction of the United States and, at times, other key contracting parties.

Amending the GATT to prohibit particular forms of subsidization was all but impossible because of the extraordinary majorities required.[23] Dispute settlement was a prolonged affair that increasingly dissatisfied all parties.[24] This problem may also have had its roots in the assumption at the time GATT was drafted that it would soon be superseded by the Havana Charter, which promised a relatively well-staffed, powerful International Trade Organization. Article XXIII of the GATT provides only the vaguest outline of a dispute settlement procedure where bilateral consultations have failed. To fill the void, there developed a GATT practice of appointing a few officials from disinterested nations to hear the positions of both sides to a dispute. Yet these "panels" never seemed quite sure whether their role was to mediate, to adjudicate, or both. This confusion was perhaps grounded in Article XXIII itself, which seems to favor dispute settlement by consensus of the parties but also contemplates "rulings" by the Contracting Parties. Yet, by the terms of Article XXIII itself, a ruling on whether a nation had violated the terms of the GATT was insufficient, because the standard to be applied was whether there had been "nullification or impairment" of benefits reasonably expected by a party, regardless of whether another party had contravened a GATT provision. In any event, problems arose at each step of the way: Months or even years elapsed before a panel was constituted, the panel often vacillated between its two roles, and rulings were rarely forthcoming as disputes dragged on.

Although the inadequacy of Article XVI was not remedied through institutional management of disputes, GATT proceedings were not the only avenue open for a nation aggrieved by another's subsidies. The Havana Charter[25] and the GATT[26] each provided for the unilateral imposition of countervailing duties "for the purpose of offsetting any bounty or subsidy bestowed, directly or indirectly, upon the manufacture, production or export of any merchandise."[27] Article VI:4 forbids imposition of countervailing duties on products exempted from indirect (i.e., sales or value-added) taxes in the country of exportation. Article VI:7 provides for special rules for the primary commodity price stablization schemes mentioned earlier. Otherwise, a nation is effectively free to countervail against subsidized imports based on its own understanding of "subsidy," subject only to the Article VI:6(a) requirement that the subsidization causes or threatens to cause "material injury" to a domestic industry. Because of the odd circumstances under which the GATT was given effect, even this injury requirement did not apply to U.S. countervailing duty impositions. The GATT exempted national legislation which existed in 1947 from its requirements, and since the United States had maintained a countervailing duty law without an injury requirement since 1897, it was not required to begin one. As we shall see, this peculiarity played a major role in negotiations for the Subsidies Code.

To recapitulate briefly—the GATT subsidies and countervailing duties provisions that evolved between 1947 and 1962 provided very few prohibitions or guidelines on the "conduct" of contracting parties. Instead, they generally focused on the effects of particular national conduct (i.e., subsidy programs), quite apart from the inherent nature of the conduct itself. Thus, consultations and *ad hoc* accommodations in GATT forums were the contemplated mode of dispute resolution. At the same time, nations were permitted to take countervailing measures against imports that benefited from subsidies which were in themselves not prohibited. The scheme was never very satisfactory; events of the 1960s would render it almost unworkable.

(b) The Impetus to Negotiation

The GATT Panel on Subsidies had, as early as 1961, explained why subsidies were increasingly prominent in catalogues of world trade issues; the Panel had also hinted at some of the friction that would develop later.[28] As tariffs were lowered and the use of quantitative import restrictions reduced, other possible trade distortions such as subsidies were bound to attract more attention. The Panel found a "wide-spread" use of subsidies and concluded, rather gloomily, that Article XVI "has clearly not resulted in any general abandonment of subsidies which affect imports and exports."[29] Indeed, the Panel suggested that the number of disputes over the use of subsidies had been held down largely by the reluctance of governments granting significant subsidies to object to the subsidies granted by another government.[30]

By the end of the decade, two important and related developments had transformed a latent problem into an active one. First, the use of subsidies continued to increase. The Common Agricultural Policy of the

European Community, with its integral role for export subsidies, was substantially implemented during the 1960's.[31] It was also during the 1960's that a number of LDC's began to replace or supplement their development programs of import substitution with programs of export promotion, including subsidies.[32] These LDC subsidy programs often benefited not "primary" products, but manufactured goods. Moreover, for both social welfare and industrial policy reasons, Japan and several Western European nations were granting domestic subsidies to auto, computer, steel and other industries.[33] Thus the GATT Panel's observation in 1961 that "the great bulk of . . . subsidization measures relate to primary products"[34] was no longer valid.

The second development placing great strain on the GATT scheme for subsidies regulation was the erosion of U.S. economic hegemony and the ensuing U.S. reaction. The U.S. share of world exports, which stood at 23 per cent in the early 1950s, had declined to 20 per cent in the early 1960's and further still to 16 per cent by 1970.[35] In absolute terms U.S. exports rose through this period, but the relative decline suggested to U.S. officials that major changes had taken place in the world economy:

> It was natural and expected that our share of world trade would have declined during the fifties with the economic recovery and rapid growth in Europe and Japan. However, the continued deterioration in the U.S. trade position during the sixties is not a natural consequence of postwar recovery, but appears to be a reflection of fundamental structural changes in the U.S. and the world economies.[36]

By 1969, these economic shifts, coupled with U.S. government efforts to finance a prolonged foreign war without significant tax increases, had reduced the substantial U.S. merchandise trade and current account balances of the early 1960's to less than a billion dollars each. In the early 1970's the United States experienced its first balance of trade deficits since World War II.

One major U.S. government response to these changes was the Nixon Administration's "New Economic Policy" of 1971, which included the suspension of U.S. dollar convertibility into gold, a 10 per cent import surcharge, and domestic wage/price controls. U.S. business leaders and government officials had already concluded that foreign trade barriers and other trade distortions shared responsibility for the relative decline in U.S. export performance.[37] Subsidies (or practices understood by some to be subsidies) consequently received much attention, most of it focused on two developments in the European Economic Community (EEC)—the implementation of the Common Agricultural Policy (CAP) and the harmonization of border tax adjustment policies.

The CAP was an important source of new export subsidies in the 1960's. The CAP set EEC prices at levels high enough to assure secure supplies and adequate farm incomes. Because these prices were substantially above world prices, the EEC paid export subsidies on the inevitable surplus production. During the 1960's, the CAP grew to include grain, poultry, pork, eggs, fruits and vegetables, beef, milk, rice, fats and oils, and sugar.[38] The result was considerable U.S. concern both with domestic subsidies and protection that effectively limited imports of U.S. farm products and with the possible displacement of U.S. exports to third countries by subsidized EEC exports. U.S. exports to the EEC of products covered by CAP regulations rose only 12 per cent between 1962 and 1972, while exports of unregulated agricultural products rose 134 per cent during the same period.[39] With Great Britain, Ireland, Denmark, and Norway then looming as new entrants into the EEC and the CAP, U.S. agricultural and trade officials found still greater cause for concern.

The second major concern of U.S. officials was the EEC's harmonization of the indirect tax systems of member countries, an event which also occurred largely during the 1960's.[40] Systems of indirect taxation (i.e., taxes levied on products, such as a sales or value-added tax) are commonly based on the so-called "destination principle," whereby the tax is borne only by products sold in the taxing state. Exports are thus exempted from the tax, and imports are assessed with it. During the 1960's, the EEC member states harmonized their indirect tax systems by adopting the destination principle and moving toward common rates for a general value-added tax (VAT). In some cases—notably that of West Germany—harmonization entailed substantially higher rates. This development concerned U.S. officials and business executives, who believed that the United States was already disadvantaged by its predominant use of direct taxes (e.g., those levied on corporate profits). The U.S. exporter, so the argument went, must pay to the U.S. government tax on his profit on sales to the EEC, where his products would *then* be assessed with the EEC indirect tax. The EEC producer, on the other hand, paid little in the way of income taxes; its exports were exempted from indirect tax; and the United States levied few taxes beyond customs duties on the producer or its products. The traditional rationale that indirect taxes were fully shifted forward and paid by the consumer was unconvincing to U.S. business and increasing numbers of economists. It seemed that U.S. products effectively bore one tax at home and two in the EEC, whereas EEC products bore no tax in the United States and one at home.

In short, many in the United States believed that EEC exports were, in effect, subsidized. Yet, in theory, exchange rate adjustments would negate any advantage to EEC producers from the VAT, but in the 1960's exchange rates were still fixed on the basis of "par values." Even with the demise of the Bretton Woods regime of fixed rates in 1973, floating exchange rates were still "managed" by governments to a great degree. Many in the United States concluded that exchange rates would not quickly or perhaps ever compensate fully for the VAT. Yet Article VI:4 of the GATT expressly forbade a country from applying counter-vailing duties against products exempted from indirect taxes, and the 1960 GATT working group list of illustrative export subsidies explicitly *excluded* indirect tax exemption or rebate.

Official expressions of U.S discontent with this situation were heard repeatedly in the late 1960's and early 1970's. In announcing his 1968 program to meet U.S. balance of payment difficulties, President Johnson addressed the issue:

> American commerce is at a disadvantage because of the tax systems of some of our trading partners. Some nations give across-the-board tax rebates on exports which leave their ports and impose special border tax charges on our goods entering their country.
>
> International rules govern these special taxes under the General Agreement on Tariffs and Trade. These rules must be adjusted to expand international trade further.[41]

A year later Special Trade Representative William Roth declared that "the United States cannot continue to tolerate the trade disadvantages arising out of the GATT rules."[42] Similar complaints would reverberate for the next several years.

Thus, the business and government leaders in the United States saw a proliferation of subsidy practices at a time when the United States seemed increasingly vulnerable to international competition generally: Less-developed countries were subsidizing the export of basic manufactures in their efforts to industrialize, creating problems for industries such as the U.S. textile industry. The European Economic Community's Common Agricultural Policy denied the United States many export opportunities and even created problems for U.S producers in some domestic markets. The EEC's value-added tax system seemed to disadvantage *all* competing U.S. industries. Finally, many in the United States were troubled by the growing acceptance of state intervention in microeconomic matters in the rest of the industrialized world. Governments subsidized, or even owned, important enterprises, creating the fear in U.S. minds of a bottomless state pocket of loss-sustaining capital. Because worries over subsidies were but part of a broader concern with the nation's international economic performance, U.S. responses were appropriately broad-gauged. However, the United States did take several actions directed specifically at the subsidies problem. These actions made subsidies and countervailing measures a central subject of negotiations when the Tokyo Round began.

First, and in a quite straightforward fashion, the United States called for international discussions of the border tax adjustment issue and the spread of various subsidies, with a view toward elaborating or modifying the GATT rules. In his balance-of-payments program quoted earlier, President Johnson indicated that the United States would seek a solution to the border tax adjustment problem through international talks.[43] A GATT working party on this subject was established two months later, in March 1968. But when it issued its report in December 1970,[44] the working party showed no signs of progress. It had no substantive suggestions to offer and could not even agree to a proposal for a regular review of changes in tax adjustments by member countries.[45] A similar fate of inaction fell upon Ambassador Roth's call in 1969 for "negotiations in the GATT with the objective of strengthening the present prohibition against subsidies on industrial exports with a clear definition of industrial subsidies."[46] Finally, in 1972, a GATT working party was formed at U.S. request to study domestic subsidies that stimulate exports, to try further to define subsidies, and to consider GATT rules to cover subsidizations in third country markets.[47] This effort would be overtaken a year later by the start of the Tokyo Round.

Experience with the Common Agricultural Policy led U.S. policymakers to conclude that the "ambiguity in GATT language concerning export subsidies on primary products has come to cause special problems."[48] Ironically, of course, the United States itself was responsible for this ambiguity, as U.S. trade officials admitted.[49] The 1969 Special Trade Representative Report recognized that the United States must be prepared to change its own agricultural subsidy and quota practices, reflecting a growing sense that U.S. agriculture stood to gain more than it lost from increased GATT discipline on agricultural subsidies and protection.

By the beginning of the Tokyo Round negotiations in 1974, U.S. desires for increased discipline on subsidies had congealed into specific negotiating objectives, as listed by Congress in the Trade Act of 1974:

> the revision of GATT articles with respect to the treatment of border adjustments for internal taxes to redress the disadvantage to countries relying primarily on direct rather than indirect taxes for revenue needs, . . . any revisions necessary to define the forms of subsidy to industries producing products for export and the forms of subsidy to attract foreign investment which are consistent with an open, nondiscriminatory, and fair system of international trade.[50]

In reporting out the Trade Act, the Senate Finance Committee added that "comparable treatment should be given to primary and nonprimary products."[51]

Another U.S. response to what it saw as the proliferation of unfair subsidy practices was increased resort to its countervailing duty law. This "response" was really an aggregation of actions by three groups: Private businesses began to file more petitions asking for countervailing duties to be imposed on allegedly subsidized imports; the Executive Branch began to take quicker action on these petitions; and, in the Trade Act of 1974, Congress removed much of the administrative discretion that had previously allowed the Executive to bury disagreeable countervailing duty petitions. Coloring this development was the absence of a requirement in U.S. law that a domestic industry be injured by the subsidized imports before countervailing duties could be imposed. Thus, any imports benefiting from subsidies as defined under U.S. law (as opposed to GATT rules) were vulnerable.

From the GATT's inception in 1948 through the mid-1960s, the United States had applied countervailing duties against fewer than a dozen products. In 1968 a number of petitions were filed, including several directed against EEC agricultural products. In September of that year, U.S. Steel Corporation filed petitions against steel products from all six ECSC member states. A variety of subsidies were alleged, but one allegation attracted particular attention—that rebate of the value-added tax upon export of a product constituted a subsidy for purposes of U.S. law. Also in 1968, the United States applied a countervailing duty of 2.5 per cent on all imports from France, in response to a French decree granting export subsidies on most products to compensate for wage increases forced by the general strike earlier that year.[52] Reduction[53] and elimination[54] of the countervailing duties followed within six months, as the French reduced and then eliminated the subsidies. However, the quick and broad imposition of duties—unaccompanied by any injury test—had demonstrated the potential for trade disruption by the U.S. law.

Between 1969 and 1972 the old ways returned, and only a handful of products were subjected to countervailing duties. Yet even this period produced anxiety for U.S. trading partners when, in 1970, Zenith Radio Corporation filed a countervailing duty petition against a number of consumer electronics products from Japan. Echoing U.S. Steel's complaint, Zenith claimed that the Japanese government's remission of indirect taxes upon export of the products constituted a subsidy for purposes of U.S. law.

In early 1973, the U.S. Treasury entered a countervailing duty order against radial tires from Canada,[55] the first time that the United States had countervailed against products that had benefited only from domestic (as opposed to export) subsidies.[56] Federal, provincial, and local governments had bestowed certain grants, loans, and tax advantages on the Michelin Tire Corporation so that it would locate two plants in economically depressed Nova Scotia. One apparent factor in the Treasury decision was the large proportion (approximately 75 per cent) of the plants' production exported to the United States. Thus, the reasoning might be, the subsidies were effectively export subsidies. Still, a kind of formal barrier had been broken by the U.S. action, and Western European nations with substantial programs for developing economically depressed areas shared Canadian concerns.

The rejuvenation and growth of the U.S. countervailing duty law prodded the rest of the world to the bargaining table. Through a GATT peculiarity—the "grandfather" right to maintain all national legislation existing at the time of the Protocol of Provisional Application—the United States could "legally" act against what it considered subsidies without establishing significant adverse effects on its own industries. An attitude of free-market self-righteousness that prevailed in some quarters combined with growing insecurity over U.S. competitiveness and an unquestionable increase in world subsidy practices to produce a host of trade disputes involving U.S. countervailing measures. After the Tokyo Round negotiations began, the pressure increased. In 1976 the United States entered fifteen countervailing duty orders; in 1977, eight; and in 1978, twelve. During the negotiations duties were imposed on several EEC agricultural products: canned hams, dairy products, beef, and sugar. Nearly half of the orders during the Tokyo Round were entered against products benefiting from LDC export subsidy programs.[57] These were concentrated against a small group of LDCs, because once a program as applied to one product was proclaimed a subsidy for purposes of U.S. law, petitions against other exports of that country tended to follow. Thus a few LDCs were particularly motivated to participate in the negotiations to obtain an injury test in U.S. law. Brazil, identified by the U.S. negotiators of the Subsidies Code as principal spokesman for LDCs,[58] was also the LDC with the most countervailing duty orders entered against it during the negotiations—six.

The specter of substantial disruption in their exports to the United States doubtless induced many countries to negotiate. Yet if friction is severe enough, bad feelings may override an interest in accommodation, and negotiations may break down. The United States contained the ill-will arising from its spate of countervailing duty orders by "waiving" the duties during the duration of negotiations on a subsidy code. This option had been provided for in the Trade Act of 1974.[59] Most countervailing duty orders during this period were waived, thus avoiding inflammatory restrictions while maintaining a silent threat that the restrictions would be forthcoming if the negotiations did not reach a satisfactory conclusion.

Another potential disruption of the negotiations was avoided when the U.S. Supreme Court upheld in 1978 the Treasury Department's decision that rebates of indirect taxes were not subsidies, as Zenith had claimed.[60] A lower court had found in favor of Zenith a year earlier,[61] creating a furor that threatened to end the negotiation, since the application of U.S countervailing duties against such practices would have clearly violated the GATT Article VI:4 obligation.

A number of codes negotiated during the Tokyo Round seem informed by a belief that each country would profit if all participants reduced a certain kind of trade distortion. The Government Procurement Code, for example, rests on the willingness of many countries to alter their national procurement policies in exchange for like action by their trading partners. There was general agreement that national policies should be constrained. No such consensus attended negotiation of the Subsidies Code. As we saw, the GATT rules had never rested on such a consensus. This shortcoming was manageable for twenty years, but more recent developments and attitudes had rendered the GATT rules unsatisfactory to all. The United States complained that the rules unfairly advantaged countries with indirect tax systems and failed to contain rampant violations of market principles. Much of the rest of the world, in turn, objected that the continued absence of an injury requirement in U.S. law made the U.S. response to national subsidy programs quite reckless. Most industrialized countries found no fault in domestic subsidy programs or state ownership of productive enterprises. LDCs, joined by Australia and New Zealand, continued to find fault in the GATT differentiation between primary and non-primary commodities. They held that their export subsidies to manufactured goods were a necessary, if often temporary, aid to development that should be approved internationally. The negotiators who gathered in Geneva to work out a subsidy code could not hope to draft a set of principles for the use of subsidies to which all would agree. Instead, their task was to reach an accommodation that would prevent disagreement over these principles from creating international trade battles.

3. The Subsidies Code

The negotiators' efforts produced substantive rules and institutional procedures far more detailed than the GATT rules. Yet the conceptual disagreements on the use and propriety of subsidies that rendered the GATT rules so tentative have not been resolved. In fact, while modest agreements were reached in some areas, other Code provisions show that the disagreements are more significant than ever. The Code's extensive provisions on national countermeasures, bilateral consultations, multilateral dispute settlement, and the new Subsidies Committee suggest that the negotiators tried to contain the adverse effect of conflicting views on subsidies by ensuring procedural fairness in national countermeasures and by creating an institutional buffer to absorb the shocks from these conflicts.

(a) Countervailing Measures

The most significant change from pre-Code ways was U.S. agreement to apply an injury test before levying countervailing duties on subsidized imports. This, of course, was a principal stated negotiating objective of most U.S. trading partners. There was protracted negotiation over whether the injury must be "material" injury, and this adjective was eventually included.[62] The controversy was entirely out of proportion to the apparent importance of the issue, with roots in U.S. Congressional reaction to use of that term in the 1967 Anti-dumping Code.[63] To allay the fears of some in the United States that the required test would be stricter than that applied under U.S. antidumping law, the Code includes a lengthy provision of the standards and factors relevant for the material injury determination.[64] This provision is roughly compatible with the pre-Code practice of the United States International Trade Commission (USITC) under U.S. antidumping law. At the behest of the U.S. steel industry, U.S. negotiators added to the Code's list of factors indicating injury to a domestic industry "negative effects . . . on ability to raise capital for investment."[65] Even the USITC had not previously considered this factor in its injury determinations.

In the last stages of the negotiations, a number of countries expressed concern that the Code's injury test was too liberal, particularly in the required causal link between subsidized imports and injury to the domestic industry. At the behest of Canada, Japan, and some Nordic countries, Article 6:4 of the Code was revised to make clear that the injury must be tied to the effects of the subsidy (rather than simply to the quantity of imports). A list of other factors that could be causing injury, thereby exculpating the subsidized imports, was also added.[66]

The remaining significance of the Code provisions on countervailing measures[67] is simply their detail. National procedures for countervailing duty applications are required to be quite open, with frequent opportunity for comment by importing interests. The Code addresses such technical issues as the sufficiency of domestic complaints, investigative procedures, provisional measures, and removal of countervailing duties. Most, but not all, of these detailed requirements reflect prior U.S. practice, insofar as the United States was both the most frequent and legalistic user of countervailing duties. The overall effect is the creation of a procedure which gives at least the appearance of fairness. If the propriety of a subsidy cannot be resolved, the procedure at least channels the resulting conflict into an open forum with articulated standards for decision.

(b) Export Subsidies on Non-Primary Products

In a significant change from GATT rules, Article 9 of the Code flatly prohibits export subsidies on "non-primary" products.[68] The dual-pricing requirement of Article XVI:4 of the GATT is omitted, thereby disposing of a feature considered both economically unsound and practically difficult of proof.

In early drafts of the Code a proposed definition of export subsidy had been included, but this formulation seemed to raise more questions than it answered. Accordingly, the negotiators reverted to the 1960 Working Party list of export subsidies. With a few additions and substantial refinements based on two decades of experience, this list became Annex A of the Code, the "Illustrative List of Export Subsidies." Several items in Annex A, along with the lengthy footnote 2 to the Annex, respond to disagreements that existed when the negotiations began.

In some cases, an item on the Illustrative List reflects a genuine resolution of a disagreement. For example, item (g) specifies as an export subsidy the "exemption or remission in respect of the production and distribution of exported products, of indirect taxes in excess of those levied in respect of the production and distribution of like products when sold for domestic consumption." By implication the *non-excessive* remission of taxes such as the EEC value-added tax is not a subsidy, just as under the GATT rules. The remission of direct taxes is designated a subsidy in item (e), also a continuation of prior practice. Thus the U.S. aim of changing GATT rules on direct vs. indirect tax remissions was not achieved, largely because increased "discipline" over indirect tax systems would have forced fundamental changes in the tax systems of many countries. At last all parties agreed on the propriety of the rules.

In other cases, disagreements arising from national practices said to be subsidies were not resolved, but simply deferred to allow agreement on the rest of the Code. One striking example is the provision in item (e) on deferral of direct taxes related to export performance. The United States had granted just such a deferral in enacting the Domestic International Sales Corporation (DISC) provision of the Internal Revenue Code in 1971. The EEC had complained of this practice and eventually asked for a GATT ruling. In 1976 a GATT panel found that the DISC provision was an export subsidy within the meaning of GATT Article XVI:4.[69] This same panel also found GATT violations in certain French, Belgian, and Dutch tax practices against which the United States had, in effect, counterclaimed.[70] The GATT Council took no action on any of the panel reports.[71] The EEC, however, raised the DISC issue rather persistently during the Subsidies Code negotiations. In the end, "deferral" of indirect taxes was listed as a subsidy in item (e), but footnote 2 stated that the "signatories further recognize that nothing in this text prejudges the disposition by the Contracting Parties of the specific issues raised in GATT document L/4422" (i.e., the panel report on DISC). Thus the EEC had seemingly prevailed on principle, but the specific issue raising the principle was left untouched.

Another deferral of a troublesome issue is item (k) of the list, dealing with export credits. Government programs granting export credits at rates below the cost of the funds so used are designated as export subsidies. But the second paragraph of item (k) exempts official export credit programs that are consistent with the OECD Arrangement on Export Credits, even where these same programs do not conform to the test just recited.[72] Again, the troublesome issue of aggressive government export credit practices was deferred in the interests of agreement on a Code. As discussed in Section 4 of this chapter, both the DISC and export credit evasions have since threatened the legitimacy and viability of the Code.

A final note on the Illustrative List—item (l) embraces any "charge on the public account constituting an export subsidy in the sense of Article XVI of the General Agreement." Thus, it would appear, an export subsidy not specifically listed in the Annex will violate Article 9 of the Code only where the GATT Article XVI bi-level pricing requirement is met.

(c) Export Subsidies on Primary Products

The rules on non-primary products were much advanced by removing, in most cases, concern with bi-level pricing. The focus is now on the more readily identified nature of the practice. Disagreements may arise over whether a particular practice fits the definitions in Annex A. There may also be instances where, as a political matter, a country simply cannot discontinue a practice contained in the Illustrative List. Still, conciliation of these issues should be facilitated by the relative clarity of the rules themselves. The same cannot be said for the Code rule covering export subsidies on primary products.

Because the Common Agricultural Policy of the European Economic Community had become the greatest source of export subsidies on primary products, the United States sought to strengthen the very rules on this subject which it had created after World War II. Seeing the resolve of the EEC on this subject, U.S. negotiators dismissed from the start any prospect for a rule prohibiting subsidies on primary products. Thus, while Australia was arguing as late as February 1979 for stricter rules, the U.S. and EEC had already agreed to retain the language of GATT Article XVI:3. The Code's contribution was to elaborate upon the Article XVI:3 formula.

The most important elaboration is contained in Article 10 (2)(a) of the Code:

"more than an equitable share of world export trade" shall include any case in which the effect of an export subsidy granted by a signatory is to displace the exports of another signatory bearing in mind the developments on world markets.

According to U.S. negotiators, the standard of "displacement" was drawn directly from a 1958 panel decision concerning French export subsidies on wheat.[73] Displacement is certainly easier to evaluate than is "equitable share," though nice questions of causality are likely to be raised. Further, the "developments on world markets" language potentially opens an inquiry to every possibly relevant factor, past and present. Finally, the test is still based on effects rather than conduct. Export subsidies on primary products are themselves legitimate, so long as they do not produce certain effects—sure to be disputed.

The Article 10(3) prohibition on export subsidies resulting in sales to particular markets at "materially" lower prices than those of other suppliers is a bit closer to a rule of "conduct." Here too, though, is an ambiguity—what is "material"? Here also are questions of causality—did prices drop over time simply because of the increased supply of the product or were the lower prices set "intentionally" by the supplier? In economic terms, of course, there is little if any difference between these phenomena.

(d) Domestic Subsidies

The absence of international consensus on the proper role of government subsidization is nowhere more apparent than in the Code rules on domestic subsidies. Negotiators could not agree on prohibiting or permitting particular kinds of subsidies, even presumptively. Instead, the Code focuses entirely on avoiding "adverse effects" to the interests of other signatories. Again, this approach contemplates *ad hoc* accommodations once "adverse effects" are felt. By this time, a subsidy program is well-entrenched, perhaps even an integral part of a nation's economic policy. Changes are politically more difficult. If the program's effect on exports is part of a general effect on production, changes may not be feasible. The potential for friction between countries is obvious.

The negotiating history of the Code reveals an awareness of these problems on the part of at least some negotiators. The United States unsuccessfully attempted to proscribe certain kinds of domestic subsidies by proposing their inclusion in the Annex A Illustrative List. While the distinction between domestic and export subsidies would be maintained, certain practices commonly considered "domestic"measures would be legally denominated "export" subsidies. Thus, for example, the U.S proposed as an item for inclusion in Annex A "government procurement policies which provide an assured domestic market for producers of certain industrial products . . . thus enabling such firms to realize economies of scale and permit quotation of competitive prices in export markets." Earlier U.S. proposals had reached even further to include as possible "export" subsidies such measures as government-sponsored research and development, special depreciation allowances for plant modernization, and government sales of electricity at preferential rates.

The United States also proposed a "Supplemental Understanding" to the Code which would enumerate in considerable detail certain domestic subsidies that might cause serious prejudice to other countries' interests. By the admission of the U.S. negotiators, this proposal was intended to evolve into a standard of "acceptable or unacceptable behavior" despite its express disavowal of this function.[74] Fearing just such a result, other delegations rejected the U.S. proposal.

Another version of this approach was contained in a mid-1978 draft of the Code, which contained a second annex, this one a list of "internal subsidies." The relevant Code provisions identified these practices as possibly having adverse effects on the trade and production of other countries and directed that these effects "be taken into account by signatories in drawing up their policies and practices." While hardly ideal, this formulation would have placed planners in signatory countries on notice that certain forms of domestic subsidies were particularly likely to cause trade problems. It would, in a general way, have required these planners to modify subsidy proposals in light of international obligations and sensitivities. Of course, forecasting when and where adverse effects would occur would be a very speculative undertaking. But this approach did, at least, recognize the flaw of rules whose applicability cannot be known until they have been breached.

The final form of the draft provision just mentioned shows the inconclusiveness of the negotiations on domestic subsidies. There is no Annex B; the Code instead reads:

> [S]ignatories, when drawing up their policies and practices in this field, in addition to evaluating the essential internal objectives to be achieved, shall also weigh, as far as practicable, taking account of the nature of the particular case, possible adverse effects on trade.[75]

The number of subordinate clauses in this provision is representative of the Code's handling of domestic subsidies. Two antithetical themes run parallel throughout Articles 8 and 11:

> Signatories recognize that subsidies are used by governments to promote important objectives of social and economic policy. Signatories also recognize that subsidies may cause adverse effects to the interests of other signatories.[76]

The succeeding provisions elaborate upon each theme but never offer a resolution. Thus Article 8(4) lists ways in which subsidies may adversely affect other countries. Article ll(l) lists important social objectives served by subsidies and declares that signatories "do not intend to restrict the right . . . to use . . . subsidies to achieve these . . . objectives." Article ll(2) states that these same subsidies can harm other signatories' interests and recites the familiar undertaking of signatories to "seek to avoid causing such effects through the use of subsidies."

The Code does not specify which subsidies are more likely to serve important social objectives (and hence are legitimate) and which are more likely to adversely affect others. Of course, the underlying problem is that many subsidies have both effects. The Code negotiators could not take the next step of even presumptively legitimating or condemning certain forms of subsidies. An effects-based standard—with all its problems—was the recourse.

(e) Less Developed Countries

The kind and degree of preferential treatment for developing countries were at issue in most areas covered by the Multilateral Trade Negotiations. In the negotiations on a Subsidies Code, the earlier mentioned reliance by LDCs upon extensive subsidy programs to propel development squarely presented the issue. From the start the United States and the EEC acknowledged that some measure of special treatment for LDCs was appropriate.[77] Again, though, basic disagreement over the legitimacy of subsidies led to difficult negotiations and, eventually, ambiguous Code provisions on the subject.

The Subsidies Code provides for no special treatment where a signatory applies unilateral countervailing measures upon LDC exports. Also, Article 14(10) specifies that Code obligations pertaining to primary product export subsidies "apply to all signatories." (This requirement does not really disadvantage LDCs, because the slippery standard for primary product export subsidies has itself existed for the benefit of *developed* countries, first the U.S. and more lately the EEC.) Article 14(7) precludes signatory complaints over domestic LDC subsidies that result in increased LDC exports to third-country markets. This language creates an LDC exception to the terms of Article 8(4)(c), which states that subsidies displacing another signatory's exports to a third-country market can be considered a nullification or impairment of Code benefits and hence grounds for complaint.

The negotiating battle royal over LDC preferences was waged on the subject of obligations to limit export subsidies on non-primary products. This struggle underscores the differences that prevailed—and prevail still—over the permissible role of subsidies in development efforts. The first formulation of special rules for LDCs appeared in a mid-1978 draft of the Code, which provided only a possibility of agreement (presumably by the Code Committee) to individual LDC deviations from general Code rules. However, LDC representatives had played little role in the negotiation to this point. Brazil finally began serious negotiations in late 1978, after suffering five impositions of U.S. countervailing duties on its products during the Tokyo Round to that point and facing three more pending cases. To obtain an injury test Brazil was willing to talk and to try to bring other major LDCs along to the negotiating table. By December 1978, a negotiating draft included the LDC provisions earlier discussed. It also allowed LDC use of export subsidies, but stated:

> A developing country signatory should agree or commit to reduce or eliminate export subsidies when the use of such export subsidies is inconsistent with its competitive needs.

Though this formulation survived into a February 1979 draft Code, it evoked the displeasure of several large LDCs whose participation in the Code was considered key to hopes for substantial LDC accessions. In March and early April 1979, two small but significant changes were made to obtain the agreement of India and Mexico. First, the final phrase was amended to include "development" needs, thereby dissipating any notion that once an LDC product was price competitive, export subsidies would be improper. The second, and crucial, change was conversion of the export subsidy provision from a mandatory obligation to a discretionary action. Article 14(5) of the Code reads that a developing country signatory "should endeavor to enter into a commitment," thus rendering the provision essentially hortatory.

Though the United States had agreed to these changes to obtain accession by India and Mexico (which, in the event, came late and never, respectively), it was not prepared to abandon its position that LDCs should "graduate" to full Code obligations as they became more prosperous. This general position was undermined by the strictly hortatory provision phasing out export subsidies, which reflected victory for the LDC position that the matter was solely for the sovereign determination of an individual LDC. Domestic political constituencies and parts of the Congress would have objected strenuously if the Executive abided by the language to which it had agreed. And so, even as they agreed to the changes, United States negotiators announced in Geneva that their nation would take advantage of the Article 19(9) possibility of non-application of the Code between two signatories: it would refuse to apply the Code (and hence apply an injury test in countervailing duty actions) to any LDC that did not make a "satisfactory" commitment under Article

14(5) to phase out its export subsidies. The United States stated its flexibility in the matter—that the terms of the commitment would depend on the prosperity of the particular LDC. Still, this was a policy of dubious propriety. The U.S. had agreed to concessions in the draft Code and then sought to undo these concessions through leverage obtained by its longstanding refusal to abide by the terms of GATT Article VI. As discussed in the next section of this chapter, the U.S. policy nearly undermined the entire Subsidies Code within two years of its adoption.

(f) Institutional Considerations

With so many ambiguities and unresolved issues in its substantive rules, the Code needed well-developed institutional features. Like other MTN agreements, the Subsidies Code establishes a committee of all signatories "to carry out responsibilities as assigned to it under this Agreement or by the signatories and [to] afford signatories the opportunity of consulting on any matters relating to the operation of the Agreement or the furtherance of its objectives."[78] The committee must meet at least twice a year and must undertake an annual review of the operation of the Agreement.[79] Thus, although the GATT Secretariat provides the only staffing for the committee, an institution of sorts has been established, onto which may fall the burden of developing the Code rules and settling disputes between signatories.

The Code invites the committee to elaborate upon two particular provisions.[80] Whether and how the committee might develop other standards is left unclear. Article ll(3), for example, requires periodic review of the Illustrative List of export subsidies, but does not specify a procedure for adding or deleting items. Adoption of clearly new obligations is probably subject to the Article 19(7) paragraph on amendments, which specifies that the Committee may establish its own procedures for approving an amendment but that no signatory will be bound by an amendment it does not accept.

The Code's provisions on dispute settlement are considerably more detailed and, in fact, are the best defined of any such procedures in the GATT and the various MTN agreements. Earlier drafts had adopted the skeletal GATT procedures for dispute settlement panels, with a few modifications. In the Subsidies Code negotiations, the legalistic perspective of the United States and the anxieties of the economically weaker LDCs over power-oriented diplomacy eventually overcame the predisposition of the EEC and Japan to favor political and perhaps secret accommodations. Thus, any signatory has the right[81] to a dispute settlement panel of three or five impartial individuals. The panel is generally limited to determining the facts and legal obligations of the disputants,[82] rather than becoming involved in mediation efforts and perhaps slanting its report in an effort to procure a mediated solution. There are time limits on the selection and deliberations of a panel,[83] thereby prompting expedited resolutions. Recommendations and sanctions are reserved to the Committee of signatories, which is not required to use either.[84] However, where action is appropriate, the Committee must move quickly.[85]

The Code has moved closer to a rule-oriented model for dispute settlement. As to export subsidies, the guide for a panel or the Code Committee is whether the export subsidy "is being granted in a manner inconsistent with the provisions of this Agreement."[86] Articles 8(4) and 13(4), however, present a standard of injury, serious prejudice, a nullification and impairment in considering domestic subsidies. Moreover, footnote 4 to Articles 8(4) seems to suggest that even as to export subsidies, violation of the Code provisions is only a prima facie "case," which can be rebutted by the subsidizing nation.

Those familiar with GATT dispute settlement procedures will recognize the Code's approach as considerably clarified, though by no means completely so. Yet as the substantive conflicts glossed over in the Code reemerge in concrete circumstances, procedures alone will not likely preserve a cooperative spirit among the signatories.

4. Operation of the Code

(a) Formal Implementation

In the most narrow sense, implementation of the Subsidies Code begins with the obligation of signatories "to ensure . . . the conformity of [national] laws, regulations and administrative procedures" with the Code.[87] Although this requirement seems applicable to national subsidy programs, as well as to national laws on countervailing measures, in practice only the latter have been changed and reported to the GATT. Because only Canada, the European Communities, and the United States have traditionally invoked these laws with any frequency, changes in their laws have been of principal concern. The Communities[88] and the United States[89] amended their laws prior to the January 1, 1980 effective date of the Code. Certain aspects of the new U.S. law—such as the very brief time periods for processing countervailing duty complaints—concerned some signatories. Canadian legislation on countervailing duties has not been amended since the Code was signed. In July 1980 the Canadian Department of Finance issued a series of proposed changes to Canadian import legislation, including the countervailing duty law.[90] Several of these proposals appeared to some EEC and U.S. interests to be inconsistent with the Code. As of this writing, the Canadian Parliament has not acted on the proposals.

A broader construction of Code "implementation" includes the task of adding signatories. Prospects for imposing greater discipline on national subsidies affecting international trade are obviously enhanced as more countries subscribe to the Code rules. Certain subsidies of nonsignatories might induce signatories to deviate from Code principles as the only available means of counteracting the non-signatory subsidies. Such a response is particularly likely where sales to third country markets are subsidized. As of July 1982, though, only twenty-nine countries (including all ten EEC member states) had accepted the Subsidies Code.[91] This figure includes less than a dozen LDCs, most of whom appear to believe that the Code does not adequately address their development needs. The chief motivation for an LDC to sign the Code has been to obtain an injury test on its subsidized exports to the United States. Some LDCs held back to await the outcome of the U.S.-India dispute over the commitment obligation of Article 14(5), which presented the question whether the GATT Article I most-favored-nation obligation required the U.S. to extend its injury test to imports from *all* GATT countries. As explained below, the actual dispute has been settled. However, the commitments issue has not receded and, while discussions are underway with a number of LDCs, the pace of LDC acceptances remains slow.

In one of its first actions, the Subsidies Code Committee authorized a number of non-signatories to attend Committee meetings as observers. These countries, all of which participated in the MTN negotiations and most of which are LDCs, are obviously possible additional signatories. The Committee has apparently recognized the shortcomings of a limited membership propounding international norms. In creating an observer status, it has broadened participation in the Code.

(b) Institutional Developments

Few international agreements are substantially amplified through regular additions or alterations to the text of the agreement itself. The Herculean effort often necessary to muster the required unanimity of views most often leads either to inaction or to diluted amendments that fail to affect important obligations. Vehicles for rule elaboration more frequently take the form of dispute settlement procedures or the often painstakingly slow emergence of a consensus through discussion and practice. Though both these methods are valuable, they are not usually sufficient to cope with widespread departures from an existing norm or with new practices unaddressed by the agreement but relevant to its operation. Some government officials and academics, particularly in the United States, had hoped that the Multilateral Trade Negotiations would yield one or more codes that supplemented the traditional methods with a stronger "statutory" option for rule development. The Subsidies Code was a likely candidate. In the end, though, the statutory approach remained more a wish than an accomplishment. The Code provisions analyzed in Section 3 and Committee practice since the Code took effect suggest that traditional methods will continue preeminent. Signatories were unwilling to be bound by future decisions in which they did not specifically concur.

(1) RULE DEVELOPMENT.   There have been no amendments to the Code during its first two years of operation. However, U.S. officials have suggested "clarification" of the provision on primary product export subsidies. For reasons already explained, such an effort would entail great difficulties if the "clarification" proposed looks like a significantly more restrictive standard. In a less ambitious vein, the Code Committee has accepted the invitation in footnote 15 to develop an understanding "setting out the criteria for the calculation of the amount" of a subsidy subject to countervailing measures. The Committee established an "experts" group to consider over a dozen issues subsumed under this general topic. Some issues pertain to the calculation of particular subsidies affecting identified imported products. For example, one discussion paper focuses on the amount of subsidization on a product whose manufacture has been advanced through research and development subsidies. Other issues considered by the experts group more nearly resemble determinations of what practices can be considered subsidies at all.

The experts group itself consists of technically competent representatives from each signatory wishing to participate. (Most signatories do.) Meetings are off-the-record, and participants understand that any individual's comments or suggestions are not binding on his country. The resulting atmosphere has reportedly been one of cordiality and cooperation among the participating officials, some of whom are directly involved in administration of their national countervailing duty laws. As of July 1982 the group has agreed upon a few reports concerning relatively technical issues.

The early success and promise of this group is apparently due in part to its informality. The group's limitations spring from this same attribute. First, it is unlikely that an experts group of this sort will address the difficult questions left over by the Code negotiators. Indeed, it is probably inappropriate for such a group to wrestle with these essentially political questions. During the recent dispute over U.S. preliminary determinations of subsidies on a large proportion of EEC steel exports to the United States, issues of how to calculate subsidies have assumed great importance. EEC officials have declared that these questions must be answered by the Subsidies Committee itself, not by a subordinate group.[92] Second, the group's method rather resembles the emergence of a consensus approach to rule development that has often characterized GATT groups. The process has been accelerated, but the method is the same. This method does not generally produce interpretations or elaborations that become hard legal obligations, a matter of some concern to those who believe in a rule-oriented approach. In fact, there has been considerable confusion over what precisely the Code Committee will do with reports it receives from the experts group—"adopt" them, "note" them, or something else entirely. It may be that standards, consensually adopted, on relatively technical (though important) issues should not be transformed into legal obligations. Reliance might best be placed on the cooperation of the bureaucracies that administer the various national laws.

Neither the experts group nor the Code Committee as a whole has formally considered several interpretive problems arising from Annex A, the Illustrative List of export subsidies. Because rules on export subsidies are the clearest in the Code, interpretive issues here are both more important and more likely. The current problems result from provisions in which the Code negotiators were apparently trying to include or exclude particular national practices from the general definitions of export subsidies in the Annex. Perhaps for diplomatic reasons, the negotiators did not identify the specific practices; instead they attempted definitions of general application that in reality covered only the specific practices in mind. Problems have arisen where another country argues that *its* practices also fit within the general provision. For example, item (e) of the Illustrative List defines as an export subsidy the "deferral specifically related to exports, of direct taxes." Footnote 2 adds that the "signatories further recognize that nothing in this text prejudges the disposition by the Contracting Parties of the specific issues raised in GATT Document L/4422" (the panel report on the U.S. DISC legislation). The negotiators had apparently intended by this footnote only to defer the DISC question. Yet at least one other country has suggested that its deferral of direct taxes related to exports is sufficiently similar to U.S practice that the item (e) prohibition would not apply pending resolution of the DISC issue.

Another interpretive problem is raised by the somewhat imprecise drafting of items (g) and (h), which deal with remission of indirect taxes. Item (g) specifies that the "excessive" remission of indirect taxes is an export subsidy. By implication and GATT practice, the "non-excessive" remission (i.e., not more than the domestic tax actually levied) of indirect taxes is not an export subsidy. This provision was apparently meant by the negotiators to exclude the EEC value-added tax from the definition of export subsidies. A distinguishing feature of the EC value-added tax is that it is paid at each stage of production and carefully documented. Each producer receives credits for the tax on earlier stages of production. The amount remitted on export of a product covers only the final stage of production. Any country adopting a similar value-added system would also benefit. Item (h) addresses the so-called "cascade" tax systems in which all indirect taxes levied at any stage of production—whether on material inputs or on items such as electricity—are remitted upon export. Under such a system the documentation on actual prior stage taxes and credits may not exist. In any event the allocation of indirect taxes on power, water, and other utility taxes paid by a manufacturer is difficult to trace accurately. Item (h), therefore, allows remission of "prior" stage indirect taxes only when those taxes have been paid on items "physically incorporated" into the exported product. However, several countries with cascade tax systems have argued that they simply remit "indirect taxes" in "nonexcessive" amounts. Therefore, they argue, item (g) legitimizes their practices, with recourse to item (h) being unnecessary. The problem, of course, is that item (g) does not specify that it applies only to final stage remissions. And, while an impartial tribunal examining Annex A and the negotiating history would likely disallow the claim of cascade countries, the interpretive problem in item (g) raises an institutional question as to what body is competent to decide such issues and how.

(II) DISPUTE SETTLEMENT.   For its first two years there were no formal dispute settlement procedures under the Subsidies Code. Then began a flurry of activity, most of it involving the United States and the European Communities. The U.S. has requested panels to consider alleged EEC export subsidies on certain fruits, poultry, pasta and wheat flour. As of this writing the panel decision on wheat flour is several months overdue; the others are in earlier stages.[93] The United States has joined the chorus of complaints against EEC sugar subsidies. Two pre-code GATT panels determined that EEC sugar subsidies seriously prejudice the interests of other exporters.[94] Thus a full-scale confrontation over the Common Agricultural Policy seems to be developing. EEC officials have complained that the U.S. seems to be provoking a confrontation intentionally, insofar as it has engaged in only *pro forma* consultations before requesting a panel.

In the fall of 1981, the United States and India settled their dispute arising from the U.S. refusal to apply the Code to India. In the end, In-

dia provided a "best endeavors" commitment under Article 14(5), and
the United States recognized Indian membership in the Code. However,
U.S. demands for additional LDC commitments under Article 14(5) to
eliminate export subsidies may continue and lead to more friction in the
Code. Meanwhile, India still complains that its products have been subject to countervailing duties without an injury determination.

The U.S.-India dispute threatened to knock out from under the Code
one of the legs on which it rests. As mentioned earlier, the United States
has insisted that an LDC accepting the Code make an Article 14(5) commitment to phase out its export subsidies, despite the hortatory character of that provision. India made such a commitment when it accepted
the Code in early 1980, but U.S. officials eventually rejected it as insuffi-
ciently precise. The United States invoked Article 19(9), which allows
any signatory to decline to apply the Code to any other signatory. The
most important consequence was that the United States did not, before
levying countervailing duties, apply an injury test on subsidized imports
from India. India requested consultations with the United States under
Article XXIII of the GATT after a final countervailing duty order
against Indian fasteners was entered.[95] When those consultations
predictably failed, India requested that a GATT panel be established to
consider the matter. India maintained that, in refusing to apply an injury test to its subsidized exports, the United States had violated its
GATT Article I most-favored-nation obligation toward India.

The basis for India's complaint struck at the conditional MFN approach which had been the very heart of the U.S. negotiating
strategy—an injury test in return for discipline covering at least export
subsidies. Article l of the Code seemed to approve the conditional MFN
approach:

> Signatories shall take all necessary steps to ensure that the imposition of a
> countervailing duty on any product . . . of any *signatory* imported into the
> territory of another signatory is in accordance with the provisions of Arti-
> cle VI of the General Agreement and the terms of this Agreement. [em-
> phasis added]

While other nations maintained or enacted a single countervailing duty
procedure to cover products of both signatories and non-signatories, the
United States added an injury test (thereby giving up its GATT "grandfather" rights) only for signatories. And, as India learned, the executive
branch of the U.S. Government could withhold the injury test from a
country which had signed the Code but had not "accorded adequate
benefits" to the United States.[96] Yet the Indian complaint threatened to
produce a GATT determination that the unconditional MFN obligation
of Article I required the U.S. to apply an injury test to subsidized
imports from all sources—including non-signatories—because it had applied such a test to the imports of some countries.

Most observers found the Indian case strong, though not airtight. It also appeared that the United States had badly handled the issue of an Indian commitment and was too strident in its insistence on something not required by the Code. A GATT decision against the United States would likely have been resisted in some Congressional and private quarters, with resulting reactions against the United States in Geneva. A panel was convened in the late spring of 1981, a delay which suggested to some that India would prefer to settle the matter with the United States. Indeed, by late September a settlement was reached, with India offering an Article 14(5) commitment that was somewhat stronger than its original offering. It is difficult to believe, however, that the Indians would not have offered this same modification a year earlier had the United States quietly pursued the matter.

(c) Prospects for the Code

Just three years after the Code took effect, the agenda of nettlesome issues is lengthy. There remain issues such as DISC and export credits, relatively discrete matters deferred during the negotiations and still not completely resolved. There will doubtless be similarly circumscribed disputes in the future: whether a particular practice falls within a definition in the Illustrative List of export subsidies, whether some detail of national countervailing duty law is being applied inconsistently with the Code. One or even several of these disputes will not likely threaten the Code's basic utility as a mechanism to blunt conflicts over the use of subsidies. The Code established procedures for extensive discussion and mediation to reduce further the corrosive potential of such disputes. The spirit of mutual accommodation and compromise on which the Code largely depends may prevail in these cases.

Yet it seems as though no subsidies issue completely disappears, even as others develop. The DISC, for example, continues to provoke disagreement. After two years of sparring over what to do with the panel report, it was finally accepted. Still, U.S. officials labor under the political pressure applied by those corporations enjoying the tax breaks provided by DISC. Meanwhile, many U.S. tax experts favor its repeal because they doubt that the program actually increases exports. This national ambivalence meets European determination to have the program modified or eliminated, based on the panel finding of its inconsistency with the GATT. Recent developments include charges in the Committee that the U.S. has failed to identify the program as a subsidy (as required by GATT Article XVI:1 and Code Article 7) and an EEC request for authorization to take compensatory measures.[97] The issue left by the Code negotiators has thus far eluded resolution by a later generation of officials, although U.S. officials have agreed in principle to repeal DISC.

A series of disagreements can strain the Subsidies Code or any international agreement, even where each dispute in isolation appears manageable. The Code machinery seems better able than most GATT arrangements to handle these disagreements. However, major disputes implicating the long-standing rifts over the proper role of subsidies and government intervention have already developed. These disputes could lay bare the absence of a consensus behind the Code and threaten the uneasy order created by the Code.

The Common Agricultural Policy of the EEC has come under increasing attack.[98] Examination of the GATT panel report in the EEC Sugar (Australia) case mentioned earlier confirms the difficulties in applying the rules on export subsidies for primary products. In fact, that panel found no violation of these rules (i.e., Article XVI:3) but did find "serious prejudice" to Australia within the meaning of Article XVI:1. Predictably, Australia (joined by Brazil and the U.S.) has since claimed that the EEC should alter its program, while the EEC counters that it has done nothing "wrong." The spate of U.S. complaints against EEC products may have forced an eventual confrontation. Whatever the disagreements over it among member states, the CAP is obviously basic to the operation of the EEC, and changes to accommodate world opinion will be hard to extract. Yet considerable commerce is affected, and world opinion is in some respects coalescing against the EEC.

A second confrontation, in which the U.S. and EEC are again the protagonists, began in early 1982 when the U.S. steel industry filed major countervailing duty cases against most imports of steel from the EEC (and other nations). The U.S. Government found subsidies on most, though not all, of these imports. The International Trade Commission made the requisite injury determination in most of the cases. The U.S. Government and EEC Commission had agreed during the summer on an export quota to "settle" the cases, but the U.S. industry rejected this settlement. The EEC, meanwhile, alleged in the Code Committee that some of the U.S. countervailing duty determinations were inconsistent with Code provisions defining subsidies. Finally, only a day before the U.S. Department of Commerce would have been required by law to issue countervailing duty orders, the U.S. industry agreed to withdraw its complaints in favor of a revised U.S.-European Commission agreement on export quotas.[99]

The steel cases did not lead to a "trade war," though perhaps only through the grace of an eleventh-hour settlement. Perhaps the CAP cases can be mediated successfully within the Code Committee or, less probably, panel decisions will be accepted by the losers. Yet the text of the Code itself reveals the conflicting attitudes toward subsidies that will outlive particular disputes. The conflict seems not to be susceptible to a rule-oriented approach precisely because no one can formulate a standard that convincingly distinguishes legitimate state intervention from illegitimate state intervention. "Implementation" of the Code may finally mean development of the Code's accommodating mechanisms and an appeal to the interests of the major Code signatories in preserving the remnants of the postwar world trading order.

Notes

1. The formal, and cumbersome, title of the Code is "Agreement on Interpretation and Application of Articles VI, XVI and XXIII of the General Agreement on Tariffs and Trade," done Apr. 12, 1979, MTN/NTM/W/236, reprinted in *Agreements Reached in the Tokyo Round of the Multilateral Trade Negotiations*, H.R. Doc. No. 153, 96th Cong., lst Sess., pt. 1 (1979).

2. "GATT" refers to both an international agreement and the international institution that oversees that agreement. The GATT, which became effective in 1948, was the international trade portion of the postwar economic arrangements begun at Bretton Woods with the creation of the International Monetary Fund and the World Bank. An "International Trade Organization" was supposed to replace GATT, but that organization's charter never took effect. The result was that both a rather sketchy set of rules and a very weak institutional structure were left to "govern" world trade.

3. Two recent contributions with a specifically legal focus are Barcelo, *Subsidies, Countervailing Duties and Antidumping after the Tokyo Round*, 13 *Law & Pol'y Int'l Bus.* 257 (1980) and Schwartz, *Zenith Radio Corp. v. United States: Countervailing Duties and the Regulation of International Trade*, [1978] Sup. Ct. Rev. 297.

4. See Bhagwati & Ramaswami, *Domestic Distortions, Tariffs, and the Theory of Optimum Subsidy*, J. Pol Econ. 71 (1963); Kelkar, *Export Subsidy: Theory and Practice*, 15 *Economic and Political Weekly* [India] 1010 (1980); Schwartz & Harper, *The Regulation of Subsidies Affecting International Trade*, 70 Mich. L. Rev. 831 (1972).

5. See K. Dam, *The GATT: Law and International Economic Organization* 135 (1970).

6. See J. Gresser, *High Technology and Japanese Industrial Policy*, House Ways and Means Committee Print 96–74, 96th Cong., 2d Sess. (1980).

7. Indeed, a number of American observers do not decry the Japanese model, but commend it to their fellow citizens. See J. Gresser, *supra*; G. Schwartz & P. Choate, *Revitalizing the U.S. Economy* (1980). See generally E. Vogel, *Japan as Number One* (1979).

8. For a more detailed history see J. Jackson, *World Trade and the Law of GATT* 365–399 (1969).

9. U.S. Dept. of State, *Proposals for Expansion of World Trade and Employment*, Pub. No. 2411, Commercial Policy Series 79, 15–17 (1945).

10. See Potter, *Trade Barriers Imposed by Governments*, in U.S. Dept. of State, *American Trade Proposals*, Pub. No. 2551, Commercial Policy Series 88, 1,5 (1946).

11. See, e.g., W. Brown, *The United States and the Restoration of World Trade* 116–119 (1950).

12. See, e.g. K. Dam, *The GATT: Law and International Economic Organization* 132 (1970).

13. U.N. Doc. ICITO/1/4 (April 1948).

14. Articles 25–28 of the Havana Charter covered subsidies.

15. An account of the demise of the Havana Charter is contained in R. Gardner, *Sterling-Dollar Diplomacy* 348–380 (1956).

16. An interpretive note defining "primary products" was also added in 1955: ". . . any product of farm, forest or fishery, or any mineral, in its natural form or which has undergone such processing as is customarily required to prepare it for marketing in substantial volume in international trade." Note 3.2. to Article XVI.

17. GATT Doc. L/1864 (1962).

18. See J. Jackson, note 8 *supra* at 373.
19. *Ibid.* at 369, 399.
20. GATT Doc. L/1381 (1960). Reprinted in *GATT, Basic Instruments and Selected Documents*, 9th Supp., at 184. The list was as follows:

(a) Currency retention schemes or any similar practices which involve a bonus on exports or re-exports;
(b) The provision by governments of direct subsidies to exporters;
(c) The remission, calculated in relation to exports, of direct taxes or social welfare charges on industrial or commercial enterprises;
(d) The exemption, in respect of exported goods, of charges or taxes, other than charges in connection with importation or indirect taxes levied at one or several stages on the same goods if sold for internal consumption; or the payment, in respect of exported goods, of amounts exceeding those effectively levied at one or several stages on these goods in the form of indirect taxes or of charges in connection with importation or in both forms;
(e) In respect of deliveries by governments or governmental agencies of imported raw materials for export business on different terms than for domestic business, the charging of prices below world prices;
(f) In respect of government export credit guarantees, the charging of premiums at rates which are manifestly inadequate to cover the long-term operating costs and losses of the credit insurance institutions;
(g) The grant by governments (or special institutions controlled by governments) of export credits at rates below those which they have to pay in order to obtain the funds so employed;
(h) The government bearing all or part of the costs incurred by exporters in obtaining credit.

21. (Emphasis added). Professor Jackson has pointed out that the curious language of XVI:3 seems to make the "equitable share" standard applicable to any subsidy that results in increased exports of primary products. See J. Jackson, *supra* note 8 at 393.
This language seems all the more curious when one considers that paragraph 3 appears under Section B, which is entitled "Additional Provisions on *Export* Subsidies" (emphasis added).
22. GATT Doc. L/334, reprinted in *GATT, Basic Instruments and Selected Documents*, 3d Supp. at 222, 224 (1955).
23. See GATT Art. XXX.
24. See R. Hudec, *The GATT Legal System and World Trade Diplomacy* 216-29 (1975).
25. Havana (ITO) Charter Art. 34.
26. GATT Art. VI.
27. GATT Art. VI:3.
28. See Panel Report adopted on 21 November 1961, GATT Doc. L/1442 & Add. 1-2, reprinted in GATT, *Basic Instruments and Selected Documents—UNK,52–*, 10th Supp., at 201 (1962).
29. *Ibid.* at 208.
30. There were only half a dozen GATT complaints or consultations concerning subsidies between 1948 and 1961. *Ibid.* at 207.
31. See Executive Branch GATT Study No. 12—The Common Agricultural Policy of the European Community, in *Subcomm. on International Trade of the Sen. Comm. on Finance, Executive Branch GATT Studies* 161, 163 (Comm. Print 1974).
32. See I. Little, T. Scitovsky, & M. Scott, Industry and Trade in Some Developing Countries (1970).
33. The United States had, in the eyes of its trading partners, subsidized its aerospace and computer industries for years through substantial government procurement and R & D assistance.
34. Panel Report, note 28 *supra*, at 203.

35. Staff of Senate Comm. on Finance, 92d Cong., lst Sess., *A Survey of Current Issues to be Studied by the Subcommittee on International Trade* 1–2 (Comm. Print 1971).

36. *Ibid.* at 2.

37. See generally *Foreign Trade: Hearings Before the Subcomm. on International Trade of the Senate Comm. on Finance*, 92d Cong., lst Sess. (1971); *U.S. Office of the Special Representative for Trade Negotiations, Future United States Foreign Trade Policy* (1969) [hereinafter cited as *STR Report*].

38. During the 1970's a number of other products were added—wines, tobacco, fish, flax and hemp, seeds, and hops. See *Commission of the European Communities, The Common Agricultural Policy* 18–28 (1977).

39. Executive Branch GATT Study No. 12, note 31 *supra*, at 215.

40. For a more complete treatment of this issue see Butler, *Countervailing Duties and Export Subsidization: A Re-emerging Issue in International Trade*, 9 Va. J. Int. L. 82 (1969).

41. Balance of Payments, Statement by the President Outlining a Program of Action, 4 *Weekly Comp. of Pres. Doc.* 20, 25 (Jan. 1, 1968).

42. *STR Report* at 25.

43. See note 41 *supra*.

44. Border Tax Adjustments, Report of the Working Party adopted on 2 December 1970, GATT Doc. L/3464, reprinted in GATT, *Basic Instruments and Selected Documents*, 18th Supp., at 97 (1972).

45. *Ibid.* at 107.

46. *STR Report* at 21. The report also recommended consideration of "seeking the inclusion in the GATT of a provision under which importing countries would be required to apply countervailing duties against subsidized industrial exports if the GATT Contracting Parties find that they materially injure a competing export industry in another GATT country."

47. Executive Branch GATT Study No. 2, note 31 *supra*, at 29.

48. Executive Branch GATT Study No. 3, The Adequacy of GATT Provisions Dealing with Agriculture, note 31 *supra* at 31, 34.

49. *Ibid.* at 33.

50. Trade Act of 1974, Pub. L. No. 93-618, §121(a)(5), (ll), 88 Stat. 1978 (1975).

51. *S. Rep. No. 1298*, 93d Cong., 2d Sess. 85 (1974).

52. *Treasury Decision* 68–192 (Aug. 10, 1979).

53. *Treasury Decision* 68–270 (Oct. 25, 1978).

54. *Treasury Decision* 69–41 (Jan. 24, 1969).

55. *Treasury Decision* 73–10 (Jan. 4, 1973). On appeal to the Court of International Trade, the Treasury position was affirmed in principle, but modified in some particulars. *Michelin Fine Corp.* v. *United States*, 3 ITRD 1187(Oct. 26, 1981).

56. For a description and analysis of the case see Guido & Morrone, *The Michelin Decision: A Possible New Direction for U.S. Countervailing Duty Law*, 6 Law & Pol'y Int'l Bus. 237 (1974).

57. Non-rubber footwear from Uruguay, *Treasury Decision* 78–32; Leather wearing apparel from Uruguay, *Treasury Decision* 78–154; Leather handbags from Uruguay, *Treasury Decision* 78–33; Leather handbags from Columbia, *Treasury Decision* 78–125; Certain textiles from Uruguay, *Treasury Decision* 78–444; Certain textiles from Argentina, *Treasury Decision* 78–445; Certain textiles from Brazil, *Treasury Decision* 77–87; Handbags from Republic of China, *Treasury Decision* 77–151; Handbags from Republic of Korea, *Treasury Decision* 77–152; Scissors from Brazil, *Treasury Decision* 77–64; Carbon steel plate from Mexico, *Treasury Decision* 76–7; Castor oil products from Brazil, *Treasury Decision* 76–80; Non-rubber footwear from Republic of Korea, *Treasury Decision* 76–340; Leather handbags from Brazil, *Treasury Decision* 76-3; Non-rubber footwear from Brazil, *Treasury Decision* 74–233.

58. See Rivers & Greenwald, *The Negotiation of a Code on Subsidies and Countervailing Measures: Bridging Fundamental Policy Differences*, 11 Law & Pol'y Int'l Bus. 1447, 1480 (1979) [hereinafter Rivers & Greenwald].

59. Pub. L. No. 93-618, §331(a), amending Tariff Act of 1930, §303, 19 U.S. C.A. §1303 (1976).

60. *Zenith Radio Corp.* v. *United States,* 437 U.S. 443 (1978).

61. Zenith Radio Corp. v. United States, 430 F. Supp. 242 (Cust. Ct. 1977).

62. Article 2(l), fn. 6.

63. See Rivers & Greenwald at 1483–87.

64. Article 6.

65. Article 6(3).

66. Some U.S. Congressional interests objected to these provisions, which might be read to give a semblance of rigor to the injury test. Out of political expediency, the Executive simply omitted them from the U.S. implementing legislation.

67. Articles 2–6.

68. "Signatories shall not grant export subsidies on products other than certain primary products." Footnote 29 of the Code removes minerals from the category of "primary product" and includes them in the Article 9 coverage.

69. GATT Doc. L/4422.

70. GATT Docs. L/4423, L/4424, L/4425.

71. For a full discussion of these cases see Jackson, *The Jurisprudence of International Trade,* 72 Am. J. Int. L. 747 (1978).

72. See John Moore's chapter in this book for extended consideration of the export credit arrangement.

73. Rivers & Greenwald at 1478.

74. Ibid. at 1473.

75. Subsidies Code Article ll(2).

76. Subsidies Code Article 8(l).

77. In this December 1977 "Outline of an Approach" the U.S. and EEC declared that the "special situation of the developing countries and their development needs should be taken into account." GATT Doc. MTN/INF/13, reprinted in Rivers & Greenwald at 1466, 1469.

78. Article 16(l).

79. Article 19(6).

80. (1) "An understanding among signatories should be developed setting out the criteria for the calculation of the amount of the subsidy." Article 4(2), fn. 15. (2) "The Committee should develop a definition of the word 'related' as used in this paragraph" (pertaining to the definition of "domestic industry" where domestic and foreign producers are related. (Article 6(5), fn. 21.

81. See Article 17(3).

82. See Article 18(l).

83. Article 18(2).

84. Article 18(9).

85. *Ibid.*

86. Article 13(4). Cf. Article 8(2): "Signatories agree not to use export subsidies in a manner inconsistent with the provisions of this Agreement."

87. Art. 19(5).

88. Council Reg. (EEC) No. 3017/79 of 20 December 1979, 22 O.J. EUR. COMM. (No. L 339) l (1979); Commission recommendation No. 3018/79 of 21 December 1979, 22 O.J. EUR COMM. (No. L 339) 15 (1979).

89. Trade Agreements Act of 1979, Title I, P.L. 96-39, 93 Stat. 150, adding Title VII to Tariff Act of 1930, 19 U.S.C. 1671 *et seq.*

90 Canada Department of Finance, Proposals on Import Policy (1980).

91. The twenty-nine are: Australia, Austria, Brazil, Canada, Chile, the EEC ten, Finland, India, Japan, South Korea, New Zealand, Norway, Pakistan, Spain, Sweden, Switzerland, United Kingdom (for Hong Kong), United States, Uruguay, and Yugoslavia.

92. See BNA Int. Trade Reporter, U.S. Import Weekly, 7/2⅛2 at 476.

93. See U.S. Import Weekly, April 7, 1982 at 8; May 5, 1982 at 118.

94. GATT Doc. L/5011 (1980) (Brazil); GATT Doc. L/4833 (1979) (Australia), reprinted in 20 International Legal Materials 862 (1981).

95. Certain Fasteners from India, 45 Fed. Reg. 48607 (July 21, 1980).

96. Trade Agreements Act of 1979, P.L. 96-39, §2(b)(2), 19 U.S.C. 2503.

97. See J. Commerce, May 3, 1982, at 9A, col. 3; J. Commerce, July 23, 1982, at 3A, col. 5.

98. U.S. Secretary of Agriculture Block has publicly stated that the U.S. "will not accept" the EEC's present export subsidy practices. J. Comm., Sept. 22, 1981, at lA, col. 4, a sentiment perhaps masked behind the recent U.S. call for "clarification" of the primary product Code provision.

99. See N.Y. Times, Oct. 22, 1982, at Al, col. 5. The text of the U.S.-EEC agreement is reproduced in U.S. Import Weekly, Oct. 27, 1982, at 125–133.

SIX

The UN Code of Conduct of Transnational Corporations: Problems of Interpretation and Implementation

A. A. FATOUROS

The effort to draft a UN Code of Conduct on transnational corporations must be seen both in its own historical and institutional frame of reference and in the broader world-wide political and economic context. Only then is it possible to approach the issue of interpretation and implementation and ask the right questions, questions that are not wide of the mark.

The present paper begins by examining the historical and institutional origins of the Code; it proceeds to a brief description of the Code of Conduct, as it is presently emerging; and then turns to the principal focus of study, the problems of interpretation and implementation.

1. Origins of the Code

The distant origins of the UN Code of Conduct on transnational corporations may be found in the denunciations of activities by American enterprises in Chile in the early seventies.[1] Debate in the United Nations led to an ECOSOC resolution asking the UN Secretary-General to appoint a group of "eminent persons" to study the impact of multinational (or, as they came later to be called, transnational) corporations on world development and on international relations.[2] When appointed, the

A. A. Fatouros is Professor of Law, Faculty of Law and Economics, Aristotelian University of Thessaloniki. While the author has served as consultant to the Secretariat of UN agencies on matters related to the preparation of international codes of conduct, this article reflects solely his own perceptions, positions, and opinions.

Group conducted a series of hearings and eventually submitted a report, in which, responding to its charge "to submit recommendations for appropriate international action," it picked up and amplified a number of suggestions made in an earlier UN Secretariat report.[3] The creation of a Commission on Transnational Corporations and an Information and Research Centre was proposed.

Closer to our present concerns, the Group expressed a positive, though qualified, reaction to the idea of a code and included its preparation among the terms of reference of the Commission to be created.[4] In its 1974 resolution establishing the Commission, the UN Economic and Social Council followed suit.[5] The Commission, when created, proceeded to proclaim this task as its highest priority.[6] An Intergovernmental Working Group was established which started meeting in January 1977. After five years and seventeen Working Group sessions, an advanced draft of a Code has emerged, but this draft cannot be considered final, since it is in no way free of gaps and brackets.[7]

To explain the efforts that have gone into the preparation of a Code of Conduct on Transnational Corporations, we must separate the broader compelling concerns regarding the need for international control of transnational corporations from the choice of the particular form of a code of conduct. The broader concerns are, of course, far more important than the particular choice.

The internationalization of production and trade during the past two decades has complex economic, political and technological roots. One of the factors that allowed it to flourish has been a favorable legal and institutional environment, created through deliberate public and private decisions, leading to legal action. It is not surprising therefore that the widespread concern which focused on transnational corporations (as the most visible manifestation of this process of internationalization) turned to legal and institutional remedies. Another major reason for the emphasis on legal methods is that most governments, while fearful and therefore resentful of transnational corporation power, are not prepared to cut off, or radically decrease, their contacts with transnational corporations. Appreciating the possible advantages from transnational corporations operations in their territories, they seek instead to increase the benefits to be derived and to perfect their methods of control. When looking for "acceptable" ways to influence corporate behavior, legal and institutional means are highly appropriate.

Much of what governments can do and are doing to cope with transnational corporations involves legal action at the national level. Such action, however, is inadequate for the effective control of transnational corporations since they have created for themselves a new, transnational economic space, which transcends traditional legal, i.e., territorial boundaries. The corporations possess an increased capability to evade, disregard or subvert national law and policy in any one of the countries in which they operate, a capability based on their possession of financial, technological and other resources which are in each case extra-national. Governmental cooperation across national borders is thus indispensable for the effective control of transnational corporations.

Concern with controlling the power of transnational corporations is by no means found exclusively among the developing countries. It is shared by many developed countries; the latter, however, do not allow these concerns to dominate their policies, in part because they are able to exercise relatively more effective control through their national law and in part because they are often interested in protecting the interests of transnational corporations based in their territory. Neither of these offsetting considerations carries force in the case of the governments of the developing countries. The proposals for international action have thus come chiefly from the developing countries, although they have found open support from some of the smaller developed countries and from labor unions and other groups within most developed countries.

The point in time at which most of the proposals were formulated has its own importance. The early 1970's was the historical moment at which the developing countries had an enhanced ability to obtain a favorable reception for their demands. Circumstances have changed considerably since then. Nevertheless, proposals for the preparation of codes of conduct presented at that time have slowly moved toward some mode of realization.

The choice of the particular form of the code of conduct as a major means for establishing international standards cannot be accounted for with any certainty or precision. The earliest of the recent codes of conduct, the one concerning liner conferences, was proposed in 1972, but the original proposal and to some extent the actual result are not of the same scope or character as the other codes discussed here.[8] Yet, use of the term "code of conduct" in that case led to its adoption in 1973 in the context of transfer of technology.[9] Later that same year, the term was also used in a UN Secretariat study on transnational corporations.[10] Since then, the term has made its fortune.

What is a "code of conduct," however, and what form does it take? The term itself did not have a definite meaning barely ten years ago. Indeed, it has gone through a variety of meanings even in the brief history of the UN exercise. A summary rehearsal of these transformations may be instructive.

The 1973 UN Secretariat report just mentioned noted that an international multilateral agreement on transnational corporations "might be considered too ambitious at this stage." It went on to state

Nevertheless, some general agreement on a code of conduct for multinational corporations is not beyond reach. Although such a code might be mostly in general terms and its enforceability might be limited by unwillingness to establish a strong agency to administer it, it would at least have an educational value.[11]

The report of the Group of Eminent Persons added further qualifications to the idea. It stated:

> A code may be the assembling in one document of laws, decrees and rules which are already adopted and being enforced. A comparable attempt would be the drafting of an international agreement which, as mentioned above, we hope can be ultimately negotiated and ratified. The same term is also used for a set of rules established by negotiations in international organizations . . . all or only some of which each country chooses to accept and apply . . . . Finally, a code of conduct may be a consistent set of recommendations which are gradually evolved and which may be revised as experience or circumstances require. Although they are not compulsory in character, they act as an instrument of moral persuasion, strengthened by the authority of international organizations and the support of public opinion.
>
> It is the last-mentioned form of code of conduct that the Group has in mind; namely, a set of recommendations which could be prepared by the Commission, and considered and approved by the Economic and Social Council. They should be addressed to both governments and multinational corporations.[12]

As a result, the Group's report included two versions of a possible code in its proposed terms of reference for the Commission on Transnational Corporations. According to the report, the Commission should:

(e) Evolve a set of recommendations which, taken together, would represent a code of conduct for governments and multinational corporations to be considered and adopted by the Council, and review in the light of experience the effective application and continuing applicability of such recommendations.

(f) Explore the possibility of concluding a general agreement on multinational corporations, enforceable by appropriate machinery, to which participating countries would adhere by means of an international treaty.[13]

These terms of reference were largely repeated in the ECOSOC resolution stating the functions of the Commission on Transnational Corporations.[14]

It is hard to determine exactly what the authors of these recommendations had in mind. What seems clear is a definite distinction between two kinds of instruments covering essentially the same areas: one a gradually evolving set of "recommendations" and the other a legally en-

forceable international treaty. It would seem that the "recommendations" would not at the very start be embodied in a unitary instrument,
but no criteria are provided for distinguishing between the various subjects that would ultimately be assembled into a code. A number of possible approaches come to mind: starting with broad and general
recommendations which gradually become more specific; a division by
categories of problems (along the lines of the chapters and sections of
the current draft, e.g., ownership, finance, restrictive practices, etc.); or
a division based on economic sectors.

Given these fundamental ambiguities, it is no wonder that the Commission on Transnational Corporations, while adopting the idea of a
code of conduct, paid little heed to the specific meanings attached to the
term by its predecessors (and creators). From the very start, the Commission and the Centre appear to have operated on the assumption that
there would be a comprehensive, unitary instrument, whatever its precise form and legal character. Their conception of a code thus turned
out to be very similar to that prevailing in UNCTAD (e.g. the Code of
Conduct on Transfer of Technology), a conception which has by now
become widespread. According to this now established definition, a code
of conduct is a legal instrument adopted by states which embodies principles and rules establishing standards for the behavior of international
actors. These principles and rules are normative in that they prescribe
desirable modes of behavior and condemn undesirable ones, although
the entire instrument typically lacks formal binding legal force and is instead adopted as a "declaration" or "recommendation."

Two lines of explanation, neither of them fully persuasive, may be offered to account for the popularity of the term and the instrument. In
the early 1970's, the developing countries sought to establish international development as the principal goal of the world community. The
formulation of legal (at least normative, even if not formally binding)
propositions was a major element of this strategy. The ploy may have
reflected a particularly Latin American penchant for the formulation of
abstract legal norms on a "programmatic" basis, as conscious reflections
of ideals to be realized in the future rather than as positive law for the
present. But it went much further than that. It made possible the formal
statement by a surprisingly united "Group of 77" of a series of claims for
the restructuring of the international economic and therefore political
and legal order in authoritative (albeit not binding) form, through the
resolutions of the UN General Assembly and other international organization organs in which the G-77 has a large majority.

In the second place, it would be a mistake to regard codes of conduct
as would-be legal formulations that happen to have failed to acquire legal force. In fact, it is highly doubtful if, at this stage, any of the devel-

oping states that took the initiative in proposing codes of conduct would be willing to accept a strict binding instrument. But codes of conduct can have a variety of functions which are by no means irrelevant to the law, but which do not involve the possession of legal binding force, at least not in the first instance. A code of conduct adopted by a large number of states in some formal manner, even if expressly declared to be nonbinding, may have several functions and consequences. In an earlier study,[15] I have tried to summarize these functions, starting with the hypothetical possibility of legal force:

  a. A code adopted in legally binding form (e.g., as an international convention) would, it may be presumed, impose on states party to it legal duties calculated to enhance national control of TNCs; to put it another way, states party to the code would normally undertake the binding obligation to carry it out. The numerous qualifications and caveats that should be attached to this oversimple statement will be discussed later.
  b. A formally adopted code, even if not in legally binding form, may have important consequences in national and international law. This topic too will reappear later in other contexts. Here it may be laconically noted that such consequences may include a "legitimizing" effect (i.e., expressing the world community's approval of particular policies and measures directed at national control of TNCs) and a role as a "source" of domestic and international legal developments, possibly at the behest of domestic groups (e.g., labor unions), particular states or international agencies.
  c. The code may have a demonstration effect; it may serve as a model for national action. It brings to the fore possibilities of national (and international at the regional level) control measures, which may be independently adopted by states.
  d. The code may have an educational function. The process of its preparation gives opportunities for studying related issues, focuses attention on particular problems and concerns, and generates potentially useful debate among countries and among individuals and groups.

While codes of conduct remain fundamentally an objective of the developing countries, their concerns appear to have been met half-way by another set of concerns, advanced by developed countries. Long before the idea of a "code of conduct" was brought forward by the developing countries, various private groups within developed nations, and eventually some of their governments, had suggested the adoption of a "code," in the form of an international convention, to assure the protection of foreign investors from nationalization of their properties and generally from "mistreatment" by host countries. These proposals were given a decent burial in a 1964 OECD Council resolution presenting a draft convention on the protection of foreign property.[16] When, several years later, the current code of conduct proposals came up, with provisions calculated to assure control and regulation of transnational corporations by host countries, the governments of developed countries exhumed those earlier suggestions and presented a set of "balancing" norms directed at the protection of transnational corporations. These norms, circumscribing the rights of host countries and the corresponding obligations of transnational corporations, have found a place in codes of conduct, considerably tempering the developing countries' initial proposals.

2. The Emerging Code

A group charged with preparing a comprehensive text, a "code"—even a "code of conduct"—is faced at the very start with the simple question of where and how to begin. In the case of the UNCTAD Code of Conduct on the Transfer of Technology, this question was providentially answered by a Working Group of the Pugwash Conference on Science and World Affairs which prepared, in April 1974, a draft code. Its text was adopted by the Group of 77 and submitted as its own proposal at the very start of the negotiations. Eventually, the two other groups of states, Group B (the developed market-economy countries) and Group D (the socialist countries), submitted competing drafts of their own. All three drafts were initially incomplete, often obscure, and sometimes extreme in their positions. They were supplemented and perfected during the negotiations that ensued. The process of preparing the code consisted essentially of bargaining among the three groups regarding the substance and language of the drafts, chapter by chapter and provision by provision, with the chairmen of the various working groups submitting, with the help of the UNCTAD Secretariat, compromise proposals. As is well known, the process is not quite over. Nevertheless, agreement has been reached on a substantial part of the code text.[17]

When starting its own operations in early 1977, the Intergovernmental Working Group on the Code of Conduct on Transnational Corporations chose to follow a different approach, based on the principle of a single text rather than competing drafts. At the time, certain steps had already been taken which, if followed to their logical conclusion, would have led in the opposite direction. Each geographical group had submitted more or less formal lists of "areas of concern," which manifested their differing positions on the content and direction of the projected code of conduct. But the Working Group reversed direction at that point and adopted the single-text approach.

The text was built up gradually from an initial skeleton. A Centre report on the "major issues involved in the preparation of a code of conduct" offered a survey of the entire topic.[18] Largely on the basis of that report, the Chairman of the Working Group, proposed a "list of headings" for the code, essentially a table of contents.[19] These were discussed within the Group, which then requested that the Centre prepare "tentative annotations" to the headings. After another round of discussions, a set of "suggestions for an annotated outline" of the code was prepared by the Chairman.[20] More discussions ensued; then, at the request of the Working Group, the Centre prepared a working paper which tentatively formulated so-called "common elements" that had emerged from all these discussions, along with some commentary and a list of points on which agreement was lacking.[21] This was the first text in which normative language was, hesitatingly and somewhat inconsistently, used. Yet, all these successive texts were treated as only "a basis for discussion"; they did not formally commit the participating delegations to their language or substance. Still, certain informal understandings, initially on the identification of an issue and gradually on the direction the related provision should adopt, were reached during these discussions. Although inchoate, these informal understandings could not easily be renounced.

After further discussions, the Chairman prepared and presented to the Working Group, in December 1978, a set of formulations, which were gradually supplemented so as to cover ultimately the entire area of concern of the code.[22] The final round of lengthy general discussion on this text marked the end of the first phase of the code's preparation.

The second phase, now just completed, involved the actual preparation of a draft. The Group still eschewed full use of international conference procedures; for example, it has never resorted to a vote. It now did have recourse, however, to the submission of competing proposals by groups of states (or sometimes individual states) on particular paragraphs. Indeed, the Group of 77 eventually presented a complete text of proposals, which follow largely the structure of the Chairman's formulations, although with some significant differences in the language. The other groups offered no such complete proposal. The Working Group thus labored through long discussions, managing slowly to formulate several "concluded" provisions, that is to say, provisions which had been tentatively agreed upon, subject to reconsideration (on terms never fully clarified) when the entire code was completed. Where agreement on the language of a provision proved impossible, the traditional square brackets were used. Bracketed language appears in about half the paragraphs. In some cases, the brackets indicate fundamental disagreements among delegations; in others, the differences appear less serious and removal of the brackets without too much trouble at some future stage can be envisaged.

The issue of the legal character of codes of conduct, more precisely of their being legally binding or "voluntary," has plagued general debate on codes. In the case at hand, the question was left at the beginning formally open and appears to have been tacitly settled in favor of a nonbinding code. The importance of the issue has been much exaggerated.[23] No doubt, an ideal code, properly drafted, in clear and specific language, would be much more effective if it took the form of a multilateral international convention. Such a code, however, is more than improbable, it is by any realistic standard wholly impossible. A code designed to have binding force would surely be drafted in such a manner as to deprive it of any actual effect. A nonbinding code stands a better chance of being couched in relatively specific and unambiguous language. Moreover, a nonbinding code need not necessarily be deprived of legal or political effect, as the listing of possible "roles" quoted above tried to indicate. The code's nonbinding character is by no means solely a handicap; it can also be an element of strength, or at least "effectiveness." A nonbinding code offers to those willing to use it (states or other international actors) opportunities for action unhampered by the kinds of difficulties a formally binding instrument would normally face. Precisely because the processes involved are not strictly legal, they are not limited by such considerations as rules of evidence or rigid requirements of standing. The code's nonbinding character has, furthermore, a significant impact on the questions of interpretation and implementation, but these will be dealt with in the next section.

In addition to an introductory section, which is to include a Preamble and a statement of objectives, but which was not drafted by the Intergovernmental Working Group, the Code of Conduct is divided into five main parts or chapters: definitions and scope of application; activities of transnational corporations; treatment of transnational corporations; intergovernmental cooperation; and implementation.

While a number of brackets remain in the chapter on definitions, principal differences center on two issues: the coverage of state-owned transnational corporations (the socialist bloc insisting that they should not come under the Code, while both the developed market economy countries and the developing countries hold that they should) and the precise formulation of the scope of application of the Code. There is general agreement on the criteria for the definition of a transnational corporation: entities in two or more countries; a system of decision-making permitting a common strategy among entities; links "by ownership or otherwise" which enable one or more entities to exercise "a significant influence over the others."

The chapter on activities of transnational corporations is the longest in the Code, consisting of about forty paragraphs, and will probably prove the most influential. It is essentially a fairly detailed statement of the obligations of transnational corporations toward the countries in which they operate, that is to say, toward both home and host countries. A first set of paragraphs restates in a number of differing contexts the duty of transnational corporations to respect the sovereignty, laws and policies of the countries in question. When formulated in broad terms, this prescription is unexceptional and unopposed. The more specific the formulation, however, the more explicit the connection to particular interests or activities of states or corporations, the less agreement there is. For instance, in the case of transnational corporation involvement in political activities, there is agreement on the general principle of non-involvement, while differences persist with respect to specific aspects of the principle. Somewhat out of place in the midst of these rather general provisions is a paragraph on review and renegotiation of contracts between governments and transnational corporations, which affirms the need for good faith negotiation and implementation of contracts, recommends the inclusion of renegotiation clauses and suggests the cooperation of the corporations in the renegotiation of contracts in cases of fundamental change of circumstances. Disagreement is marked on the laws applicable to such renegotiation, whether the host country's laws only or "relevant international legal principles" as well.

The majority of the provisions in this chapter (about twenty five paragraphs) deal with a variety of particular issues regarding transnational corporations, from ownership and control to financing and balance of payments, and from transfer pricing to protection of consumers and the environment, as well as long provisions on disclosure of information. While some of the provisions are phrased in such vague and general terms that their actual import remains doubtful, other provisions are reasonably specific as well as original—for instance those on consumer protection, the environment and information disclosure. In this entire set of provisions, moreover, there are very few diverging formulations and brackets.

The next chapter of the draft Code of Conduct is probably the most controversial. Although rather short (about twelve paragraphs—and suggestions of deletion have been made as to several of them), it is replete with brackets and alternative proposals. The fact is hardly surprising, since these provisions seek to delimit the power and authority of host governments vis-à-vis transnational corporations, something which, for the past forty years, has been at the very center of international legal controversy. What is indeed surprising is that on such issues as the national treatment of transnational corporation entities or even nationalization, agreement on compromise formulations was almost reached in the International Working Group, even though in the end it proved too elusive. Some of these attempted formulations, it is true, were mere verbal evasions of the disputed issues; this seems unavoidable, for it cannot be expected that a code of conduct will provide genuine solutions to such difficult and long standing problems as the nationalization of foreign property. Yet, this was not the case in all instances; some of the compromises that failed were genuine attempts at finding midway points between opposing positions and—sometimes through astute reformulations of established propositions—involved real concessions on both sides. Be that as it may, the chapter has ended up, especially after a flurry of extreme proposals and uncompromising formulations at the very last session of the Working Group, with a dismally large number of brackets.

3. Interpretation and Implementation

The draft Code of Conduct deals with its own application in the last two chapters, one of them concerning intergovernmental cooperation on a bilateral or multilateral basis and the other covering action at the national level and by international institutions. This division of topics is not particularly logical or consistent; it is in fact largely accidental and may be altered at some later stage.

The chapter on intergovernmental cooperation starts with an affirmation of the necessity of cooperation "in accomplishing the objectives of the Code." Its more specific provisions, considerably weakened from earlier proposals, deal with consultations between governments "on matters relating to the Code and its application" and the exchange of information between governments, but only "on the measures they have taken to give effect to the Code and on their experience with [it]," and not on activities of transnational corporations or problems arising in specific cases involving the regulation of such corporations. Still between brackets is language calling for consultations concerning, according to one view, "conflicting requirements" imposed by governments on transnational corporations and conflicts of jurisdiction and, according to the other, "conflicting requirements imposed by parent companies" on affiliates operating abroad. This chapter further provides that "the objectives of the Code as reflected in its provisions" should be taken into consideration in the negotiation of international agreements which in some manner concern transnational corporations.

The chapter on implementation deals first with state activities at the national level. There is no gainsaying that action at this level is indispensable for the legal regulation of transnational corporations and for the effective application of the code. But this is an area where states, be they developed, developing or socialist, are most reluctant to promise anything specific as to the measures they will take or even the attitude they will adopt. As a result, the relevant provisions of the code are few and weak. It is characteristic that an undertaking that states "should take no action contrary to the objectives of the Code," which had been included in the text proposed by the Chairman, has been deleted from the "concluded" draft. The draft now mentions the duty of states to publicize the code and to "follow" ("monitor" was deemed too strong) its implementation within their territories. States are to report to the UN Commission on Transnational Corporations "on the action taken . . . to promote the Code and on the experience gained from its application." In view of the limited scope of these provisions, the most interesting one, because of its relatively open-ended character, is the paragraph which requires (requests) states to "take actions to reflect their support for the Code" and to take the Code's objectives into account when dealing with matters covered in the Code.

The establishment of institutional machinery for interpreting and implementing the Code at the international level has great potential significance. The actual significance depends on the precise role assigned to that machinery, its exact terms of reference. Early suggestions and drafts for the code referred to a wide spectrum of possible tasks for the competent organs. A 1978 paper, prepared by the UN Centre on Transnational Corporations,[24] distinguished four main types of functions for such organs: administrative and technical, policy-making, interpretative and advisory, and dispute settlement. The Secretariat would handle the first type of function, the UN Commission the second, an independent panel of experts the third, and *ad hoc* arrangements could be made for the last. Subsequent debate showed total lack of support among governments for an independent panel and the idea disappeared from later drafts. Gradually, moreover, most of the other explicit references to interpretation or "clarification" of the code, as a function of some organ of the institutional machinery, disappeared from the provisions on implementation. At this moment, inclusion of a reference to "clarification," among the terms of the UN Commission on Transnational Corporations, formally remains an open question, within brackets. It seems likely that whatever related language finds its way into the final text will be severely restrictive.

What has remained in the "concluded" text is a series of provisions designating the UN Commission on Transnational Corporations as the organ charged with oversight of the implementation of the code and as the "focal international body within the United Nations system for all matters related to the Code." The Commission's terms of reference include discussing matters related to the Code, facilitating intergovernmental consultations on related issues, assessing periodically the Code's implementation, and reporting annually to the UN General Assembly. Finally, there is provision for eventual "review" (i.e., revision) of the Code by the UN General Assembly on the recommendations of the UN Commission, on the basis of procedures to be established. The Centre on Transnational Corporations is charged with assisting the Commission in any way the latter sees fit, particularly through the collection and analysis of information and the preparation of studies.

When approaching the multifaceted problem of the application of the Code of Conduct, a distinction should be made at the outset between the situation of governments and that of the transnational corporations.[25] Most of our discussion here focuses on the former, yet this does not mean that identical considerations apply in the case of transnational corporations. While the States remain formally not bound by the Code, the corporations may find themselves under legal compulsion, in the directions established by the Code, whether because of legislative action by States or because the Code norms may, formally or informally, directly or indirectly, be given legal effect.[26] Other quasilegal or paralegal considerations, beyond that of binding force, may also obtain in the case of transnational corporations as they do in the case of States.

The lack of any reference in the Code to the modalities of its interpretation is no doubt a serious defect. The provisions of the Code are formulated in such a manner that, with very few exceptions, they cannot be applied so to speak automatically, without doubts or disputes. The language is far from specific; even when obscurity and ambiguity are not the obvious result of compromise, the language is frequently too inclusive to allow for ready application.[27] There is certainly need for interpretation and the lack of an established authoritative interpretative process is a significant gap in the code. It is possible, however, to go beyond this finding and suggest a slightly different perspective which usefully complements the view just stated.

To begin with, the traits of the Code's provisions just described, combined with the nonbinding character of the entire instrument, make any strict distinction between the implementation and application of the Code and its interpretation totally meaningless. Even when implementation is formally discussed, at issue is a process of interpretation and further development of the provisions and the entire system of the Code. We are aware by now that, contrary to the images in positivist doctrine, the outcome of an interpretative process depends largely on the context—the "what," the "who," the "what for"—in which it occurs.

Problems of interpretation must thus be seen in a number of possible lights. Different questions, requiring different answers, arise with respect to specific situations. First, the Code contains many kinds of provisions. Some are couched in very broad language, others in deliberately ambiguous formulations, still others are relatively specific or use technical terms. All of them need interpretation, but the interpretation problems arising with respect to each kind of provision vary considerably. In the second place, there is the problem of the person (or persons) charged with (or somehow involved in) interpreting the Code in each particular instance. Closely linked with this issue is the specific context in which a question of interpretation arises. A wide variety of possibilities exist in all these cases.

The implementation provisions of the code of conduct give an indication, although not an exhaustive one, of the contexts in which interpretation of its provisions will occur. A comprehensive listing of possible interpretation contexts might be tedious, but an illustrative catalogue—a baker's dozen—of possibilities may be instructive. The listing roughly follows the sequence of the Code chapter on implementation, adding along the way some related possibilities. The Code and any one of its provisions will be interpreted:

1. by a government in its effort to "publicize and disseminate" the Code of Conduct. Such publicity may only involve reprinting (or translating and publishing) the text of the Code, but it may go beyond mechanical reproduction; in summaries or paraphrase elements of interpretation are often present, through emphasis, omission, etc.;

2. by a government when monitoring ("following") the application of the Code in its territory.

3. by a transnational corporation (or one of its affiliates) when reporting or responding to a government official concerning the application of the Code, or in annual reports to stockholders and the public at large;

4. by a government when responding to the UN Commission on Transnational Corporations;

5. by a government when taking action through legislation or otherwise to give effect to the Code or on topics covered by the Code;

6. by a government official, especially but not exclusively a judge, when dealing with cases where the Code is invoked in domestic disputes or negotiations;

7. by a trade union or other group or association when presenting a grievance to a government or a transnational corporation;

8. by a trade union and a transnational corporation affiliate when settling a dispute or concluding a collective agreement;

9. by two governments when settling a dispute or dealing with any other related matter on the basis of the code;

10. by a government in an "exchange of views" within the Commission;

11. by the Commission as a whole in its "assessments" of the application of the Code and in its annual reports to the UN General Assembly;

12. by the UN Commission on Transnational Corporations in a possible "clarification" proceeding. Reference to such a possibility has not been definitely included in the current draft of the Code. Presumably, even in the absence of such provision, the Commission may still be able to offer "clarifications," perhaps under another name, where there is no objection to its doing so;

13. by a nongovernmental organization or association when presenting or answering a "case" before the Commission. The exact role of such associations is still undecided.

The authoritative value of the interpretation issuing from each of these contexts is by no means the same; these are not all legally equivalent situations. However, the nonbinding character of the code eliminates the usual sharp dichotomy between authoritative and nonauthoritative interpretative processes. Since no interpretation is formally binding, all interpretations are, if not equal, at least close to being equivalent. Differences still persist, no doubt; some are too obvious to require extensive analysis: An interpretation agreed to by all participants in a collective process (e.g., a conclusion of the UN Commission on Transnational Corporations) is, of course, more authoritative (i.e., more valuable as precedent, closer to being binding in effect, if not in law) than an interpretation offered by a single state or transnational corporation in argument during a dispute. Still, the differences are less sharp than otherwise; what matters is far less the formal process and far more the substantive content and the persuasiveness of the particular position. All interpretations, given in any kind of situation, will constitute the background for positions eventually adopted by each one of the international actors involved in the transnational corporation drama.

What we are talking about, of course, is something very far away from the formal certainty of a private contract, or even of many international treaties. In classical private law, (at least in doctrine, as distinguished from the realities of a complex economy) a contract negates the existence of the time dimension; a meeting of minds which has occurred at a particular moment is frozen (i.e., made binding) for the predictable future, and is thus placed outside time. In theory, the same is true of a treaty. In practice, a margin for reconsideration is allowed in many treaties (except, for instance, in the case of the so-called "dispositive" treaties). This is done mainly through careful drafting of the treaty text itself (e.g., the exact language describing the parties' obligations, the possibility of denunciation, etc.). Only in exceptional cases must states rely on principles outside the treaty itself in order to find the flexibility they may need. In some cases, moreover, the international agreement itself contains no hard (i.e., certain) obligations on substantive issues and constitutes essentially a procedural framework for future negotiations.

It is in that last direction that we must try to locate the effects of the instrument we are studying. The interpretation and application of the Code of Conduct can be best understood as involving a continuous process of negotiation. That the outcome of this process is not predetermined does not mean that the Code makes no difference. The process of negotiation would not have been the same, had there been no Code of Conduct. The Code provides both a procedural framework and a substantive frame of reference. The procedural framework is strict neither in terms of jurisdiction (its "competence" is not exclusive) nor in terms of certainty. Yet it still serves to channel some, possibly most, of the related debates, disputes, and claims. The substantive frame of reference involves the invocation of a number of broad principles and some not very clear substantive and procedural norms. It affects all discussion in the sense that all arguments now have to be couched in reference to certain terms and concepts. The Code thus delimits the area of debate and negotiation; certain borderlines are established, even though they are often imprecise and highly inclusive.

The actual effectiveness of this complex and confused process (that is to say, the degree to which it will influence the behavior of relevant actors) will depend in any particular case on a number of considerations, for example, the actual degree of consensus reached among the states involved (and possibly other actors) and the inherent reasonableness of the interpretation, not by reference to some metaphysical "ratio" but in view of the concrete legal practices and political and economic conditions of the moment. Neither the usefulness nor the uselessness of such an instrument should be exaggerated.

Notes

1. The history of this and other codes is usefully summarized in H. Baade, "Introductory Survey," in N. Horn & E.R. Lanier eds., *Legal Problems of Codes of Conduct for Multinational Enterprises* 407 (1980). For the particular antecedents and history of the UN Code discussed here, see A.A. Fatouros, "Le projet de Code international de conduite sur les entreprises transnationales: essai preliminaire d'evaluation," 107 *J.Dr. Int'l* (Clunet) 5, 7–15 (1980).

2. ECOSOC Res. 1721 (LIII), 28 July 1972.

3. UN, Department of Economic and Social Affairs, *The Impact of Multinational Corporations on Development and on International Relations* (New York, 1974, E.74.II.A. 5) (hereinafter cited as U.N., *Impact*). For the earlier report, see note 10 *infra*.

4. UN, *Impact, supra* note 3, at 54–55. And see the introductory report of the UN Secretary General, *ibid.* at 7.

5. ECOSOC Res. 1913 (LVII), 5 December 1974; and cf. ECOSOC Res. 1908 (LVII), 2 August 1974.

6. UN Commission on Transnational Corporations, *Report of the Second Session* (March 1976), UN Doc. E/5782 (E/C.10/ 16) 3–4, ll–12. And see, UN, Centre on Transnational Corporations, *Transnational Corporations: Issues Involved in the Formulation of a Code of Conduct*, UN Doc. E/C.10/17, July 1976; ibid., *Transnational Corporations: Material Relevant to the Formulation of a Code of Conduct*, UN Doc. E/C.10/18, December 1976.

7. See the Working Group's last report, UN Doc. E/C.10/ 1982, May 1982.

8. See, UNCTAD, *The Regulation of Liner Conferences (A Code of Conduct for the Liner Conference System)*, Geneva, 1972, E.72.II.D.13; UN Conference of Plenipotentiaries on a Code of Conduct for Liner Conferences, Final Act, 6 April 1974, UN Doc. TD/CODE/ll/Rev.l, April 1974, repr. 13 *Int'l Legal Materials* 910 (1974).

9. See, UNCTAD, Intergovernmental Group of Experts on Transfer of Technology, Res. l (II), para. 17 (February 1973), in UN Doc. TD/B/424 (Annex I), February 1973. And cf. Res. 104 (XIII) of the UNCTAD Trade and Development Board, September 1973.

10. UN Department of Economic and Social Affairs, *Multinational Corporations in World Development*, UN Doc. ST/ECA/190, New York, 1973, at 92-93.

11. *Ibid.* at 93.

12. UN, Impact *supra* note 3, at 55.

13. *Ibid.* at 57.

14. ECOSOC Res. 1913 (LVII), 5 December 1974.

15. A.A. Fatouros, "The UN Code of Conduct on Transnational Corporations: A Critical Discussion of the First Drafting Phase," in Horn & Lanier eds., *supra* note l, 103, at 107–08.

16. OECD Council Resolution on the Draft Convention on the Protection of Foreign Property, adopted on 12 October 1967 (with draft convention text annexed), 7 *Int'l Legal Materials* 117 (1968).

17. UNCTAD, Draft International Code of Conduct on the Transfer of Technology, UN Doc. TD/CODE.TOT/33, 10 April 1981. For some discussions of this code, see, G. Wilner, "Transfer of Technology: The UNCTAD Code of Conduct," in Horn & Lanier eds. *supra* note l, 177; A.A. Fatouros, "International Controls of Technology Transfers," in T. Sagafi-nejad, R. Moxon & H.W. Perlmutter eds., *Controlling International Technology Transfer: Issues, Perspectives, and Policy Implications* 478, 489–98 (New York, etc., 1981); D. Thompson, "The UNCTAD Code on Transfer of Technology," 16 *J. World Trade L.* 311 (1982).

18. UN Centre on Transnational Corporations, *Transnational Corporations: Issues Involved in the Formulation of a Code of Conduct*, UN Doc. E/C.10/17, July 1976.

19. UN Commission on Transnational Corporations, Report of the Intergovernmental Working Group on a Code of Conduct, UN Doc. E/C.10/31, May 1977, at 2–3.

20. *Ibid.* at 5–15, repr. in *The CTC Reporter*, No. 2 (June 1977), 10–12.

21. UN, Commission on Transnational Corporations, Intergovernmental Working Group on a Code of Conduct, Working Paper No. l (March 1978).

22. UN Commission on Transnational Corporations, Intergovernmental Working Group on a Code of Conduct, "Transnational Corporations: Code of Conduct: Formulations by the Chairman," UN Doc. E/C.10/AC.2/8, December 1978, repr. in *The CTC Reporter* No. 6 (April 1979) 5–8.

23. Cf. J. Davidow and L. Chiles, "The United States and the Issue of the Binding or Voluntary Nature of International Codes of Conduct regarding Restrictive Business Practices," 72 *Am. J. Int'l L.* 247 (1978); H.W. Baade, "The Legal Effects of Codes of Conduct for MNEs," in Horn & Lanier eds. *supra* note l, at 3; A. A. Fatouros, "On the Implementation of International Codes of Conduct: An Analysis of Future Experience," 30 *Am.U.L. Rev.* 941, at 949–52 (1981).

24. UN Commission on Transnational Corporations, "Transnational Corporations: Certain Modalities for Implementation of a Code of Conduct in Relation to Its Possible Legal Nature," UN Doc. E/C.10/AC.2/9, December 1978.

25. See, Baade *supra* note 23, at 21-24; Fatouros, *supra* note 23, at 968-69; and the more detailed discussion in P. Sanders, "Codes of Conduct and Sources of Law," pages 281-299 of *Le droit des relations commerciales internationales, Etudes offertes a Berthold Goldman,* Publishers: Librairie Technique, Paris (1983).

26. For instance, through their incorporation in the *lex mercatoria* governing private and semi-private international transactions; see Sanders *supra* note 25; N. Horn, "Die Entwicklung des internationalen Wirtschaftsrechts durch Verhaltensrichtlinien—Neue Elemente eines internationalen Ordre Public," 44 *Rabels Zeitschrift* 423 (1980).

27. For some indications on the role of language in such instruments, see Fatouros, *supra* note 23, at 955–57.

SEVEN

The Implementation of International Antitrust Principles

JOEL DAVIDOW

At least since protectionism and cartelization contributed to world depression and the rise of dictatorships in the 1930's, many western nations, particularly the United States, have sought to expand and protect a liberal world trading order. That order is based on lowering tariffs to the point where they do not impede international trade, developing the principles of nondiscrimination and reciprocity in trade and investment, eliminating all significant nontariff barriers to trade and investment, and creating rules that differentiate fair international competition from unfair competition.

Almost from the outset, it has been clear that rules controlling restrictive business practices are an important part of the ideal liberal world economic order. Private cartelization negates free trade as surely as public protectionism. Nevertheless, progress in the antitrust dimension was for many years very slow and very controversial. United Nations antitrust codes were proposed in 1948 and 1953, but in both instances failed to gain adoption, particularly because of U.S. opposition. The adoption of OECD antitrust guidelines in the late 1970's and of U.N. principles and rules concerning the control of restrictive business practices in 1980, are significant developments in this evolving area of international economic "soft law."[1] But major controversies remain, and implementation procedures are still in their infancy. Before considering what can be achieved in adopting and implementing antitrust principles and rules at the international level, it is useful first to survey the antitrust

Joel Davidow is a Partner, Mudge, Guthrie, & Alexander, New York City; former Director of Policy Planning, Antitrust Division, U.S. Department of Justice; and U.S. Delegate to U.N. Conferences on Restrictive Business Practices and Transfer of Technology.

policies now in force at the national level, noting variations in their purposes, scope and methods of enforcement. It is these differences, combined with conflicts of national interest, which have caused nations to be shy of binding norms and full cooperation in this field.

1. National Approaches

Under the political pressure of the Granger movement, Canada and the United States adopted antitrust laws in 1889 and 1890.[2] In practice, the United States law has been much more effectively developed and applied, though the Canadian statute continues in force and has been slightly strengthened in recent years. The United States has supplemented its antitrust laws on numerous occasions, but most enforcement has arisen under four provisions: Section 1 of the Sherman Act, which condemns all agreements, combinations or conspiracies in restraint of trade; Section 2 of the Sherman Act, which condemns monopolies or attempts to monopolize; Section 7 of the Clayton Act of 1914, which condemns mergers and acquisitions which may substantially lessen competition; and Section 2 of the Clayton Act of 1914 as amended by the Robinson Patman Act of 1936, which condemns anti-competitive price discrimination.[3]

After an auspicious early period when the Sherman Act was used successfully to break up the oil trust and the tobacco trust among others, the law gradually became quiescent during the pro-business period of the 1920's and the pro-cartel and regulation period of the early 1930's.[4] The U.S. turned strongly to a pro-antitrust policy in the late 1930's and this continued during World War II, supported by revelations that international cartels may have contributed to the depression and to the rise of dictators.[5] After World War II, the United States insisted on the adoption of antitrust laws and policies in Germany and Japan, and was influential in installing similar laws in liberated countries such as France and the Philippines.[6] A committee on restrictive business practice legislation was established in the Marshall Plan organization in Europe in 1954, and became a permanent part of the Marshall Plan's successor, the OECD, in 1961.[7] By the mid-1970's, twenty-two of twenty-four OECD member nations had an antitrust law of some kind. About a dozen developing countries have also adopted such laws.[8]

In general, most laws followed the U.S. model; having one section dealing with multi-firm conduct such as agreements or combinations that unduly restrain competition, and one dealing with single firm conduct such as acquiring or abusing a dominant position of market power. Eight of twenty-two OECD countries adopted a system of merger control, though only the German law was as stringent as the U.S. law.[9] In about half a dozen OECD countries, price discrimination is specifically controlled by a competition statute.[10] Criminal penalties are authorized in only a few states.[11] Private damage actions are allowed in about ten countries, though treble damages are authorized only in the United States.[12]

2. Variations in the Purposes, Scope and Approach of National Laws

The purposes of most antitrust laws are similar, though there are some important variations and unresolved contradictions. It is generally agreed that the major single purpose of antitrust rules is to further economic efficiency, for the benefit of consumers, through the encouragement and preservation of competition. A second purpose that often motivates such laws, but is not fully consistent with the first purpose, is to ensure that competition is fair as well as vigorous, that powerful firms do not crush weaker ones and that a multiplicity of firms is preserved. A third purpose, really a corollary of the first, is to ensure that private restrictive arrangements do not restrain or distort patterns of trade, particularly of international trade.

A fourth purpose, not always recognized by economists, is to ensure that the control of markets or regulation of trade remains solely a prerogative of sovereign states. To protect the principle that sovereign action does not violate the antitrust laws but that unauthorized private action does, courts have developed special defenses such as the act of state, state action, and foreign compulsion doctrines in the United States, as well as the rule that the delegation of unfettered cartel discretion to self-interested groups will not justify exemption.[13] The distinctions required by these rules, however, can become very fine and controversial, particularly when many enterprises are state owned or managed, or when government involvement in industrial decision-making is very informal and involves large delegations of power.

A fifth purpose of most antitrust laws is to further the national interests of the enacting country, including its trading interests. Such purposes underlie all laws affecting commerce. However, in the antitrust field whether or how to take such factors into account has led to considerable debate. A national interest standard is not always written into antitrust laws. Moreover, it is debatable whether such laws should be enforced against almost all anti-competitive practices, as presumably being injurious to the national interest, except for limited exemptions (such as for export promotion), or whether national officials should undertake a case-by-case analysis of whether prosecution in a specific instance would further national political or economic goals. In general, most nations ex-

empt all purely outward bound conduct from the coverage of their antitrust laws, but most of them do not engage in case-by-case analysis as to
whether other practices might serve some national interest purpose even
while limiting competition. But specific responses vary considerably
from nation to nation, particularly in regard to merger control.[14]

Generally speaking, there are four major methods of antitrust enforcement: criminal actions, civil actions, administrative actions before a
specialized tribunal, and injunctive and damage actions by private citizens. The United States is unique in providing for all four methods. The
European Common Market in contrast, provides expressly only for
administrative enforcement by a government agency, though private actions seem possible in some member state courts.[15]

Overall, the United States remains the world leader in the severity of
its antitrust sanctions. Criminal violations can lead to fines of up to one
million dollars per offense for a corporation and one hundred thousand
dollars for an individual. Individuals may also be sentenced to up to
three years in prison for each offense. Treble damage recoveries in private actions have led to recoveries of over $1 billion.[16] Recently, the Eu-
ropean Communities Commission has levied administrative fines even
more severe than the criminal fines of the United States, penalizing
firms over $6 million for a scheme of market allocation that was de-
signed to enforce resale price maintenance.[17] Many countries object to
the use of criminal sanctions against antitrust violations and to the
trebling of damages.

Nations vary in theory and in practice concerning the international
coverage of their competition rules. The Sherman Act outlaws all restraints on U.S. commerce among the states or with foreign nations.
This has been interpreted and enforced to mean, at the extreme, that a
restrictive agreement made entirely outside the U.S. and entirely by foreigners may be held to violate the Sherman Act if the scheme is likely to
produce a restrictive effect on U.S. foreign or domestic commerce.[18]
Other jurisdictions, such as the European Common Market and
Germany, have also concluded that their law is applicable to extraterritorial activities by foreigners, but they have brought fewer cases of that
nature, and they do not apply criminal or treble damage sanctions to
such conduct.[19]

Some nations, such as the United Kingdom and Australia, have con-
tended that it is not legal for a nation to apply its domestic law to a foreign corporation unless at least some significant overt acts by it have
taken place on national soil.[20] They object particularly strongly to the
employment of severe sanctions against their nationals in cases where
they believe jurisdiction is improper or doubtful.

The issue of permissible jurisdiction is complicated because a number of distinct jurisdictional issues can be presented in the course of an antitrust matter: (i) jurisdiction over the offense; (ii) jurisdiction over the persons involved, including the possibility of jurisdiction over a foreign parent or subsidiary corporation; (iii) jurisdiction over information located abroad that is relevant to investigation or trial; and (iv) jurisdiction over relevant assets located abroad for purposes of effective relief. Because of strong theoretical differences concerning the appropriate limits of each type of jurisdiction, conflicting national interests perceived in international antitrust cases, and important differences as to appropriate exemptions from antitrust rules, there have been continuing pressures to develop international rules that would set limits on the exercise of national antitrust enforcement, or would require notification, consultation, conciliation or even arbitration. In the meantime, countries that object to the "long arm" aspect of U.S. antitrust jurisdiction have refused to follow international recommendations urging cooperation in eliminating restrictive business practices, and have devised measures to hinder U.S. investigations or cases.[21]

A different but equally important complaint about the enforcement of antitrust and related laws to foreign or foreign-owned enterprises is that such enforcement, particularly in developing countries, may be unfair or discriminatory. Some LDCs in fact use antitrust type rules only in the context of foreign investment or transfer of technology regulations, and thus apply them only to foreign firms. Many LDCs write strict rules but grant an administrative official broad powers to allow exceptions.[22]

These disputes and concerns have produced at least as much pressure for international norms to limit antitrust enforcement as for norms to limit cartel practices. In fact, the development of international mechanisms for states to consult with each other concerning antitrust enforcement efforts, though still limited, has far outpaced the development of international mechanisms for states to help one another investigate, prevent, or punish anticompetitive practices.

3. Early Efforts at International Antitrust Codification

In addition to the adoption of antitrust laws at the national level in some nations, particularly Germany and Japan, there were important efforts to create such laws or policies at the international level after World War II. In 1948, under U.S. leadership, over fifty nations agreed at Havana to a charter for an international trade organization that would be headquartered in Geneva and that, among other things, would implement a code against classic types of restrictive business practices. For a variety of reasons, a conservative incoming U.S. Congress refused to support this effort, and it was postponed.[23] The project was revived under the auspices of the United Nations Economic and Social Council in New York in 1952, when a committee of ten nations drew up a limited program of investigation and voluntary national enforcement against a similar list of restrictive practices to that contained in the Havana Charter. Again, conversative opposition in the United States led to abandonment of the effort, on grounds that too few nations had adopted competition laws and policies around the world to guarantee uniform implementation, and that further development at national and regional level should precede international or worldwide efforts.[24]

In the early 1950's, competition rules of a binding nature at a multinational level were adopted for the first time, as part of the European Coal and Steel Community regime. Those rules have been enforced successfully ever since to control steel mergers and consolidations, though hardly to stop them.[25] In 1958, the European Common Market, then a federation of six nations, now of ten, was created by the Treaty of Rome. Articles 85 and 86 of the treaty condemn all restrictive agreements or abuses of a dominant position that have the effect of injuring competition within the Common Market and thus interfering with attainment of free trade among its member states.[26]

Regional antitrust rules were also adopted as part of the European Free Trade Association charter and as part of the Caribbean Compact, but neither set has had significant application. The Andean Pact, adopted by five Latin-American states as part of their common market efforts in the early 1970's included in its charter the so-called "Decision 24," which condemns certain restrictive practices involved in the transfer of technology to member states.[27] Those rules were enforceable only at the national level, though the Pact did have the effect of unifying the law of member states at a fairly high level of stringency.

4. OECD Codes and Their Implementation

So far, the most effectively implemented international norm in regard to antitrust is the OECD notification recommendation first passed in 1967 and recodified in 1979. Under that recommendation, all OECD nations with an antitrust enforcement program are asked to notify other member nations in advance of any investigation or prosecution that is likely to affect important interests of the other nations. Such notifications are provided by the U.S., Germany and other major countries with religious regularity. OECD studies indicate that over two hundred notifications are made every year.[28] The U.S. alone gives about forty or fifty notifications a year and receives about a dozen notifications from other nations.

The U.S. Justice Department and Federal Trade Commission (FTC), for instance, notify foreign governments before beginning antitrust investigations involving their firms, or as soon as a domestic investigation changes focus to offshore conduct by foreigners, and again about ten days before prosecution. Notification is normally by letter or cable, to whatever foreign agency the foreign government has listed with the OECD, usually its foreign office.

One obvious purpose of such notifications was to facilitate government-to-government consultations concerning controversial matters that were of strong interest to both nations. It soon developed that consultations were held in almost every case where they were requested after notification, which occurred in approximately 10 per cent of the notified situations. In 1979, the obligation to consult was itself codified into an OECD recommendation, which reads as follows:

Consultation and Conciliation

3.(a) a Member country that considers a restrictive business practice investigation or proceeding being conducted by another Member country to affect its important interests should transmit its views on the matter to or request consultation with the other Member country;

(b) without prejudice to the continuation of its action under its restrictive business practices law and to its full freedom of ultimate decision, the Member country so addressed should give full and sympathetic consideration to the views expressed by the requesting country, and in particular to any suggestions as to alternative means of fulfilling the needs or objectives of the restrictive business practice investigation or proceedings.[29]

Although OECD recommendations are ostensibly voluntary, there have been few instances in which a nation has declined to follow them. However, since most nations will consult about almost any matter of common interest with other friendly countries, the statistical record of cooperation does not necessarily indicate a development of international norms or procedures extending very much beyond the normalities of ordinary diplomatic relations. It is likely, however, that regularizing the procedures makes it more probable that notifications will occur, will be prompt and thorough, and will lead to meaningful consultations.

Since 1967, the OECD has had a recommended procedure for antitrust conciliation as well as for notification and consultation. The idea of the conciliation procedure is that, when an OECD member nation believes itself injured by a restrictive business practice occurring on the territory of another member nation, it should request conciliation and seek redress by the home country of the enterprises involved. Further, when two member nations are unable to conciliate their differences, it is suggested that they should submit the problem to a committee of experts from other member nations, in the hope that the committee can recommend an acceptable solution. However, neither part of this procedure has ever been used.

In 1979, when the notification/consultation procedure was revised and clarified, the United States suggested that the conciliation procedure should be eliminated because it appeared to be useless. A few smaller nations clung to the view that even the threat of conciliation might be persuasive in some situations. There being no consensus to eliminate the conciliation recommendation, it was reconfirmed in the 1979 formulation, though it continues to be studiously avoided by all member nations. The new text reads:

> 4.(a) a Member country that considers that one or more enterprises situated in one or more other Member countries are or have been engaged in restrictive business practices of whatever origin that are substantially and adversely affecting its interests may request consultation with such other Member country or countries, recognizing that the entering into such consultations is without prejudice to any action under its restrictive business practices law and to the full freedom of ultimate decision of the Member countries concerned;
>
> (b) any Member country so addressed should give full and sympathetic consideration to such views and factual materials as may be provided by the requesting country and, in particular, to the nature of the restrictive business practices in question, the enterprises involved and the alleged harmful effects on the interests of the requesting country;
>
> (c) the Member country addressed which agrees that enterprises situated in its territory are engaged in restrictive business practices harmful to the interests of the requesting country should attempt to ensure that these enterprises take remedial action, or should itself take whatever remedial action it considers appropriate, including actions under its legislation on restrictive business practices or administrative measures on a voluntary basis and considering its legitimate interest.[30]

There are a number of difficulties with the conciliation idea. Nations that are prepared to apply their antitrust laws to extraterritorial conduct usually find no need to seek the assistance of foreign governments. The foreign governments, in fact, are often unable or unwilling to provide assistance in suppressing the restrictive practice. If the practice produces no adverse effect on their domestic market, they may be unable to control it because it does not constitute a violation of their law. If the practice is export-related and earns foreign exchange for their enterprises at the expense of the complaining government, or has the blessing of the exporting state, that state is not likely to interfere with it. Lately, most antitrust investigations concern conduct that has already occurred, or that ceases when the investigations become intense. In such cases, the relevant remedies are penalties or damages, neither of which can normally be obtained through diplomatic consultation with a foreign government.

As to conciliation by neutral third parties, no OECD member seems prepared to submit its antitrust enforcement decisions to the review and judgment of foreigners, no matter how expert or disinterested. The actual or symbolic surrender of sovereignty is simply too great to be made voluntarily.

In general, studies by the OECD Restrictive Business Practice Committee have dealt with past enforcement experience or possible directions for legislation, rather than with the behavior of enterprises. However, by 1976 the issue of multinational enterprise behavior had become so politically intense that it was decided that the OECD should formulate appropriate guidelines. These guidelines numbered twenty-nine, four of them relating to restrictive business practices. In brief, the four competition principles for multinationals provided that such firms should (i) avoid abuses of dominant positions of market power; (ii) allow distributors and licensees reasonable freedom to purchase and re-sell; (iii) avoid participation in international cartels lacking government approval; and (iv) provide needed information to national antitrust officials.[31]

There was no prescribed enforcement mechanism for the Guidelines, beyond the understanding that OECD governments would recommend them to their enterprises. A working Group of the Committee on Investment and Multinational Enterprise (CIME) does consult about issues arising under the Guidelines, with the assistance of the Business and Industry Advisory Committee (BIAC) and the Trade Union Advisory Committees (TUAC) of OECD, and with the possible participation of interested companies.[32] However, the CIME is prohibited from examining or commenting on the behavior of individual enterprises. The Guidelines are to be reviewed every three years. Such a review was conducted in 1979, and resulted in the inclusion of one additional guideline in the labor relations area.[33]

Apparently the competition guidelines have not yet been consulted about, interpreted or used in any decisive way, though some nations report that they have referred to the guidelines in discussions with enterprises or with other nations. This is not to say that the OECD Guidelines are incapable of actual effect. The labor guidelines have resulted in at least five consultations and have twice been cited by national courts or administrations in situations where a multinational enterprise eventually agreed to conform its behavior to the international standard. Thus, it seems conceivable that the competition guidelines will ultimately have some practical effect, though they appear to offer less fertile pastures for potential complainants than the norms on labor relations.

5. United Nations Codes and Their Implementation

In the mid-1970s, political issues arose in the United Nations concerning the investment behavior of multinational corporations. This concern was increased by particular scandals involving bribery and political interference, and the issues presented ranged from labor relations to 'restrictive business practices. Developing countries sought to codify a "new international economic order" in which international trade, investment, competition, and technology transfer would be restructured to assure the weaker nations fairer and more favorable treatment.[34]

While a newly created U.N. Center on Transnational Enterprises worked on a general code of conduct, the United Nations Conference on Trade and Development (UNCTAD) in Geneva was assigned the task of gathering experts to negotiate a set of principles and rules for the control of restrictive business practices and a code of conduct for the transfer of technology.

Although both exercises involved antitrust-type issues, the restrictive business practice principles proved significantly easier to negotiate than the code on technology transfer. Both negotiations commenced in 1975. The restrictive business practice rules were adopted unanimously by a U.N. conference in the spring of 1980 and endorsed by the U.N. General Assembly in December 1980.[35] The transfer of technology negotiation reached nearly total impasse in 1980 and 1981, with about 40 per cent of its provisions still in dispute, particularly those relating to restrictive licensing practices and to choice of law and forum for the settlement of licensing disputes. The final meeting in 1981 ended with so little progress that the delegates could not even agree on when or whether to hold another negotiating conference. A new conference schedule has been formulated, but it remains unlikely that agreement will be reached on the full code. One reason for this is that the Reagan Administration has adopted even more conservative attitudes toward patent-antitrust issues than its predecessors.[36]

Initially many of the most controversial issues in the restrictive business practice ("RBP") and transfer of technology ("TOT") negotiations concerned issues of legal nature and implementation, but these were generally resolved with very moderate compromise solutions. It was largely differences in background, purpose and perception that explain the disparate results of the two negotiations.

The idea of an RBP code found support in the United States and other western nations from the days of the Havana conference, long before the developing countries came to favor the approach. Antitrust laws in the developing world were largely copied from developed country antecedents, and had no special relation to investment or trade issues, nor to the political side of disputes about multinational enterprises. The TOT code, on the other hand, was a project solely of the developing countries. The leaders of this movement, Mexico, Brazil and India, had copied a few strategies from post-war Japan and a few rules from U.S. antitrust cases, but they had mixed these into a stringent form of investment control and contract interference that was generally not used in developed nations. Moreover, the developing countries saw the TOT code as a way of weakening international norms protecting the rights of technology suppliers, while the U.S. and a number of other major western nations saw their own interests as contrary, since they were major technology suppliers and were fully committed to the protection of patent and know-how rights.

The first general issue in regard to both codes was whether they should be cast as potentially legally binding international conventions, or merely as voluntary recommendations.[37] The position of the western nations was clear and consistent: The codes must be voluntary and not legally binding. In fact, western delegates took this position long before the substantive provisions of the codes were known.

Developing countries delegates engaged in some political confrontation with the West on this issue, but their position was not nearly as far in the other direction as preliminary rhetoric made it appear. Shortly into the negotiations on an RBP code, the Group of 77 dropped their quest for a binding code and contented themselves with seeking express assurances of each nation's "commitment" to a nonbinding one. They also insisted that the word "voluntary" not appear in the document, though they agreed to a text stating that the text consisted of "recommendations" to states. The legally binding issue was pushed harder by the G-77 in the TOT code negotiation, though it was eventually surrendered in exchange for language implying that the question could be revived at a review conference five years after adoption.

In both negotiations, the G-77 were vague and cautious about what their legal nature proposals might entail. At no time did they suggest an international investigative and enforcement agency, or an international court, modeled after the institutions that have been so effective in making Common Market competition rules an international reality. Their concept, at most, called for a convention which nations would interpret or enforce as they saw fit after adoption.

If the RBP Code is to have any practical effect on the behavior of en-

terprises, its meaning will have to be interpreted. There are some codes
of conduct which, although voluntary, are so clear, direct and simple
that their mere promulgation will have significant effect, particularly if
political pressure is applied. For instance, the OECD Guidelines for
Multinational Enterprises state in regard to labor relations that a parent
company should assist an insolvent subsidiary in paying severance wages
to the former employees of the subsidiary.[38] When such a situation
occurred in Belgium after the adoption of the OECD Guidelines, political pressure was brought to bear on the parent company, Badger Corporation, and it eventually provided additional funds.[39] It is very doubtful, however, that the antitrust rules in the RBP Code could be used in
the same way. A rule stating that a firm should not abuse a dominant
position of market power by restricting exports when not justified by
reasons of adequate distribution and service is so full of arguable and
vague terms that a company would seldom acknowledge voluntarily that
its conduct contravenes the rule. Only a tribunal capable of discovering
facts and interpreting rules could be expected to apply these broad principles to an actual or illustrative case.

Initially the only group capable of implementing or interpreting the
United Nations' RBP Code will be an intergovernmental group of experts created by Section G of the Code. That section provides that a
group of experts operating within the framework of a Committee of
UNCTAD should provide a forum for consultations and discussions
among states on matters relating to the Principles and Rules—
particularly their operation, the advancement of their goals, and the
steps states have taken to promote them.[40] This work includes periodic
studies of restrictive business practices, and examination of studies produced by other groups or of data obtained upon request. The group
may make reports and recommendations to states on matters within its
competence, including the application and implementation of the Principles and Rules. However, all these functions are to be carried out
within the strict limits of Section G(4), which mandates that:

> In the performance of its functions, neither the Intergovernmental Group
> nor its subsidiary organs shall act like a tribunal or otherwise pass judg-
> ment on the activities or conduct of individual Governments or of individ-
> ual enterprises in connection with a specific business transaction. The
> Intergovernmental Group or its subsidiary organs should avoid becoming
> involved when enterprises to a specific business transaction are in dispute.

What can one realistically expect from a group so new and diverse,
with such broad responsibilities and limited powers? It is most unlikely
that the group will achieve anything approaching antitrust enforcement
or will even provide much interpretation of the Principles and Rules.

The absence of implementation and interpretation will probably not disappoint the developed countries. Their position, based on OECD experience and fear of developing country domination, was that the group of experts should devote itself primarily to discussions of national legislative and enforcement experience, rather than attempt to turn the Principles and Rules into international law or transform UNCTAD into an antitrust enforcement agency.

The weaker developing countries on the other hand have often doubted whether national antitrust laws suited their stage of economic development or their social philosophy. They question whether they can staff and operate an effective antitrust enforcement program against large foreign corporations. Accordingly, they believe they would benefit if the Principles and Rules were treated seriously by developed countries and their enterprises, and if UNCTAD were capable of using publicity and discussion as an instrument for change. Even before adoption of the Principles and Rules, UNCTAD had published studies of restrictive business practices by certain industries, such as chemicals and heavy electrical equipment. To add meat to some of these studies, developing countries provided UNCTAD with government studies documenting the prevalence of certain restrictive practices. A number of developing countries, for instance, provided data concerning the percentage of licenses to their countries that included partial or complete export prohibitions or tying clauses.

Western nations and industries have attacked some of these UNCTAD studies as simplistic or biased. Possibly the power of the new group of experts to issue its own studies will give national delegates, particularly from the West, greater influence over the accuracy and neutrality of such investigative efforts than was available in the past.

The other implementation device included in the RBP Code is the consultation procedure outlined in Section F(4):

4. Consultations:

(a) Where a State, particularly of a developing country, believes that a consultation with another State or States is appropriate in regard to an issue concerning control of restrictive business practices, it may request a consultation with those States with a view to finding a mutually acceptable solution. When a consultation is to be held, the States involved may request the Secretary-General of UNCTAD to provide mutually agreed conference facilities for such a consultation;

(b) States should accord full consideration to requests for consultations and upon agreement as to the subject of and the procedures for such a consultation, the consultation should take place at an appropriate time;

(c) If the States involved so agree, a joint report on the consultations and their results should be prepared by the States involved and, if they so wish, with the assistance of the UNCTAD secretariat, and be made available to the Secretary-General of UNCTAD for inclusion in the annual report on restrictive business practices.[41]

This consultation procedure is in every possible sense voluntary. Because of mutual suspicion between developed and developing nations, the procedure is even weaker than its analogue in the OECD.[42] The developed countries would have liked a rule requiring notification of all antitrust proceedings against their enterprises in developing countries. The LDCs were unwilling to agree to this, out of concern that larger, stronger nations would pressure them to drop investigations.

The LDCs would have liked three additional provisions allowing the Secretary-General of UNCTAD to invite nations to consultations, authorizing the UNCTAD secretariat to provide substantive technical assistance to a developing country engaged in a consultation, and allowing recourse to the Trade and Development Board of UNCTAD for any party to a consultation who was dissatisfied with its outcome. The West strongly resisted these suggestions on the grounds that they would place undue pressure on the home governments of multinational corporations. The proposals were eventually abandoned as part of a general compromise under which the West abandoned the idea of notification of national proceedings.

The final result is a seemingly innocuous text stating not much more than what is obvious, that most nations are prepared to consult with most other nations on almost any subject that is raised in a diplomatic manner. On the other hand, it is possible that the existence of this text may embolden some new or small nations to raise antitrust issues with nations they would not previously have thought to approach, and may add a little pressure on the consulting nation to take the discussion seriously. If nations do agree to consult on restrictive business matters in Geneva at UNCTAD, the forum may lend a little greater weight to the proceedings than would be accorded to more ordinary consultations. Lastly, the possibility that there may be a written report summarizing the consultation and its result (this, too, is voluntary), and the possibility that this report may be included in the annual RBP report of UNCTAD, increase somewhat the incentives for a serious consultation and a mutually acceptable outcome.

However, in light of OECD experience, it remains doubtful that the home country of an enterprise will be willing to consult about the firm's conduct abroad or to promise to seek to alter that conduct, by law, persuasion, or otherwise. The consultations that have been most frequent under the OECD procedure—those relating to treatment of foreign firms under local antitrust laws—are unlikely to be popular in the UNCTAD context, since developing countries want to initiate the consultations and they generally want to complain about enterprise behavior rather than about antitrust prosecution.

In 1981, sixteen states reported to the Secretary General of UNCTAD that they had met their "commitment" to the Code.[43] In two cases, those of Korea and Argentina, the action reported was adoption of a national antitrust law. In a few other cases, strengthening amendments to national antitrust laws were reported. In many developed countries, the only implementing activities reported were letters to national business organizations calling the new code to their attention. This was the case in the United States, where the State and Justice Departments co-authored a letter to eight hundred business leaders combined with a question and answer sheet explaining the Code and emphasizing its voluntary nature.[44]

In October 1981, the first meeting of the permanent U.N. committee of experts on restrictive business practices was held at UNCTAD. There, developed country delegates established the principle that they could control which antitrust topics the secretariat would study. The delegates agreed that studies would be made concerning exclusive distribution, tying and resale price maintenance, but rejected studies of multinationals and of contract notification systems, due to western opposition. Developed country delegates also established the principle that a model antitrust law previously drafted by the secretariat and opposed by the West as draconian should be modified to conform to the Principles and Rules.

Korea was the only developing country to send antitrust officials, rather than Geneva diplomats, to the experts' meeting. Apparently, questions of finances and interest will limit the educational value of the UNCTAD meetings for some time to come.

6. Conclusions

The control of restrictive business practices remains essentially a national or regional activity, not an international concern. As late as 1975, the question of implementation of international antitrust rules would have been moot, as there were almost no rules to enforce.

Thus, the major development of the last five years has been the formulation of international principles. This paper has highlighted how, time and again, the price of agreement has been strict limitation of the legal nature and implementation procedures of the codes. Yet, progress has been made. In 1976, the OECD officially condemned enterprise participation in cartels or use of abusive anticompetitive practices. In December 1980, the United Nations adopted the same principles.

In attempting to predict the extent of implementation of the United Nations antitrust Principles and Rules, it is well to keep in mind that the code is addressed to three different types of actors: enterprises, states and U.N. secretariats.

Despite rhetoric suggesting that the primary purpose of antitrust codes is to control the behavior of multinational corporations, it seems very likely that the weakest implementation of the Principles and Rules will be that addressed to enterprises. The code applies to companies only indirectly, through states. The rules for enterprises are clearly not legally binding. Prohibitions of cartel behavior are relatively clear and direct, but private international cartel activities are rare in modern times, due to strong policing and heavy penalties under United States and European Community's antitrust laws. Most modern cartels are sponsored or authorized by one or more governments. Since the Principles and Rules exempt cartels resulting from intergovernmental agreements and tolerate restrictive practices authorized by single governments for public purposes (such as furtherance of economic development), the application of the code to many modern cartel practices is neither simple nor clear, and thus is unlikely to produce a significant amount of voluntary change in corporate conduct.

The principles for states are primarily of three kinds: (i) those urging adoption, improvement and vigorous enforcement of antitrust laws, (ii) those favoring non-discriminatory treatment of enterprises and respect for the confidentiality of their business secrets; and (iii) those suggesting cooperation and exchange of information between governments engaged in antitrust enforcement.

The recommendation of stronger and better enforced antitrust laws is not likely to have significant effect in the near future. A few countries have adopted or will adopt new or improved antitrust laws contemporaneously with the adoption of the U.N. code, but only a few. It does not appear that the passage of the code or the nature of its recommendations was really a significant factor in the legislative plans of any country. For the great bulk of developing countries, there are so few enterprises competing in their markets, and such a high degree of state involvement in the enterprises and their markets that antitrust laws can play almost no significant role for them. Even in those developing countries which do adopt a law, the lack of trained legal and economic personnel available for antitrust enforcement would usually ensure an inactive program.

The code principle of non-discrimination could be implemented through diplomatic and political channels. There is some vagueness, however, in understanding or determining just what it means to treat enterprises "fairly, equitably and on the same basis for all. . . ." Given the necessary flexibility of prosecutorial discretion and the economic realities in many developing countries, it would not be surprising to find that most of the firms that were sued for abusing dominant positions of economic power were foreign multinationals. The developing countries may well defend such a result as not unfair and certainly "equitable," as they understand the political connotations of that word.

Antitrust cooperation and exchange of information among nations is a reality, evidenced not only by formal agreements between the United States and Canada and the United States and Germany but also by the regular practice of many other antitrust agencies. A new agreement between the United States and Australia points toward compromise of previous issues. Nevertheless, most cooperation is hampered by national secrecy laws, and some cooperation is directly prohibited by blocking statutes aimed particularly at United States enforcement in the international sphere. Thus the principle of cooperation is likely to be implemented, at most, only when there are no conflicts of national interest or jurisdiction involved.

The principles addressed to the U.N. secretariats are likely to be the most extensively implemented. The mandates to issue annual reports on antitrust, to study special topics, to gather information, and to form a permanent experts' committee are all being implemented fully. The recommendation to arrange conferences at regional level will probably be implemented. Technical assistance programs have not yet been funded or staffed, but it seems likely that modest programs will eventually be created.

Interpretation of international antitrust rules can be expected primarily to follow interpretation of the national law standards that served as models for the international text. Thus, as United States courts explicate the meaning of the comity defense, or the European Court of Justice clarifies what constitutes an abuse of a dominant position, most scholars and enterprises will assume that U.N. or OECD texts based on the same concepts should be deemed to have the same meaning.

It seems certain that nations will not, in the foreseeable future, give the U.N. the power to investigate or adjudge alleged anti-competitive behavior, or to condemn the antitrust policies of a particular nation. Instead, UNCTAD will, as it has in the past, make studies, usually based on the work of consultants or on records obtained in national proceedings. The developing countries hope that such studies will embarrass companies or their governments into action.

Some harmonization of policy can be expected, as more nations gradually adopt and strengthen antitrust laws and accept the principle that even state-owned enterprises are separate from the state. Harmonization, combined with consultation, may lessen conflict sufficiently to allow the precatory norms of cooperation to be followed more frequently. But an effective international antitrust regime is unlikely to precede the development of free trade and evolution of free markets which would provide it with a raison d'être.

Notes

1. See generally, S. Benson, "The U.N. Code on Restrictive Business Practices: An International Antitrust Code is Born," Am. U. L. Rev. 30:1031 (1981); J. Davidow, "International Antitrust Codes: The Post Acceptance Phase," Antitrust Bulletin, 26:567 (1981).

2. For the background of the antitrust laws of Canada (The Combines Investigation Act R.S.C. 1952, c. 314) see generally R. Roberts, *Anticombines and Antitrust (Ontario: Butterworth, 1980)* pp. 5–31. For a discussion of the events leading to the passage of the Sherman Act, 15 U.S.C. §1–7, see generally H. Theoretti, The Federal Antitrust Policy (Stockholm: Norstedt and Soner, 1954) pp. 143–152.

3. The Clayton Act is codified at 15 U.S.C. §12–27. It was passed in 1914 in the wake of the Supreme Court decision in the Standard Oil case, 221 U.S. 1 (1911), and was an attempt to clarify the scope of the Sherman Act. See generally P. Areeda and D. Turner, 1 Antitrust Law ¶ 229 (1978).

4. See E. Hawley, *The New Deal and the Monopoly Problem* (Princeton, N.J.: Princeton Univ. Press, 1966).

5. See generally Berge, "Cartels as Barriers to International Trade," Law & Contemporary Problems, 11:684 (1946).

6. See generally W. Friedmann (ed.), *Antitrust Laws: A Comparative Symposium* (Toronto: Univ. of Toronto, 1956), France at p. 91, Germany at p. 138, and Japan at p. 257.

7. See generally B. Hawk, *U.S., Common Market and International Antitrust: A Comparative Guide* (New York: Harcourt, Brace, Jovanovich, 1981) pp. 782–842.

8. See UNCTAD, *Control of Restrictive Business Practices in Latin America*, pp. 9–28, U.N. Doc. ST/MD/4 (1975); UNCTAD, *Laws and Regulations Relating to Restrictive Business Practices*, pp. 9–41, 56–58, 69–75, U.N. Doc. TD/B/C.2/AC.5/Misc. 1 (1975) (India, Pakistan and Yugoslovia).

9. See OECD, *Comparative Summary of Legislations on Restrictive Business Practices* (Paris, 1978), Table X (hereinafter cited as *Comparative Legislations*); Adler and Belman, "Antimerger Enforcement in Europe: Trends and Prospects," Journal of International Law & Economics, 8:31 (1973).

10. For a brief review of the antitrust statutes of the OECD countries, see OECD, *Buying Power and the Law*, Report of the Committee of Experts on Restrictive Business Practices (Paris, 1980).

11. See *Comparative Legislations*, *op. cit.* note 9, at Table XXI.

12. *Ibid*, Table XXII.

13. Schecter Poultry v. United States, 295 U.S. 495, 534–537 (1935). See also A. Schlesinger, *The Age of Roosevelt*, Vol. 3, *The Politics of Upheaval* (Boston: Houghton, Mifflin, 1960) pp. 280–283.

14. See J.D. Gribben, "Review of the OECD Export Cartels, Report of the Committee of Experts on Restrictive Business Practices, 1974," Antitrust Bulletin, 21(2):343 (1976).

15. See generally B. Hawk, *op cit* note 7, pgs. 411–424; Bebr, "Article 177 of the EEC Treaty in the Practice of National Courts," International and Comparative Law Quarterly, 26:241 (1977).

16. See "MCI Wins Record $1.8 Billion Treble Damage Award in Metropolitan Suit Against A.T. & T.," BNA Antitrust & Trade Regulation Reports, 969:A-3.

17. Pioneer Hi-Fi Equipment, CCH Common Market Reporter, 10,1¶5. (Commission decision Dec. 14, 1979).

18. United States v. Aluminum Company of America, 148 F.2d 916 (2d Cir., 1945). See generally J. Davidow, "Extraterritorial Antitrust & the Concept of Comity," J. of World Trade Law 15:500 (1981).

19. See Bellamy and Childs, *Common Market Law of Competition* (London: Sweet and Maxwell, 1978) pp. 384-388; See also OECD *Comparative Legislations, op. cit.,* note 9.

20. See generally the remarks of S. Silkin, "The Perspectives of the Attorney General of England and Wales", in J. Griffin (ed.), *Perspectives on the Extraterritorial Impact of the U.S. Antitrust and other Laws* (Section on International Law, American Bar Assoc., 1979). Mr. Silkin argues that certain applications of U.S. antitrust law in the United Kingdom are invasions of U.K. sovereignty.

21. For an overview of the blocking statutes of the United Kingdom, Canada, Australia, South Africa, The Netherlands, Italy, Germany, France, and Belgium, see P. Petit and C. Styles, "International Response to the Extraterritorial Application of the United States Antitrust Laws," Business Lawyer, 37:697 (1982).

22. See, e.g., J. Davidow, "Developing Countries and U.N. Rules Regarding Restrictive International Licensing," Address to American Patent Law Association (Feb. 5, 1980); UNCTAD, *Annual Report 1981 on Legislative and Other Developments in Developed and Developing Countries in the Control of Restrictive Business Practices*, U.N. Doc. TD/B/RBP/9 (Geneva, 1982).

23. See Sigmond Timberg, "Restrictive Business Practices as an Appropriate Subject for United Nations Action", Antitrust Bulletin, 1:411 (1955); Furnish, "A Transnational Approach to Restrictive Business Practices," International Law, 4:13 (1970).

24. See generally J. Davidow, "The Seeking of a World Competition Code: Quixotic Quest," in O. Schacter and R. Hellawell (eds.), *Competition in International Business* (New York: Columbia Univ. Press, 1981), pp. 362–365.

25. This treaty is known as the Schuman Plan (Treaty Establishing the European Coal and Steel Community, Feb. 10, 1953). For a discussion of its history see W. Diebold, *The Schuman Plan* (Clinton, Mass.: Colonial Press, 1959).

26. Treaty of Rome (Treaty Establishing the European Economic Community), March 25, 1957, Articles 85, 86; *See also* Bellamy and Child, *supra* note 19, chapters 6 and 7.

27. See generally ELB, "Transfers of Technology in Latin America: The Birth of Antitrust Law," Fordham Law Review 43:719 (1974); UNCTAD, *Recent Developments in the Control of Restrictive Business Practices*, U.N. Doc. TD/B/C.2/AC.6/17 (1978); *Control of Restrictive Business Practices in Latin America*, U.N. Doc. UNCTAD/ ST/ MD/4 (1975), chapters 6 and 7.

28. See generally OECD, *Report on the Operation of the 1967 Council Recommendation Concerning Cooperation Between Member Countries on Restrictive Business Practices Affecting International Trade During the Period 1967–1975*, reprinted in Antitrust Bulletin, 22:459 (1977).

29. OECD Recommendation of the Council Concerning Competition Policy in Regulated Sectors, C (1979) 155 (Final) 1979).

30. OECD Recommendation of the Council concerning Cooperation and Consultation (1979).

31. OECD Guidelines for Multinational Enterprises (Paris, 1976). (Hereinafter cited as *OECD Guidelines*). See also, J. Davidow, "Some Reflections on the OECD Competition Guidelines", Antitrust Bulletin 12:441 (1977).

32. See R. Kauzlarich, "The Revision of the 1976 Declaration of International Investment and Multinational Enterprises", Am. U. L. Rev. 30:1009 (1981).

33. OECD, *International Investment and Multinational Enterprises: Review of the 1976 Declaration and Decision* (Paris, 1979).

34. *See* Declaration and Programme of Action on the Establishment of a New International Economic Order. G.A. Res. 3201 & 3202, S-7 GAOR, Supp. (No. l) 3, 5, U.N. Doc. A/9559 (1974), American Journal of International Law, 68:798 (1974); International Legal Materials, 13:714 (1974).

35. UNCTAD, *The Set of Mutually Agreed Equitable Principles and Rules for the Control of Restrictive Business Practices*, U.N. Doc. TD/RBP/CONF/10 (1980). (Hereinafter cited as *Principles and Rules*).

36. See "Current Antitrust Division Views on Patent Licensing Practices," Address by Depty. Assistant Att. Gen. Lipsky, Wash. D.C. (Nov. 5, 1981).

37. See generally, Davidow and Chiles, "The United States and the Issue of the Binding or Voluntary Nature of International Codes of Conduct Regarding Restrictive Business Practices", American Journal of International Law, 72:247 (1978).

38. *Op. cit.* note 31, ¶8.

39. For a thorough review of the important Badger Case *see* R. Blanpain, *The Badger Case and the OECD Guidelines for Multinational Enterprises* (The Netherlands: Kluwer, 1977). One commentator argues that the issue of foreign parents' responsibility for their subsidiaries is becoming increasingly important as U.S. subsidiaries continue to disinvest in Europe due to changing economic circumstances there. See R. Kauzlarich, note 33 *supra*, pp. 1021–22.

40. *Op. cit.* note 35, *Principles and Rules*, provision G-3.

41. *Ibid.*

42. *Op. cit.* note 30, ¶11.

43. *Op. cit.*, note 31,¶ 11. The *OECD Guidelines* include a requirement that member governments "will cooperate in good faith" regarding consultation requests.

44. The letter is reprinted in Dept. of State Bulletin, January, 1982.

EIGHT

Export Credit Arrangements

JOHN L. MOORE, JR.

1. Background and Rationale

(a) The Berne Union

In 1934, the Export Credits Guarantee Department (ECGD), a department of the Government of the United Kingdom, and three private credit insurance companies in France, Italy and Spain met to form an organization, initially called the Union of Insurers for the Control of International Credits, a name changed in 1957 to the Union of Insurers of International Credits, and again in 1974 to the International Union of Credit and Investment Insurers. Throughout its history it has more commonly been called the Berne Union.

ECGD had been established in 1919, reflecting the concern of the British Government for the loss of export markets during the First World War.[1] Under its first program, ECGD made advances of cash to exporters against shipping documents for exports to a limited number of countries in Eastern Europe: Finland, Latvia, Estonia, Lithuania, Poland, Czechoslovakia, Serb-Croat-Slovene State, Romania, Georgia and Armenia. Losses were heavy under that limited scheme and it was not long before the program was broadened to include cover in stabler markets.

The founding French member is Societé Française d'Assurances pour Favoriser le Crédit, founded in 1927. The Spanish founding member is Compañía Española de Seguros de Crédito y Caución, founded in 1929. Both the French and Spanish charter members oper-

John L. Moore, Jr. is a Partner, Surrey and Morse, and former Chairman, U.S. Export-Import Bank

ate credit insurance on the home market only and are private organizations.

The Italian founder, Società Italiana Assicurazione Crediti, was founded in 1927, is a private company and operates commercial credit insurance programs both domestically and abroad.

The Union was organized and governed under Swiss law as an organization domiciled in Berne but with the Secretary General's office in London. The original purpose of the Union was to work for "the international acceptance of sound principles of export credit insurance and the establishment and maintenance of discipline in the terms of credit for international trade. . . ."[2] The members also agreed to exchange information and furnish the Union with the information necessary for the accomplishment of its tasks.[3]

At the initial meeting of the Berne Union, prior to the Second World War, the members were not so much concerned with standardizing credit terms as they were with exchanging their own credit information and sources of reliable credit information. Prior to the Second World War the principal concern of the members of the Berne Union was with commercial risks rather than political risks.[4] In the language of the trade, "commercial risk" is the risk that the foreign private buyer will not effect timely deposit of local currency with instructions to its bank to make payment in foreign currency. "Political risks" are the risks arising by actions or non-actions of foreign governments, including the failure or inability to effect payment in foreign currency after deposit by a private buyer of local currency with instruction to transfer. All aspects of transactions directly with foreign governments and their agencies and parastatals are regarded as "political risk."

Membership in the Berne Union was and is open only to organizations engaged in insuring or guaranteeing export credit transaction and/or foreign investments.[5] Thus, as will be noted later, the official agency of the United States Government, the Export-Import Bank of the United States, was not eligible for membership in the early years because it did not issue guarantees or insurance but acted as a bank, lending money to foreign borrowers with which to purchase U.S. exports.

For obvious reasons the activities of the Berne Union were suspended during the Second World War but were resumed in 1946. Sweden and Canada joined the Berne Union in 1947. Compagnie Française d'Assurance pour le Commerce Exterieur (COFACE), a French Government majority-owned company, was formed and joined the Berne Union in 1947. By 1957 additional entrants were the government agencies or private companies representing governments from Norway, Denmark, West Germany, the Netherlands, Belgium, Austria, Switzerland, Australia and India. For the first decade after the Second World War the European members were still largely concerned with credit information relating to trade transactions financed in the short term. By the middle 1950's however, the industrial base in Europe had been rebuilt to the extent that the previous predominance of the United States in exporting goods for large projects was being challenged. At this time the practices of the United States in extending loans over the long term in support of projects in developing countries were having a competitive effect on European practices. The Europeans therefore approached the Export-Import Bank of the United States (Eximbank or Exim) and requested it to cooperate with the Berne Union. Eximbank took up status as an associate member of the Berne Union in 1957. This status was broadened to full membership in 1962 after Eximbank instituted export credit insurance programs in the short and medium term in 1961, thus becoming eligible for full membership.

New export credit agencies were being formed from the 1950's on in the upper tier of the developing countries and the Berne Union membership list correspondingly increased. By 1980, the Berne Union had thirty-eight members from twenty-eight countries including India, Israel, South Africa, Hong Kong, Argentina, Korea, Singapore, Mexico and Cyprus. Jamaica and Zimbabwe were elected to observer status in 1981 and Sri Lanka became an observer in 1982. Export credit agencies presently also exist in Brazil, Malaysia, Greece, Bangladesh, the Philippines, Peru, Chile, Colombia, Venezuela, Taiwan, Trinidad and Tobago, and Morocco.

A considerable debate occurred within the Berne Union in the 1970's as to whether the Union should be a club of European, North American, and Japanese members or whether it should include the agencies of the developing countries as well. As the breadth of membership of developing countries shows, it now appears fairly well established that the Union will be open for membership by an export credit guarantor or insurer meeting the requisite size, experience, and coverage requirement, and paying dues.

As more and more of the agencies in Europe began to encounter the competition from the United States and Canada in extending long-term loans for projects abroad, the pressures built within the Berne Union to broaden its scope from exchanges of credit information to the establishment and maintenance of discipline in the terms of credit for international trade. Accordingly, there were continuing discussions of "sector agreements," namely, agreements on the maximum term of repayment for loans guaranteed or insured by members of the Berne Union. Initially, the focus was on sound underwriting principles. The longer the credit term the greater the risk. Later, the focus was on reducing counterproductive competition by use of more favorable terms of repayment.

The original and present purposes of the Berne Union were dictated by the financial consequences of issuing export credit guarantees and insurance rather than broader objectives. Initially, the efforts of the Union concentrated on the collection and exchange of commercial and political risk information. The Union's work was carried out through the Office of a Secretary General in Paris until the mid-1970's and then in London, as well as by regular meetings of the general membership twice a year and of the management committee, made up of 11 members, two more times a year. Responding to the pressures of the 1950's and later, the efforts of the Union turned to the attempted limitation of runaway competition for exports by way of granting more and more favorable terms. A discernible division occurred as the United States and Canada (and usually Japan) took a lender's approach, preferring a term of repayment matching the useful life of the project, while the European agencies preferred an insurer's approach, to keep term as short as possible. The lender's approach also took the view that the rates of interest charged should be market related while the insurers either did not concern themselves with interest rates or had various schemes for subsidizing rates well below market and had, therefore, an additional incentive to argue for shorter term credits.

East-West issues have also been of considerable importance in the Berne Union. It will be remembered that ECGD was established, in the first instance, to make British exporters secure in selling to Eastern Europe after the First World War. The governments of the centrally controlled economies of the East, over the years, have insisted on operating with export lines of credit in amounts sufficient to cover all anticipated imports from a particular country for a term of years, rather than separate insurance policies for each export. As a result, the Eastern countries have been able to extract from the members of the Berne Union the lowest rates of interest and the longest terms of repayment. Exchanges of information and standardization of terms of those lines of credit have been important activities of the Berne Union.

There are also important North-South issues involved in the work of the Berne Union. More than 75 per cent of the business of the members of the Berne Union is concentrated in insuring exports to developing countries. Most exporters do not require cover for sales in the short and even medium term into Europe and North America. However, cover is needed for exports to buyers in developing countries. To the extent that the Berne Union negotiates less concessional terms it can be viewed as an agency of the developed countries to reduce assistance to the Third World.

From the point of view of the Third World, the Berne Union could be called a cartel of the Organization for Economic Cooperation and Development (OECD). This label would have been especially appropriate had the decision been made to exclude agencies of developing countries from membership in the Berne Union. But developing nations do belong, including nations that are not among the so-called "newly industrializing countries."

At the invitation of the Chairman of the Sri Lanka Export Credit Insurance Corporation, an International Conference on Export Credit Insurance Organizations in Developing Countries was held in Colombo, Sri Lanka, in November 1981. The Conference was attended by export credit insurance representatives from Bangladesh, Barbados, Egypt, Hong Kong, India, Jamaica, Malaysia, Pakistan, Philippines, Sri Lanka, and Trinidad. The overlap with the Berne Union should be noted: Hong Kong, India, Jamaica, and Sri Lanka are already members or provisional members of the Berne Union. The Conference discussed the ways and means of exchanging views and experiences among export credit insurers in developing countries and examined the feasibility of establishing a permanent forum for their benefit.

Since the Conference, the Sri Lanka Export Credit Insurance Corporation has been acting as a continuing Secretariat. The aim of the Conference is not to replace the Berne Union but to provide additional services, and a forum for export credit agencies of developing countries.[6]

Some countries in the course of their development see a temporary advantage to nonmembership in the Berne Union so as to continue to have the right to gain an export advantage by undercutting the practices of the members. Brazil, for example, appears to have an extremely active export credit program but, to date, has refrained from applying to the Berne Union for membership. Its financing offers are reported to exceed Berne Union and Arrangement guidelines (discussed below).

As the Berne Union worked through a number of sector agreements it was able to arrive at substantial agreement on limiting the term of repayment in a number of quite specific sectors. It then began the arduous business of trying to negotiate an all inclusive agreement that would apply to all insured credits without regard to sector, of course preserving the sector limitations where they existed. This led to numerous and still ongoing attempts to arrive at a uniform definition of "starting point," that point in time from which it is agreed that the timing of the first repayment of principal will be determined. Likewise, there is a continuing, and still unsettled, question of the definition of "side financing"—

uninsured private bank financing arranged by the exporter in addition to officially supported financing. It is now fairly agreed that private bank financing can occur on whatever terms are negotiated by the parties for the 15 per cent downpayment not covered by export credit insurance. But it is still not agreed whether other kinds of private bank financing, even though not insured, may be used to improve the overall package, for example by covering "local costs" incurred in the buying country or by offering refinancing after the limited term of repayment sanctioned by the Berne Union.

Over the years there developed a detailed method of advance notification of intentions to derogate from Berne Union rules, thereby giving the other members a chance to match the excessive terms. These obligations were reduced to writing and, by and large, are very well honored.

However, in the early 1960's the issue between North America and Japan on the one hand and Europe on the other was whether any export credit at all should be extended for a period beyond five years. For most countries, the agencies present at the Berne Union were not themselves the ones offering direct loans. Direct loans were usually employed for credits with a repayment term exceeding five years. Thus, the negotiation of the important differences about long term (more than five years) credit became a strain on the Berne Union.

(b) The Arrangement on Guidelines for Officially Supported Export Credits

In 1963 the OECD Trade Committee established a permanent Group on Export Credits and Credit Guarantees. This Group, in semi-annual meetings, sought to evaluate national policies relating to export finance and insurance, and to negotiate better procedures for the exchange of information on offers, and to reduce export credit competition.[7] The early debates continued the discussion started in the Berne Union over longer than five year credit terms. European nations argued for an absolute bar on longer than five year credits to developed countries or, in the alternative, for prior consultation before making a firm offer of such credits to developed countries. The United States and Canada refused to agree to prior consultation but, by 1972, an agreement was reached for prompt exchange of information after the grant of more than five year credits to developed countries. Separate longer terms of ten and twelve years in the aircraft sector and twelve years in large electric power generating plants had been customary and were excepted.[8]

Also in 1963 a special working group called Working Party 6 of the OECD began to negotiate limits on subsidization of export credits within the shipbuilding sector. In that sector fixed interest rates of 5.5 per cent were offered for credit repayment terms of up to eight years. By 1969 a Ship Understanding was finalized and adhered to by a number of the members of the OECD, but not the United States. The Understanding specified maximum term of repayment, minimum downpayment, minimum interest rate, relationship to aid programs, and reporting and matching mechanisms.[9] The United States took the position that its industry was not engaged in the export of large ships under consideration in Working Party 6. The United States, through the Maritime Administration of the Department of Commerce, had subsidization programs for shipbuilding and financing, but only to domestic shipping companies in order to neutralize the effect of the subsidy programs of Europe and Japan. The subsidy programs are not available for the export of ships from the United States to foreign buyers. Moreover, since other nations offer extensive subsidies to lower the price of exported ships as well as to reduce the finance costs, the United States simply does not win export orders in the shipbuilding industry.

During the early 1970's the United States attended the meetings of the subgroup on Export Credits of the OECD but was a rather unwilling negotiator. All through the years the domestic interest rates in the United States had been among the lowest in the world. The Export-Import Bank of the United States could borrow money at the government bond rates and relend that money at 6 per cent fixed interest rates with a comfortable spread for profit. Furthermore, the rates in the private markets in the United States were not much higher than 6 per cent. Therefore, the Export-Import Bank followed a regular practice of covering 45 per cent of export value by direct loans and another 45 per cent by a guarantee that covered private U.S. banks against commercial and political risk abroad. The banks would take the maturities of the first five years of repayment and Eximbank itself would lend the money to be repaid in the last five years of a typical total ten year credit. The combined rates in the packages for 90 per cent of export value were close to a 6 per cent interest rate on a fixed basis. The European schemes had to receive rather heavy subsidies in most instances to counter these offers from the United States. At the time the United States remained totally dominant in the export of commercial jet aircraft, the European industry not having any major plane on the market.

A sudden about-face occurred in the Eximbank and U.S. negotiating positions beginning in 1974. U.S. domestic rates began to rise. The United States and other major countries had gone off the fixed exchange rate system. Economists within the U.S. Government believed that subsidized export credit programs were unnecessary because floating exchange rates would cause export maladjustments automatically to correct as one currency or another weakened. The United States thus took a very definite leadership role in proposing restraints on the subsidization of export credit interest rates. In 1975, Eximbank unilaterally announced an increase of interest rates above those prevailing on official export credits, and expressed the hope and belief that other nations would follow. The result was some slight movement upward in customary interest rates but not as high as the level adopted by the Eximbank.

The pressures of the first increases in world oil prices in 1973–74 and the ensuing world recession subsequently pushed the OECD group nearer to agreement in early 1976. However, an important debate was developing between the European Economic Community and its constituent member countries. Until early 1976 negotiation had been carried on in the OECD subgroup by EEC nations as individual countries. The EEC insisted on its right to conduct such negotiations on behalf of the member countries and won a ruling to that effect from the European Court of Justice, a ruling handed down just as the parties were about to reach agreement on substantive rules. The matter was resolved by taking a different route. The Export-Import Bank of the United States announced that, effective July 1, 1976, it would unilaterally adhere to certain restraints in export credit, essentially involving a minimum interest rate of 7.5 per cent for credits over five years and generally limiting credits to 8.5 years in the better off countries and ten years in the developing poor countries, with important exceptions for aircraft and large power plants as well as mixed aid credits with a concessional element of more than 25 per cent. Over time, most other countries adopted the same or similar provisions as unilateral declarations.

With rising interest rates, the United States continued to press for higher minimum interest rates and clarification of the excluded sectors. By 1978, there had been no change in any of the material terms on which agreement had been reached in 1976, but a longer and more detailed uniform working document had been developed which was then adopted by all parties unilaterally. That document greatly improved and clarified procedures for exchange of information, notification of derogations, and prior consultation procedures. Important gaps remained, such as detailed understandings on aircraft and power sectors as well as mixed aid credits.

As one reviews the minutes of the subgroup on Export Credits of the OECD from 1963 to 1981, one sees a continuing process. A discussion is not soon followed by uniform and clear agreement on export credit restraint. However, discussion and exchange of information about offers being made lead to a conforming of general practice to the majority position in most cases. The exchange of information system shows decreasing derogation and then final agreement after some years on a uniform policy on a particular matter or sector. General agreement is preceded

by limited, tentative partial understandings, then sometimes by derogations to make a point, then more negotiation, and the process continues.
Finally it is possible to negotiate a detailed understanding with reference
to a particular practice which has become customary.

The pressures on the process built up at the end of the 1970's as the
great upward movement of oil prices unsettled the world economy and
interest rates in the United States climbed to and over the 20 per cent
level. From 1977 to 1981, Eximbank's borrowing rates in the bond market moved upward from 7.2 per cent to close to 15.5 per cent, making
the extension of its credits at rates between 8 per cent and 9.25 per cent
a money-losing matter. The newly agreed minimum rates of 7.75 per
cent to 8.75 per cent for credits over five years arrived at in 1980 meant
that in all countries of the world except Switzerland a nation extending
export credits at the agreed minimum rate suffered a heavy degree of
subsidy.

The Eximbank and the United States reluctantly agreed to the 1978
"Arrangement on Guidelines for Officially Supported Export Credits,"
which went into effect on April 1, 1978. By the end of May all of the
twenty-two members of the group on Export Credits of the OECD had
adopted the Arrangement. During the negotiation of the Arrangement
the United States almost walked out of the negotiations when it could get
no agreement to increase interest rates in the face of then current conditions in the financial markets. However, the Swedish delegation worked
out a compromise whereby all parties agreed that the question of interest rates would be carefully reviewed by Mr. Axel Wallen, the head of
the Export Credit Agency of Sweden. During 1979, Mr. Wallen worked,
with the assistance of the OECD's Secretariat, to develop a comprehensive analysis of the problem, the differences in currencies and interest
rates, and to suggest various new approaches.

One proposed system was called the Differentiated Rate System. By
semi-annual or annual reviews an appropriate minimum rate for each
major currency would be determined, with the idea that any country
could lend at the specified rate in any currency and all nations would
offer the same degree of subsidization. From the point of view of the
United States this was the most desirable system since it seemed fair to all
parties as any nation could lend in any particular currency. It would also
provide a convenient method of making transparent the degree of subsidy inherent in export credits and facilitate negotiation away from subsidization.

An alternative system, and the only one that received much serious
negotiation, was the Uniform Moving Matrix System. This system would
establish periodically one rate, determined by rates in a basket of currencies, to apply to all currencies. However, negotiations were constantly

stymied by differences among the members of the European Community. Any one member of the Community could veto any position for the entire Community which represented any change from existing understandings. The French continued to exercise this right. Thus, the Community generally took a position against change. The only immediate upshot of a most serious and careful piece of work, the Wallen Study, was the increase in 1980 of the interest rates in the old system by one-quarter of a percent relative to the poorest countries and by three-quarters of one percent to intermediate and rich countries.

On the North American front, both the United States and Canada threatened to derogate with respect to term of repayment at rates of interest higher than the minimum interest rates agreed in the Arrangement. This threat caused extreme displeasure in Europe where there is a profound fear of the depth and capability of the North American financial markets as compared to those in Europe. If long-term export credits are extended at close to commercial rates of interest, the Europeans tend to believe that they will lose out to the much stronger financial markets of the United States and Canada.

Negotiations continue on a regular basis at approximately semi-annual intervals. By late spring of 1982 agreed minimum rates had moved to a range of 10 per cent for relatively poor countries to 12.4 per cent for relatively rich countries. If market rates for borrowings in a particular currency are lower than the minima, lower rates can be charged, with negotiated minima applicable. A different system has developed for airplane financing where there are negotiated "starting points" dependent on currency without regard to the relative wealth of the borrowing country.

Important North-South issues surround the Arrangement. Long-term export credits to developing countries are now uniformly extended at 10 percent fixed interest in any currency acceptable to buyer and lender. Credits extended now by the International Bank for Reconstruction and Development carry interest rates above 10 per cent and are in a currency or currencies determined by the Bank. Accordingly, export credits are more favorable as to interest rate and selection of currency than the lending of the international financial institutions with the exception of the concessional loans of the International Development Association. The principal markets for export credits are the better off developing countries which are not eligible for IDA loans and, in some instances, are being phased out of IBRD loans.

To the extent that subsidized export credits on a tied basis should cause any uneconomic selection away from the most efficient technology, the subsidization of export credits probably disrupts international trade. However, it has to be stated, that with the exception of mixed aid credits, the normal bid situation will find at least five or six countries competing. It is probable, therefore, aside from mixed aid credits, that the subsidization of export credits represents a net transfer of wealth from the rich to the less developed parts of the world and not a selection of inefficient goods because of more favorable credits.

Crédit Mixte, the French words for mixed aid credits, are the words generally used to describe a French innovation. The system was initially used for developing countries in Africa which had previously been French colonies. Typically, half of the export value would be supported on normal export credit terms, 7.75 per cent for ten years repayment. The other 50 per cent would be supported on concessional terms of 3.5 per cent interest and thirteen years of repayment after seven years of grace. The combined package, if expressed all as one credit, was about equivalent to 5.5 per cent interest for thirteen years repayment. In recent years the French have extended Crédit Mixte to the upper tier of developing countries like Brazil and Mexico and to miscellaneous countries in the Mediterranean Basin in support of industries where the French would like to make a strong entry. The practice has been strongly criticized by all of the other members of the Arrangement but the French have argued: 1. that with respect to their former colonies they are unable to get untied aid programs through their own Parlement, so tied Crédit Mixte is the only vehicle for transfer of development assistance from France to developing countries; and 2. France was last of the major countries in the high technology development field and it should be allowed extra latitude to break into markets it has not previously had, particularly in telecommunications, transportation, and power generation.

Until a few years ago, the Export-Import Bank of Japan administered both the export credit and the development assistance programs of Japan and used Crédit Mixte rather widely for tied commercial purposes in seeking to dominate certain markets, particularly in Asia. After long negotiation, the Japanese agreed in principle in 1978 to untie development assistance which, by that time, was located in a different department of the Japanese Government. While it was hard to obtain untying of existing credits, it appeared that for two to three years the Japanese did not grant any substantial new Crédit Mixte lines. Unfortunately, in 1981, the Japanese announced a major new program of Crédit Mixte to counter the French program.

Other countries have reluctantly moved to counter the French Crédit Mixte system, including the United Kingdom, Canada, the United States in some instances, and the Scandinavian nations. If the system broadens it will be very difficult indeed to reverse course without most serious criticism from the Third World.

There are, of course, East-West issues discussed in the Arrangement. One principal issue related to pre-existing lines of credit to the Soviet

Union when the 1976 consensus came into effect. Such lines of credit had terminal points which kept them in effect at lower than consensus interest rates for more than two years after 1976. These were a bone of contention for some time and considerable pressure was brought to bear at Arrangement and Berne Union meetings to urge the Europeans and Japanese not to renew lines at lower than consensus interest rates. The events of Afghanistan finally disposed of that issue as all the European nations and Japan then stopped renewing the lines at lower than consensus interest rates.

In 1979, the Japanese announced a major credit to China with interest rates below 6 per cent, calling the credit an "import credit". The argument was that while the credit would pay for exports of plants and mining equipment from Japan to China, the credit was really extended for the purposes of prepaying for the resulting raw materials that would be exported from China to Japan. It is to be hoped that this polite circumvention of the Arrangement for a single large credit to China will be the only one. Again, it is clear that the governments of centrally controlled economies will always seek to negotiate the best possible terms under the Consensus, the Arrangement, or the guidelines of the Berne Union.

Mr. Axel Wallen, head of the Swedish Export Credit Agency, is as experienced as anyone on the Arrangement negotiations and the effect of the Consensus on the Arrangement. He concludes:

> Experience with the Consensus and Arrangement is not, however, completely positive. The reasons are varied. To begin with, one immediate result of agreement on common guidelines was to increase the degree of subsidization. Even countries that had not earlier subsidized interest rates or had not subsidized so extensively, felt forced by the acceptance of the guidelines to enable their exporters to offer finance at the guideline minimum rates.
>
> As market rates have become much higher over time, the general volume of subsidization has further increased. This volume might not have been so large without the Consensus and Arrangement. The rigidity of these agreements has perhaps eliminated a natural adjustment of export credit rates to market interest rates. On the other hand, in many individual cases the Consensus may have eliminated a real credit race.[10]

2. Alternatives to Codes

(a) Sector Agreements of the Berne Union

Over the years, agreements have been reached with respect to a number of sectors. The agreements are normally made for a period of three years, discussed at the end of three years, and normally renewed. The sector agreements remaining in force as of this writing are as follows: On wool exports to Greece maximum credit terms are 180 days after arrival of the carrier in Greece or 120 days after the buyer takes possession (for goods sold from stocks held in Greece). The sector agreement on buses and bus chassis call for at least a 15 per cent downpayment and repayment over no more than five years from delivery. Argentina does not participate in that sector agreement because it reserves the right to match non-conforming terms offered by the Brazilians who do not belong to the Berne Union.

Terms for breeding cattle may not exceed two years from delivery for contracts up to $150,000 and three years for larger contracts. Downpayments of 15 per cent are required. Argentina does not participate for the same reason mentioned for buses. The agreement on containers and semi-trailers applies to contracts valued at $20 million or less and stipulates 15 per cent downpayment and a maximum term of five years.

The agreement on fertilizers and insecticide limits repayment to twelve months from date of delivery. The sector agreement on highway lorries and lorry chassis calls for 15 per cent downpayment and a term of repayment not exceeding five years. The sector agreement on paper and pulp specifies maximum credit terms of 180 days from delivery. In addition, there is concurrence that only cash sales of diamonds should be covered by members of the Berne Union.

In 1966 a sector agreement was reached among the major export credit insurers to limit terms of payment for electronic sorting machines to three years credit from delivery, allowing "exceptionally" for a maximum of four years credit for orders exceeding $150,000 and five years credit for orders exceeding $250,000. The sector agreement was renewed in 1970 but allowed to expire in 1973, apparently because the agreement related to too specific an item.

There also exists a "Summary of Understandings" which provides for prompt and infallible exchanges of information between members and which also contains the following two sentences:

> Attempt to conform, particularly in the case of medium-term business, to internationally accepted terms including downpayments and normal regular payments dating from shipment with no l-year, or longer, moratorium. Attempt to maintain normal short-term credits for raw materials and consumer goods to a maximum of six months and not extend them into the medium-term field of up to two to three years.

There also exists a "General Understanding on Rules Applying to Berne Union Sector Agreements" which has been negotiated over a period of years. It provides for renewals at three year intervals. It provides for notification from members as to whether they will participate in a particular sector agreement and for the right to withdraw from any particular sector agreement after thirty days notice. More importantly, it recognizes that members of the Berne Union do not necessarily control the policies of their respective governments *in toto*, and therefore contemplates derogation when particular governments offer governmental aid on concessional terms to developing countries; where the goods are not sold separately but form an essential part of a capital project for which longer terms have been agreed; and where necessary to match officially supported competition from exporters of any other country, upon notification in advance to other participants.

During the years 1978 to 1981, an important point of discussion at each Berne Union meeting was credit terms extended to Poland. Since 1978 Poland has experienced a chronic shortage of foreign exchange. As Poland does not belong to the International Monetary Fund its only source of official support for balance of payment purposes was individual creditor countries. The Russians extended support by way of loans of foreign exchange and the provision of needed materials directly to Poland. Poland turned to the countries of Europe, North America and Japan for support largely by requesting longer than usual terms of repayment for essential supplies of raw materials and semi-manufactured materials. Because the Berne Union members had generally agreed not to exceed six months or twelve months respectively for such materials, the provisions of the General Understanding came into play and members gave notification that, on the direction of "Guardian Authorities," more concessional terms were being offered. Usually, credit lines of three years repayment were established but in some instances basic steel was provided for five year repayment. In other instances the terms called for one balloon payment at the end of the term rather than for regular payments every six months during the term of the loan. Eximbank did not exceed normal terms in its extension of credits to Poland but did notify regularly the very substantial Commodity Credit Corporation loans to buy grain in annual amounts in excess of $500 million for repayment over three years instead of the normal six months. In all, it appeared that the countries of the Berne Union members extended at least $2 billion a year of unusually long credits connected to the sale of raw materials and semi-manufactured products. In the early discussions the members of the Berne Union, for themselves, were able to agree not to set up new non-conforming credit lines after June 30, 1980. However, again, the unique position of Poland brought such political pressure on the governments of Europe, North America, and Japan that considerable additional credits were granted. Finally, in late 1980 the Poles had to ask for relief in the form of rescheduling which was completed in early 1981.

The Polish case is somewhat unique in that the United States does not extend aid or economic assistance to countries in the Communist bloc.

Therefore, assistance came in the form of trade-related lending or guarantees of the Commodity Credit Corporation.

(b) Nature of Sector Agreements

The Sector Agreements and General Understandings of the Berne Union are certainly not formal treaties. No multi-party document is initialed or signed. Sector Agreements are developed and the text of the General Understanding is extended in subcommittees and presented to the annual meetings of the general membership. Members are requested, if necessary, to consult their "Guardian Authorities" and then to notify, usually orally at the next meeting, whether they are prepared to participate in the particular agreement. Such a participation is noted in the minutes of the meeting and records are kept by the Secretary General as to the participants and nonparticipants in each Sector Agreement.

It is possible that the Sector Agreements and General Understanding could be construed to be agreements of the members subject to the right of withdrawal on thirty days notice. However, it should be noted that the documents are replete with recognition that, for particular reasons, members or related agencies of their governments may decide not to conform to the agreements and understanding. It therefore seems more proper to characterize the agreements and understanding as generally accepted rules of an international organization rather than any kind of formal agreement. Under the terms of the documents the only obligations firm enough to give rise to a claim for damages under normal contract principles are the duties to give notice of derogations. It is normal in the Berne Union to counter charges of not notifying by pleading unintentional oversight.

In any event, there is strong moral pressure on the members of the Berne Union not to derogate from usual terms. All members are required to notify the Secretary General and the other members of actual derogations by themselves or the related agencies of their governments, when known. Such derogations lead to discussion if they are important enough, discussion can lead to further moral pressure, and sometimes to the development of new sector agreements or agreements on particular issues or countries, such as diamonds or Poland.

As discussed in the first part of this chapter, considerable effort was expended within the Berne Union in the early 1960's toward developing an overall agreement limiting export credit terms to five years unless there were prior consultation or notification. No agreement was reached within the Berne Union; the discussions instead led to the formation of the Special Group on Export Credits of the OECD and eventually to the development of the 1976 Consensus and the 1978 Arrangement.

(c) Legal and Political Nature of the Arrangement

The 1976 Consensus was implemented by a series of unilateral announcements to the press and by notification to other members of the OECD Subgroup on Export Credits. The text of such announcements varied slightly and each nation carefully reserved the right to withdraw unilaterally. The initial term was for a year to end on June 30, 1977. By that time most members of the subgroup had made the unilateral declaration and all agreed to extend.

By April 1, 1978, agreement had been reached on a more detailed document which did not vary the basic terms of minimum interest rates and maximum terms of repayment but did flesh out the procedures for exchanges of information and prior consultation in some instances. The Arrangement was implemented by notifications of intention to adhere to the precise text developed in negotiations. It therefore could have been deemed to be an Agreement. However, all parties preferred to make it indelibly clear that the participants were not entering into an agreement. Therefore, the initial paragraph of the Arrangement reads as follows:

> This informal Arrangement is applicable among the Participants in the form of guidelines to officially supported export credits with a repayment term of two years or more, regardless of whether they relate to contracts of sale or to leases equivalent in effect to such contracts.

The Arrangement calls generally for the requirement of a 15 per cent downpayment and limits terms of repayment, except for special sectors, to 8.5 years for relatively rich and intermediate countries and ten years for relatively poor countries. The Arrangement calls for ten days prior notice (but no right to prior consultation) where repayment terms longer than 5 and up to 8.5 years for a relatively rich country are being agreed. Principal must be repaid in equal and regular installments not less frequently than every six months commencing not later than six months after the starting point (it will be recalled that there is no precise agreement on the definition of "starting point"). Minimum interest rates for terms of repayment of 2 to 5 years were 7.75 per cent to relatively rich countries and 7.25 per cent to intermediate and relatively poor countries. For credits over 5 years the rate was 8 per cent to relatively rich countries; 7.75 per cent to intermediate contries; and 7.5 per cent to relatively poor countries. These minimum interest rates were amended in 1980 to increase the respective rates 0.25 per cent to relatively poor countries and 0.75 per cent to intermediate and relatively rich countries. Normally payment of interest should be required throughout the term without capitalization beginning six months after the starting point.

Special sector agreements were covered allowing twelve years repayment for conventional power plants; eight years for ground satellite communication stations; and a cross-reference noting that Eximbank does not adhere to the OECD Understanding on Ships.

With respect to the nuclear power sector, no formal agreement has ever been reached although, by virtue of an OECD standstill, parties generally adhere to normal practices as of 1975 when the longest term of repayment accorded was fifteen years beginning six months after completion of the power station and the downpayment requirement was 10 per cent. No minimum interest rate was identified in the standstill.

No real agreement has been reached on the aircraft sector although 1975 practices have been noted in writing. Therefore, the terms are somewhat different from the other parts of the Arrangement in that only a 10 per cent downpayment is required and no minimum rate of interest is specified. However, it is believed that at least the general arrangement minimums on interest have been honored. The term of repayment is specified at ten years for loans to buy large turbo-jet aircraft (twelve years for leases); seven years for twin engine turbo-prop aircraft; and five years for all other planes.

Perhaps the most significant gap in the Arrangement is the inability to agree to any formal limitation on the use of Crédit Mixte. That issue is referenced only by prior notification if the degree of concessionality is 15 per cent or less and prompt notification after the fact for cases involving concessionality above 15 per cent up to 25 per cent. Loans with more than 25 per cent concessionality are considered aid and not treated as export credits. Concessionality is determined by a discounted cash flow approach using a normal interest factor of 10 per cent.

With respect to cases which are considered by members to be normal export credits (not Crédit Mixte), by 1980 the information exchanges of the Berne Union and the Arrangement were effective. Prior information concerning rumored mixed credits was much harder to obtain, the French pleading that they simply did not know when a recipient nation would designate a particular project for use of a mixed aid credit line. Under the French system annual envelopes are granted to particular nations or agencies for use in designated sectors. The final decision is made by the recipient country rather than by the French Government. Therefore, during the bidding process, the receiving nation may well tell all other suppliers that it intends to use its mixed credit line. However, the French have designed the system so they are not in a position to notify or provide confirmation until after the award of the business. This practice, used widely in many of the developing countries, considerably undermines the effectiveness of the information exchange. As a reaction, many countries notify the French of reports by exporters of the possible use of mixed credit and ask the French to state that mixed credit will not be used for the particular project. The notice goes on to say that, in the absence of a response from the French, the other nation intends to use its mixed aid credit programs. In at least one case, that of an intermediate country in the Mediterranean area, the French did reply that no mixed aid credit would be used.

The five years experience after 1976 with the Consensus (a unilateral declaration) and the Arrangement (a nonbinding agreement) has been to bring some order in the situation which, while not chaotic, had involved much suspicion, charge and countercharge. Through compliance with the procedures for the exchange of information, participants learned the procedure and practices of their competitors better than they might otherwise have done. For some countries, adherence to the Consensus and the Arrangement led to an automatic adoption of the minimum interest rates rather than a case by case approach of matching other countries' offers. Undoubtedly in many cases this led to the uniform use of the minimum interest rates rather than possibly higher rates. However, overall, as concluded by Axel Wallen, in many cases and especially in relation to some participants, the Consensus and the Arrangement may have eliminated a real export credit race.

Of course, important consequences attach under domestic law and the U.S. Constitution to the proper characterization of the sector agreements and general understandings of the Berne Union and the Consensus and the Arrangement. The Restatement of the Law, Second, Foreign Relations Law of the United States, presents this codification:

> *"Gentlemen's Agreement"* Two or more states may enter into an understanding which is clearly intended to affect their relations with each other but not to be binding legally. Such an understanding, sometimes called a "gentlemen's agreement," is not an international agreement as defined in this Section.[11]

The legal adviser of the State Department has ruled that documents intended to have political or moral weight, but not intended to be legally binding, are not international agreements and therefore it is not necessary for the President of the United States to report them to Congress under the Case Act.[12] [13]

It seems clear that none of the indices of agreements or treaty is involved in the Berne Union Sector Agreements and Understanding or in the OECD Consensus and Arrangement. Most importantly, the language always indicated the nonbinding nature of the announcements of participation. None of these has been listed or published in national treaty collections; none was registered under §102 of the United Nations Charter; and all discussions of these items and submissions to Congress and in committee hearings before the Congress always treat the agreements, understandings, Consensus and Arrangement as "understandings," "guidelines," or "gentlemen's agreements."[14]

The really important question, if the understandings could be considered contracts terminable at the will of either party, is the remedy for non-compliance.[15] Clearly this must have been the main reason for the careful language of the preamble to the Arrangement quoted above. Further, in all of the documentation, a right of derogation without withdrawal from the participation, is clearly spelled out, with remedy being limited to the right of other members to have notice and to match the derogation without themselves being deemed to be in derogation.

It is, therefore, interesting to note that nonbinding "gentlemen's agreements" which themselves do not give rise to judicial remedy among the nations, became the subject of a part of the enforcement mechanisms of the General Agreement on Tariffs and Trade approved *ad referendum* in April 1979 and incorporated by reference in the U.S. Trade Act of 1979. Listed as one item on GATT's Illustrative List of Export Subsidies giving rise to possible imposition of countervailing duties:

(j) The provision by governments (or special institutions controlled by governments) of export credit guarantee or insurance programmes, of insurance or guarantee programmes against increases in the cost of exported products or of exchange risk programmes, at premium rates, which are manifestly inadequate to cover the long-term operating cost and losses of the programmes.

(k) The grant by governments (or special institutions controlled by and/or acting under the authority of governments) of export credits at rates below those which they actually have to pay for the funds so employed (or would have to pay if they borrowed on international capital markets in order to obtain funds of the same maturity and denominated in the same currency as the export credit), or the payment by them of all or part of the cost incurred by exporters or financial institutions in obtaining credits, insofar as they are used to secure a material advantage in the field of export credit terms.

Provided, however, that if a signatory is a party to an international undertaking on official export credits to which at least 12 original signatories to this Agreement are parties as of 1 January 1979 (or a successor undertaking which had been adopted by those original signatures), or if in practice a signatory applies the interest rates provisions of the relevant undertaking, an export credit practice which is in conformity with those provisions shall not be considered an export subsidy prohibited by this Agreement.

The present posture seems to be paradoxical. The principal complaint of creation of an export credit race is levied against those nations which use Crédit Mixte. While it can be argued that a mixed credit is not "an export credit practice which is in conformity with those [i.e. interest rate] provisions," it seems to this writer that it is more logical to argue that the specific requirement of notification of mixed credits to the degree of 25 per cent concessionality imply consistency with the interest rate provisions of the Arrangement and therefore mixed credits are not subject to sanction under GATT.

In the double frustration of seeing the below market interest rates of the Arrangement and the limitation of budget authority in the case of the United States and the necessity to borrow at market rates in the case of Canada, these two nations stated in 1980 that they intended to issue credit packages with interest rates 2 per cent to 4 per cent above the minimums of the Arrangement but with terms of repayment longer than those permitted by the Arrangement. It would appear possible to argue that such offers by the United States and Canada are export credit practices clearly not in conformity with those provisions. Therefore, even though the total cost of the package is considerably greater to the offeree, those derogating offers may be prohibited by GATT and subject to the sanctions of GATT while much more concessional mixed credits may not be.

3. Participation

(a) Membership in the Berne Union

An important ingredient of the Berne Union's success in stimulating cooperative dialogue is the limited membership: membership is granted only to the agency or company that actually insures or guarantees export credits. The members range from private companies operating their own domestic credit insurance business and foreign credit programs for the Government account (the German system) to separate agencies of government (United States and Canada) to subdepartments of ministries (the United Kingdom and Japan). Thus, the members of the Berne Union themselves usually do not have the authority to make broad policies. They must consult and receive instruction from "Guardian Authorities." While the Eximbank is an independent agency of the U.S. Government and legally makes final decisions on its own behalf, it too needs to consult on the formation of broad policies among the different departments and agencies of the U.S. Government before taking its final decision. Thus, the members of the Berne Union can have fairly free wheeling discussions and temporary concordance *ad referendum* to the Guardian Authorities. Disparate positions of particular governments may well arise but through the faceless Guardian Authorities. Within their own governments the members of the Berne Union can, if they choose, argue for agreement with tentative Berne Union positions. Frequently, a resolution at a meeting of the Berne Union urges members to seek to persuade Guardian Authorities to take a particular position.

(b) Negotiations in the OECD Arrangement

Negotiations in the subgroup of the OECD are quite a different matter. Such negotiations are carried out with representatives of the Guardian Authorities present. As a result the team representing the United States will have four or five participants, including representatives of Eximbank, a representative of the Department of Treasury, a representative of the Commerce Department and possibly representatives from the State Department and the Trade Representatives Office. Because nearly all the parties necessary to arrive at the decision are present at the meeting, the negotiations move much more slowly than in the Berne Union. Even if parties are inclined to move toward agreement, it is very difficult to do anything other than state positions framed in advance. It is almost impossible to change that position in the course of a meeting both because the participants need to touch base with their superiors in the home capitol and because too many parties are involved. As a result the meeting has to adjourn for a subsequent time. This is often followed by interim bilateral or multilateral meetings of fewer parties, and finally by another round of the full meeting.

The Arrangement negotiations are further complicated by the dual representation of the European members. Each of the members of the European community sends its own delegation to the Arrangement negotiation as does the EEC itself. But since the decision of the European Court of Justice in 1976, final agreement must be made by the EEC representative and announced by him. Within the EEC, if any change from existing positions is being discussed, a unanimous vote is necessary before the EEC can announce a position. Consequently any European member can, in effect, veto any change in the EEC's position. Often only the French hold back from agreeing to change and do not seem to be bothered at being the only country in the Arrangement or in the Community clinging to the *status quo*. Negotiations have been frustrating and tedious for parties like the United States and Canada who want very much to see change. Yet one still must marvel at the amount of order and change which has developed in a five year period in a very complicated international forum.

(c) Use of Experts

In the course of developing discussion of issues in the Berne Union and negotiations in the Arrangement there have been limited attempts at the use of independent experts. The principal compromise of 1978 that made it possible for all parties to agree provisionally to the 1978 Arrangement was the naming of Axel Wallen of Sweden to head a group of independent experts from the OECD to analyze the subsidization of export credits and how subsidies might be limited by revising the interest rates charged on export credits. A first-class technical paper was developed over the course of a year. It was never questioned, because of its excellent grouping and presentation of the issues. Accordingly, the Wallen report succeeded in framing the issues although not in resolving them.

The Berne Union has a standing technical subcommittee made up of a small number of experts from among the various members. To the technical subcommittee are assigned jobs of drafting technical language which could never succeed in the larger general meetings and management committee meetings. From time to time, the technical subcommittee is also assigned fact-finding missions. It then designs relevant questionnaires for circulation to all members of the Berne Union. The technical subcommittee will compile and report the information gathered from the returned questionnaires. Sometimes the responses to questionnaires serve to settle an issue simply by showing that almost all members conform to the same policy. However, on one issue the technical subcommittee has never succeeded in producing information which will lead to a resolution. Every few years an attempt is made to determine the present position of members as to length of credit based on contract value. All members have sub-limitations within the five year overall term limitation based on the amount of contract value being supported. The practices are so different in detail, though not very different in concept, that it has been impossible to gain agreement on any set of consensus figures.

Obviously, the formal applicability of the guidelines of the Berne Union and the OECD Arrangement relate directly only to the particular members. The Berne Union includes all the members of the OECD Arrangement and also representatives of the developing countries. However, it is almost certain that the members of the Berne Union who are not a part of the OECD receive, via the exchange of information system of the Berne Union, information exchanged pursuant to the Arrangement. Those countries seem to conform to the Arrangement, although South Korea joins the United States in not participating in the OECD Ship Understanding. It is also probable that those nations, if they are signatories to GATT, keep in mind the desirability of conforming to the minimum interest rate provisions of the Arrangement.

As mentioned above, some of the export credit insurers and lenders of the world have not joined the Berne Union or the OECD Arrangement. South Korea and Brazil were invited to send observers to a meeting of the OECD Arrangement. But, to date, Brazil has not shown any interest in joining the Arrangement or the Berne Union. One of the problems for the Third World Countries with the Arrangement is its attachment to the OECD. More and more the point needs to be made that the Arrangement simply uses the good offices of the OECD for a place to meet and to have staff assistance, but it is not, and will not be, limited to OECD members.

(d) Economic Summits

The increase in oil prices in the latter half of 1973 led to a serious discussion of ministers of finance from Germany, France, Italy, Japan, the United Kingdom and the United States at the IMF meeting in Nairobi in September 1973. This instituted the beginnings of a discussion to form a "Gentlemen's Agreement." Subsequent meetings did result in a simple agreement of those countries in 1974 implying a minimum interest rate in export credits of 7.5 per cent. This was later formalized by the unilateral declarations that formed the Consensus, and led eventually to the Arrangement. At the September 1978 IMF meeting in Washington the U.S. Secretary of Treasury urged the Ministers of Finance of a number of countries to negotiate seriously toward improvements in the Arrangement.

Beginning with the first economic summit of chiefs of state of the seven major countries held in Rambouillet in 1975, and continuing in each of such summits until the Venice summit of 1980, the agreed statements issued at the end contained a brief reference to export credit competition, exhorting all members to support the establishment of agreements limiting subsidization thereof. Newspaper reports of the 1981 summit in Ottawa indicate that it was the first in which no agreed statement was made on the need to limit export credit competition. The 1982 Versailles Summit concentrated, at the urging of the United States, on export credits to Eastern Europe and the Soviet Union.

4. Interpretation

No external interpretative mechanism exists for disputes over the rather simple wording of the sector agreements, understanding, Consensus and Arrangement. Rather, interpretation arises through the regular meetings of the Berne Union and the OECD Arrangement. At these meetings complaints are registered if members have discovered a financing offer which, according to the complaining members' view, does not conform to earlier understandings. This can lead to identification of issues, if they exist, and then further negotiations. For example, several members complained that a German exporter had won a power sector case in South America by financing which exceeded the term of repayment allowed by the Arrangement guidelines. After investigation, the Germans reported that the German exporter had arranged normal export credit terms through the German Government programs. The exporter had then approached Swiss banks who, without government support or the German Government's knowledge, agreed to extend a loan at the end of the officially supported loan in an amount sufficient to repay it. The Swiss banks then agreed to repayment of the refinanced credit over two additional years. Other members argued that the entire package should not exceed the guideline limit on repayment terms. While the Germans continued to maintain that privately arranged facilities for downpayments and refinancing should not be subject to the guidelines, it is probable now that most members conform to the generally held belief that, when offered in connection with an official export credit package, private credits extended for downpayment, even though not officially supported, should not exceed the terms of the guidelines, and that extension even by unguaranteed parties leading to a total term longer than the guidelines should be prohibited.

The importance of the exchange of information by telex and telephone as well as frequent, regular meetings cannot be over-emphasized. All of the agencies are subject to pressures from exporters who bring a surprising amount of information about offers from other nations. Rumors must be confirmed or disavowed, and guidelines must be applied to particular cases. A gradual process, not necessarily challenging the integrity of the different agencies, leads to identification of different positions and practices of members. The clarification of factual situations lead to the conformation of practices, thus removing some possibilities for unintended credit races.

Bilateral meetings also take place. The larger exporting nations tend to have bilateral reviews with each other on an annual basis. The meetings will cover technical issues but may well discuss positions to be taken at the next fuller bargaining sessions of the Berne Union or the OECD Arrangement. The early negotiation of the Consensus was furthered by several meetings held at different levels by the nations which met in Nairobi. It is easier to make progress in negotiations with a smaller number of parties. Too much separate negotiation, however, could lead to resentment by those not included in the groups and, by and large, any formalized structure other than the European Community is not a continuing factor.

In a few sectors, the capacity to manufacture goods exists only in a limited number of countries. The negotiations in the aircraft sector essentially involve the United States on the one hand and the Airbus consortium—the United Kingdom, West Germany, and France—on the other. Interested observers, because of their present or possible future involvement in such manufacture, are Canada, the Netherlands and Japan.

Up to the present, only the United States and the United Kingdom compete in the manufacture and sale of new jet aircraft engines. Discussions have been held on a bilateral basis as to aircraft engines. Both with respect to aircraft and the aircraft engines a very delicate point arises because of the membership of the European countries in the European Community which insists that it has sole authority to negotiate economic issues for its member countries. For that reason the discussions on aircraft and aircraft engines have to proceed on the basis of what future policy might be adopted by each party on a unilateral basis.

5. Implementation

Aside from implementation of negotiating and informational services through the regular meetings of the Berne Union, work goes on in its technical subcommittee. In addition, the Office of the Secretariat in London compiles and distributes information derived from reports required of members on an *ad hoc* or regular periodic basis. Members are required to report, for example, all credits extended for repayment beyond five years. Members also report borrowers' defaults and certain financial data concerning claims paid and the results of operations of their export credit programs. These are compiled and distributed on a regular basis.

On the other hand, the Arrangement has no secretariat and no procedures for implementation other than the semi-annual meetings to review operations under first the Consensus and then the Arrangement. However, an important part of implementation of the Arrangement is the required openness of the United States political system. Eximbank is required to compile and publish on a regular basis a report of the comparative competitiveness of its programs with those of other nations. Since the document can be bought by anyone through the U.S. Government Printing Office the Competitiveness Report of the Eximbank has become something like the annual report of the Arrangement. The Berne Union has often discussed whether it should prepare some data describing the programs of its members to hand out to those who ask for such information. The decision has always been taken not to compile and publish such a book. The Secretary General of the Berne Union, when replying to requests for such descriptive material, simply recommends the purchase of the Eximbank Competitiveness Report. In 1982 the OECD published a comprehensive book on the subject.[16]

It is obvious that the various international arrangements governing export credits, insurance and guarantees are addressed directly to the participating government agencies responsible for the export credit facilities. While the arrangements are not directly addressed to the private or parastatal entities who may be exporting, through their influence on the official agencies there is indirect supervision of the terms of credit issued by or on behalf of exporters if official support is present in the package. Obviously, if the exporter or its bank is affording credit without guarantee, insurance or funding from a government agency, the arrangements do not govern the terms of the credit. Interesting questions arise if such financing is provided by or on behalf of state-owned enterprises receiving government subsidies in their overall operations even where there is no official support for the particular export credit.

In all countries, pressure groups are formed on issues surrounding their export credit agencies. Obviously, the most important pressure groups are those representing the exporters of manufactured goods. In most countries these are strongly supported by labor unions although, in some countries and at certain times, labor unions have been known to speak against export credit arrangements as financing the "export of jobs."

During the latter part of the Carter Administration, when Congress failed to agree on a foreign affairs budget and Exim's offering of preliminary commitments had to be severely curtailed, a strong pressure group of capital goods exporters functioned most effectively. This group appears to be continuing its effective work in the face of the Reagan Administration's decision to seek lower authorization levels for the Eximbank.

6. The Process of Internationalizing Standards

Progress to date in limiting export credit competition has relied on negotiation, exchange of information, and the opportunity to match nonconforming offers as "enforcement" tools. The parties have been unable to agree on the design, or even the need, for additional sanctions. It remains to be seen whether any other sanction can be devised under GATT. The traditional sanctions under GATT are primarily bilateral, e.g. the importing nation of import can impose a countervailing duty to prevent dumping by the exporting nation. What sanction GATT would authorize in a tripartite situation is not clear. In the field of export credits, the injury to Country A is caused by an unduly concessional credit offered by Country B to Country C; hence there is no import into Country A on which to impose a countervailing duty.

The Berne Union and the Arrangement meetings have been concerned with ensuring uniform international standards of export credits offered. Meanwhile, other important differences between the underlying national systems have not yet received substantial attention. But if national export credit schemes are truly to be neutralized or made exactly equal in the degree of subsidization, then their methods of operation need to be examined and made more uniform. Some of the issues follow.

The Export-Import Bank of Japan principally draws its funds from Japanese postal savings, made available at the rate of interest paid to the Japanese savers by the Japanese Government. The Japanese postal savings system takes advantage of the convenience of postal offices to small Japanese savers to attract funds at lower than government bond rates. This institutional feature makes other parties question the Japanese negotiating position that the rate of interest for credits extended by the Export-Import Bank of Japan should be lower than the stated rates of the Arrangement because the Bank need not rely on an explicit government subsidy.

With respect to medium and long-term export credits, the French system allows the French exporter to discount that percentage of his export paper with the Central Bank of France which allows the overall loan package to bear a fixed interest rate at the minimum rate specified in the Arrangement. The British and the Italian systems simply afford banks an interest make-up payment so they will extend credits in domestic or foreign currencies at fixed interest rates at the Arrangement level. While none of the French, British or Italian programs provides credits at lower than Arrangement rates of interest in normal export credits, the method of subsidy makes apparent the heavy transfer of wealth from developed to developing countries and, in cases of credits to rich countries, transfers of wealth from one rich to another rich country. Finally, all of the schemes utilize, to some extent, domestic government credit ratings to support private financing abroad. Presumably, in certain programs, such as the Private Export Funding Corporation in the United States (guaranteed by the U.S. Government), the rates of interest are below those which would otherwise pertain in the private financial markets, and in contrast to purely private finance, offer fixed rather than floating interest rates. The French, British, Italian and U.S. programs will all require scrutiny if a change in the GATT provisions or in the Arrangement calls for less subsidy than exists at the present time.

The process for formulating official export credit policy is similar in all countries. Perhaps it can be best explained by using the example of

the United States. The Export-Import Bank of the United States is at the
center of the activity, dealing with exporters and foreign buyers on a
daily basis. Surrounding it in the formation of policy are a number of
other departments and agencies in the Executive Branch. The formal
members of the National Advisory Council (NAC) are the Departments
of Treasury, State, and Commerce, the Federal Reserve Board, the
Eximbank, and the U.S. Trade Representative. Other agencies quite often participate in the meetings of the NAC including the Labor Department, the agencies regulating nuclear power, the National Security
Council, and the Council of Economic Advisors. Finally, there is an on-
going relationship with the Congress. The Senate and House Banking
Subcommittees on International Finance hold regular oversight hearings. Eximbank's statute requires it to report to Congress any proposed
final action to approve a credit or insured or guaranteed transaction
above $100 million; any transaction, regardless of size, relating to nu-
clear power; and any transaction over $50 million to a communist coun-
try.

The process is similar in other countries except that in most the relationship to the legislative body is much less frequent and much less pub-
licized. The developed countries of the world, with the exception of
Canada and the United States, simply do not debate the question of
whether export credits are necessary or desirable.

The development of U.S. national domestic law relating to export
credits occurs through statutes governing Eximbank. In 1974 the Bank
was directed to negotiate for the limitation of export credit terms. In
1978 Congress amended the Eximbank statute in an attempt to prevent
the use of concessional export credits in the United States domestic market. The statute directed the Secretary of Treasury to determine if any
credit offered to an American buyer violated the terms of the Arrangement. If so, the Secretary of Treasury is directed to notify Eximbank to
that effect and Eximbank, at that point, is authorized, though not directed, to extend a matching credit to the American company. It is probable that the members of Congress thought they were thereby limiting
credit offers to American buyers to market-related rates of interest and
did not realize that the statutory provision would only come into play if a
foreign exporter sought to sell in the United States with repayment
terms beyond 8.5 years after construction or at interest rates lower than
a fixed rate of 8.5 per cent for credits up to five years and 8.75 per cent
over five years.[17] With revisions of the Arrangement in 1981 and 1982,
however, the threshold rates are somewhat closer to market rates.

Presently being debated before Congress is a bill establishing a contin-
gent war chest to allow Exim additional working capital to supplement
its budget in matching interest rates offered abroad when its borrowing
costs exceed those rates of interest.

7. *Extraterritoriality*

The record is replete with attempts, through Eximbank, to impose the will of the Congress of the United States around the world.

(a) Illegal Payments

For some years prior to 1978, Eximbank required a certificate from U.S. exporters specifying what payments, if any, they had made by way of commissions or otherwise in effecting the sale to be financed by Eximbank. Until 1978 the making of illegal payments abroad did not violate the criminal laws of the United States. However, a false certificate to a government agency like Eximbank was subject to criminal prosecution. For that reason, as the United States focused on the objective of stopping illegal payments in connection with sales abroad the Eximbank certificates were the sole vehicle for the criminal prosecution of acts alleged to have taken place prior to the effective date of the 1978 illegal payments law.

The severity of penalty and the ambiguity of the 1978 statute as to the criminal responsibility of high ranking officers of multinational corporations for failure to detect information has caused the U.S. exporting community to speak out about this additional impediment to its competitiveness. The export community is concerned about the possible imposition of criminal penalties on corporate officers who did not actually know of the alleged illegal payment but could have found out if the corporate accounting system had been more perfect. The problem is exacerbated because the statute does not limit exposure by any doctrine of materiality. A bill bringing in some concept of materiality is presently before the Congress, but it is improbable that any more drastic change will be made in the 1978 law.

Up to now it is hard to say that the world has been made a better place by the United States unilateral requirement of withdrawal from markets in instances where illegal payments seem to be necessary, but it is unlikely that the United States will change its unilateral approach. At the same time, it is heard regularly that most other nations in export competition do not have the same scruples and, in fact, offer official export credit support for commissions and other payments.

(b) Human Rights

Eximbank found itself at the center of another discussion concerning the worldwide extension of American rectitude when the question of human rights arose in the 1977 quinquennial Congressional review of Eximbank's charter. Sentiment was strong, especially in the House of Representatives, to deny any kind of government program to any nation abroad which consistently and habitually violated human rights. Eximbank's statute was amended to require it to consult with the State Department and to deny support to public sector projects in countries where there was a finding of a consistent abuse of human rights. Exim and the State Department set up a procedure whereby Exim received a case-by-case report on human rights conditions in each country to which the Eximbank Board would be considering extending credits. Problems only arose in a few countries such as Chile, Argentina, and the Philippines.

Exim was requested to produce a letter of interest for a major public sector project in Argentina and worked closely with the State Department to try to adapt language to a difficult situation. In effect Exim stated that the project was the kind that it favored and would support but that at the present time, were it called on to extend support, it would be unable to do so for human rights reasons. However, the communications to the U.S. exporters noted that human rights conditions were improving in Argentina and it was hoped that by the time formal action was required Exim would be in a position to support the project's financing. The publication of this communication caused an outcry in Argentina and, while the U.S. exporters involved in the case have throughout had the support of Eximbank and may eventually win the business, it was widely perceived in the business community, and afterwards in Congress, that the human rights conditionality in Exim's statute was losing countless exports for the United States.

Subsequently, a year later, Congress reversed the language in Exim's statute and required Exim's Board not to deny credits on other than economic or financial grounds unless the President of the United States or his delegate made a finding that denial was in the national interest. During the remainder of the Carter Administration only once was that statutory provision invoked, in the case of Chile after the Chileans refused to try or extradite the alleged murderers of Ambassador Letellier in Washington. One of the early acts of the Reagan Administration was to revoke that finding.

(c) Environmental Protection

A few days before President Carter's inauguration, two environmental action groups filed suit against the Export-Import Bank seeking to construe the Environmental Protection Act as applying to all cases of loan support from Eximbank. The environmentalists argued that any loan by Eximbank was "federal action," thus extending the jurisdiction of the Environmental Protection Act of the United States to any project in the world in which Exim participated in the financing. Over about a two year period there was vigorous negotiation within the Administration on this issue. It was finally resolved by settlement of the negotiation among the different affected departments and agencies of the Federal Government and the lawsuits were dismissed upon the President's issuing an Executive Order.[18]

That order exempted Exim from compliance with the Environmental Protection Act and the filing of environmental impact statements with a few important exceptions. A special study is to be given to the export of technology which might produce the dangerous substances listed in an exhibit to the Executive Order. If a project is to affect the global commons, i.e., the high seas or Antarctica, or if a project will have a substantial environmental impact upon a country which is not a party to the project, then Exim is to prepare a brief environmental analysis. In addition, all cases are reviewed by the engineering and legal staff of Eximbank to determine whether any of the requirements for environmental analysis will come into play. Even if there is such a finding, Exim does not have to comply unless it is a very substantial lender with respect to the particular project. A few environmental analyses have been prepared and have won favorable comment from the Council on Environmental Quality. It would appear that the net impact of the environmental protection law on Eximbank is to impose a reasonably heavy burden on the engineering staff which has had to be expanded from five to seven persons. It would appear that the procedures spelled out in the Executive Order are sensible and the Eximbank Board has appreciated receiving environmental informaton during the last two years. At the same time, Exim was able to turn the matter around and, if it appeared that a developing nation was not taking enough care in reducing harmful effluents, Exim would offer an additional loan to cover the equipment necessary to bring the effluent down to U.S. standards. In the few cases where this arose the foreign buyer seemed grateful for the additional loan support and this created an additional export from the United States.

(d) Adverse Employment or Production Impact

From time to time, Congress has added particular requirements to Exim's statutes. If manufacturing technology or other productive capacity (mainly agricultural) is being exported, Exim is required to determine whether there may be an "adverse impact" to labor and industry in the United States. In all such instances (approximately 10 per cent of total cases), the cases are carefully studied by the Policy Analysis Division of the Bank. First, trade flows of the particular product are analyzed globally and bilaterally. If a re-export to the United States is likely to be involved, there will be an analysis of expected future supply and demand trends in the United States and in the world. If there is a possibility of displacement of manufacture or production in the United States by reason of re-imports, particular analysis is done of the company by company impact, if possible. An analysis is then prepared of the value of the export to be supported by Exim financing and likely follow-on exports from the United States in the way of replacement parts, etc. Then a net adverse impact, if any, is predicted. Finally, there will be an analysis of the competitive framework in which the American exporter is bidding. In most cases the plant or production will be installed in any event as several other nations with the technology will be bidding in the tender. If the plant or production is going to be installed in any event, as is usually the case, it is hard to deny support for the immediate export.

In the last four years, only a few projects have not been supported because of adverse impact. One case involved steel production in Trinidad and Tobago where all of the product was to be re-exported to the United States and the decision had to be made in October 1977, exactly at the time the Department of Treasury was struggling with dumping cases filed by United States steel companies. Other difficult projects, not yet totally resolved, are engine manufacturing facilities for the automotive industry in Mexico where the government has decreed that, by 1983, firms must balance imports with exports in the automotive sector of the industry.

(e) Nuclear Proliferation

Considerable attention is given in Exim's statute in connection with the financial support of peaceful nuclear power production aboard. Foreign countries seeking Eximbank credits must have become parties to the nuclear nonproliferation treaty and must accept special U.S. conditions imposed by the Congress for the export of peaceful nuclear technology. In addition, prior notification to Congress is required in all cases of support for the export of nuclear technology. Eximbank's competitors abroad do not have similar statutory restrictions. Disagreements have arisen between the U.S. Government on the one hand and Germany and France on the other with respect to the export of nuclear reprocessing technology which could lead to the production of plutonium. The Carter Administration sought to persuade France and Germany not to go ahead with such exports. Apparently, France agreed to revoke its proposed export of nuclear reprocessing technology to Pakistan but Germany declined to break its contract with Brazil. It will be interesting to see the developments internationally on this important issue following the Israeli air strike on the nuclear facility in Iraq.

(f) Communist Nations

Over the years Congress has been extremely sensitive to support by Eximbank for exports to Communist nations. In December 1933 the United States re-established diplomatic relations with Russia. In February 1934 President Roosevelt and his advisors decided to establish the Export-Import Bank of Washington to sponsor two-way trade with the Soviet Union. The attempt to use export credit to facilitate trade with Russia immediately foundered in Congress over the issue of the Soviet Union's honoring of tsarist bonds in the hands of private U.S. citizens. The USSR refused. Congress refused to let Exim be used for the purpose for which it had been chartered and, in point of fact, Exim's programs were only opened in Russia in the early years of detente, from 1972 to 1974.

In 1974 the Jackson-Vanick Amendment brought the issue of emigration into Exim's statute, amending it to prohibit export credits to Communist nations unless the President found that there had been satisfactory improvement in the emigration policy from the particular nations. Exim's programs for Poland and Yugoslavia were grandfathered and the requisite findings have been made and reported to Congress so that Exim's programs are now open in Romania, Hungary and the People's Republic of China. Otherwise, Exim makes no contribution by any of its programs for exports to Eastern Europe and the Communist nations of Southeast Asia.

(g) Antitrust Laws

Much has been written in the United States and abroad about the extension of the antitrust laws of the United States to its own multinationals and to foreign corporations engaging in cartels. The purpose here is not to discuss that broad issue but only that part of the antitrust laws added by the Webb-Pomerene Act[19] which exempted from the antitrust law operations by consortia engaged solely in export trade from the United States. Webb Pomerene allowed this exemption, provided that any such consortia not restrain the export trade of any domestic competitor of the consortium.

The only consortia operating abroad that have received favorable rulings from the Justice Department were those which included all interested and willing parties. For example, a favorable ruling was obtained in connection with the establishment of the Foreign Credit Insurance Association which operates in cooperation with the Eximbank to fill a vacuum in the United States market of companies wishing to issue export credit insurance. Approximately fifty insurance companies joined the consortium. Another example was the establishment of the Private Export Funding Corporation where between fifty and sixty American banks, investment banks, and manufacturing exporters formed a consortium to provide fixed interest rate financing abroad backed by financial guarantees from the Export-Import Bank. The Justice Department had to be satisfied that an opportunity had been offered to all similarly situated banks and manufacturing firms and that all who wished had a chance to acquire its stock both at the initial formation and later.

A converse situation occurred in the case of a consortium of three telecommunications manufacturers who wished to support the modernization of the Egyptian telecommunication system. The fourth American company having the capability of manufacturing did not join the consortium and chose to bid itself in cooperation with its Belgian subsidiary. The Agency for International Development of the State Department, on advice of its legal counsel, refused to support the project on the grounds that the consortium was not exempt under Webb-Pomerene since it did not have all U.S. manufacturers in the consortium. The consortium effort then collapsed.

8. Conclusions

The process of international negotiations relating to export credit programs is probably more interesting than the volume of agreements produced. Twenty years of cooperative work in the Berne Union on noncompetitive issues preceded and laid a good foundation for difficult negotiations as competition in the export credit race became the predominant, perhaps the preemptive, issue. While the meetings of the OECD Arrangement have not been totally unsuccessful in framing, reducing, and resolving difficult issues of competition, the membership is so large and all-inclusive that the more flexible atmosphere of the Berne Union meetings is missing. It would probably be helpful to return responsibility to the Berne Union for further negotiations of the Arrangement. Such a return might also make it more likely that the export credit agencies of the developing world would join the negotiations.

The use of the concept of the "gentlemen's agreement" made it possible for reluctant parties, strongly influenced by vested political and economic interests at home, to agree to nonbinding, tentative declarations of policy for a limited time. After experience with these declarations, more detailed documents have been devised and agreed to. Eventually agreement by treaty—in this instance, the GATT—can follow, making cross-reference to the guidelines established by the earlier steps in the process of gentlemen's agreements. In this manner, it is easy to foresee a body of case law building on the trilateral issues raised by excessively subsidized export credits to third country markets.

Notes

1. "A History of ECGD, 1919–1979." Export Credits Guarantee Department, London, 1979, p. 7.

2. Statutes of The International Union of Credit and Investment Insurers (Berne Union), 12 June 1974, Article 2, subparagraph 2.01(i).

3. *Ibid.*, subparagraph 3.01(i).

4. Interview with Donald Ward, Secretary-General of the Berne Union, June 24, 1981.

5. Statutes of the Berne Union, Article IV, paragraph 4.01.

6. The information on the International Conference on Export Credit Insurance Organizations in Developing Countries was graciously supplied by Dr. Wimal Wickramasinghe, Chairman of the Sri Lanka Export Credit Insurance Corporation.

7. Joan Pearce, *Subsidized Export Credit*, The Royal Institute of International Affairs, Chatham House Papers, London, 1980, p. 43.

8. Axel Wallen and John M. Duff, Jr., "The Outlook for Official Export Credits", in Hufbauer, editor, *The International Framework for Money and Banking in the 1980s*, International Law Institute, 1981, p. 413.

9. *Ibid.*, pp. 412-413.

10. *Ibid.*, pp. 464.

11. *Restatement of the Law*, Second, Foreign Relations Law of the United States, §115, Comment g. Tentative Draft No. 1 (1980) restates the comment, at § 301, Comment e, as follows:

Non-binding agreements. Since an international agreement is one intended to be legally binding and having legal consequences, this part does not apply to agreements not intended to have such legal character or conseqences. Examples of such agreements are the "gentlemen's agreements" made at various times in American history; there have been such also in the history of the United Nations organization.

12. 1 U.S.C. 112(b) (1972).

13. Schachter, "The Twilight Existence of Nonbinding International Agreements," 71 AJIL 296, 302 (1977).

14. *Ibid.*, p. 298.

15. *Ibid.*, p. 300.

16. Organization for Economic Co-operation and Development, *The Export Credit Financing Systems in OECD Member Countries*, Paris, 1982.

17. See "Financing of Subway Cars for the Metropolitan Transportation Authority of New York," Decision of the Secretary of the Treasury, July 13, 1982, for the first case arising under the Section. Secretary Regan found that the Canadians derogated from the Arrangement but that other factors were more important than the lower than Arrangement interest rate. Assistance to the Budd Co., the U.S. competitor, was denied.

18. 15 Pres. Doc. 10 (1979).

19. 15 U.S.C. § 62.

NINE

Lessons from the Codes

SEYMOUR J. RUBIN

GARY CLYDE HUFBAUER

1. Introduction

It is not surprising that, after three decades, the Bretton Woods system is experiencing certain transformations. The flourishing growth of international economic ties has required—and will continue to require—a concomitant adjustment of the international legal system. More surprising, perhaps, is the durability of the basic system. Much of the change during the last twenty years has taken the form of specific agreements to deal with limited problems, and specific exceptions to general principles, rather than attempts to reconstruct the edifice on new foundations. Thus, the emerging new order lacks its own agreed set of first principles and misses sharp definition. Indeed, to a large extent the new order is simply an outgrowth of the old Bretton Woods System.

Nevertheless, the post-Bretton woods system[1] has at least one distinguishing feature: Whereas Bretton Woods was erected on the premise that a liberal open system would achieve the greatest prosperity for all, the newer arrangements have often sought to redistribute wealth by altering the framework of commercial transactions. In a sense, these attempts at redistribution entail a search for "soft aid," by reducing the price of imports or increasing the price of exports by the developing countries. Ironically, in the decade of the 1970's, when massive amounts of wealth were transferred from creditor nations to debtor nations

Seymour J. Rubin is Executive Director and Executive Vice President, American Society of International Law; and Professor of International Law, American University

Gary Clyde Hufbauer is a Senior Fellow, Institute for International Economics; and Counsel, Chapman, Duff & Paul

The authors gladly acknowledge the contributions of their colleagues to the Lessons summarized in this chapter, while absolving those colleagues from editorial responsibility.

through negative real interest rates, and when OPEC siphoned enormous amounts of income from other parts of the globe, attempts to achieve redistribution through code negotiations had rather little impact. The post-Bretton Woods system of commercial arrangements (leaving aside monetary arrangements and development finance) can be subdivided into four major areas:

(1) Regional preference arrangements, such as The European Economic Community; The Andean Pact; and The U.S.-Canada Automotive Products Agreement.

(2) Commodity agreements organized by exporting countries, such as The Organization of Petroleum Exporting Countries; The Tin Agreement; The failed Common Fund.

(3) Multilateral and bilateral import limitation agreements, such as The Multifiber Arrangement; The U.S.-Japanese automobile agreement; and The U.S-European steel agreement.

(4) Codes of conduct,[2] principally addressed to the investment and trade policies of governments and large firms, such as The OECD Codes on Invisibles and Capital Movements; The OECD Declarations on International Investment and Multinational Enterprise; The UN Charter of Economic Rights and Duties; The UN Restrictive Business Practices Code; The UN Transnational Corporation Code; The UN Illicit Payments Code; The GATT Subsidies Code; OECD Arrangements on Official Export Credits; and The Law of the Sea Treaty (which, of course, deals with issues besides investment and trade policy).

The essays in this volume have focused on the fourth dimension of the post-Bretton Woods commercial system—the codes that address the investment behavior and trade practices of large firms and governments. It must be emphasized that many of these codes are far from "hard law." Some of them, like the UN Illicit Payments Code, are merely a gleam in negotiators' eyes; others, like the OECD Declarations, are intended at most to be "soft law"—grist, perhaps, for the evolution of customary international law but not themselves the finished sausage. In fact, the range of code results reflects the extent of pre-existing agreement among signatory nations that rules were needed to address a common problem. For example, major industrial countries agreed that the subsidy component of official export financing should be reduced— hence the OECD Arrangements on Official Export Credits. By contrast, a consensus never existed that the transfer of technology should be regulated by international agreement—hence the UN negotiations remain in the category of hopes and aspirations. Indeed a fair generalization can be made that code negotiations which can trace their descent from the original Bretton Woods system of trading rules have often come close to "hard" international law, while negotiations built on a premise of redistribution have eluded international agreement. At most, redistribution has come through the back door: for example, the tiered interest rate matrix in the Arrangement on Export Credits that favors poorer countries.

Another distinction between the latter-day codes and the earlier Bretton Woods system is that the code negotiations have labored on for many years, whereas the key features of the Bretton Woods system were put in place within a comparatively short period of time (though the negotiating time for the GATT commercial system was somewhat longer than for the IMF and the World Bank). Thus the connection between original goals and the final result was much stronger in the Bretton Woods system than the Code system. In the end the code efforts of the 1960's and 1970's combined several objectives: an educational function; demonstration effects; legitimizing certain practices; an effort to declare a future program; and finally, an effort to state rules. By comparison with the Bretton Woods system, the code system placed much less emphasis on institution building and committed very little resources to implementing the codes.

(a) Blending Systems and Filling Gaps

To a large extent, the laboriously negotiated Codes have resulted in the articulation of evolving practice, rather than in shaping a new system. Indeed, some of the codes simply fill gaps that were left when the Havana Charter was discarded. In particular, Articles 11 and 12 of the original International Trade Organization (ITO) Charter contained language that balanced "investor protection" against "decent conduct" provisions. These twin concepts were revived in subsequent OECD attempts to formulate investment codes. In 1967, for example, the OECD formulated a Convention on the Protection of Foreign Property. This Convention (and its accompanying Resolution) reflected only the "investor protection" theme. However, in the 1970's, an anti-private foreign investment and anti-MNC mood appeared in the OECD: Canada and Sweden felt the presence of foreign investment to be oppressive; and the Netherlands acted as a conduit for LDC concerns about MNC dominance. The United States, Switzerland, and the United Kingdom became alarmed that the exercise would run away with anti-MNC rules. The solution was a two-track approach balancing investor protection against decent conduct, reminiscent of Articles 11 and 12 of the ITO Charter. In a similar sense, the Berne Union and OECD Export Credit Arrangements, and the GATT Subsidies Code, all filled definitional and enforcement gaps in the original GATT framework on export subsidies.

(b) Investment Focus

Nearly all the Codes deal, in one way or another, with investment and financial practices, either by the state (as in subsidies and export credits) or by private firms (as in foreign corrupt practices and restrictive business practices). At the time of the creation of the Bretton Woods system, the central problems of the day concerned the sharp division between creditor and debtor nations, and extremely high and discriminatory trade barriers. Only later did investment issues involving MNCs come into prominence.

But the absence of international agreement on the investment-related clauses of the draft ITO Charter did not mean that there was a void in the evolution of international understandings related to investment issues. By the early 1960's, a fairly well-established pattern of standards of conduct was beginning to develop, though perhaps more among industrialized nations than between those nations and the developing countries. There was, in the first instance, a continuing insistence on the part of the major investing nations on the "traditional" rules of international law, illustrated, for example, in the projected 1967 OECD Convention for the Protection of Private Foreign Investment. Unsuccessful though that effort (and several similar ones) was, the proposition continued—and continues—consistently to be advanced that there are relevant and applicable rules of international law. Indeed, that proposition was sufficiently accepted in the early UN Resolutions on "permanent sovereignty" over natural resources so that the industrialized nations could accept those Resolutions, in contrast to their later (1974) rejection of the UN "Charter of Economic Rights and Duties of States," precisely for the reason that it seemed to question the validity and applicability of the traditional international law rules. Industrialized nations continue to press the point and, at least in the now large number of existing bilateral investment treaties with developing countries, to do so with success. Other elements in the pattern contribute to the same result. The Paris Patent Convention, though revision has been urged in UNCTAD V and will undoubtedly again be urged in UNCTAD VI (scheduled for mid-1983), continues in effect. So also do the Berne Union understandings. Early International Court of Justice cases on which investors have long relied have not been repudiated by the Court, though opportunities to reinforce doctrine have largely been avoided on jurisdictional grounds. And even in code efforts such as those of the UN Commission on Transnational Corporations, where clear recognition of the applicability of international law to investment issues has not been achieved, there has been general recognition that a code of conduct must be "balanced"—that is, must include rules with respect to treatment of TNCs and their property interests as well as standards for their conduct. The absence of a formal, global investment treaty (a "GATT for Investment") has probably made less difference than would otherwise be the case because of the complex network of bilateral agreements, informal understandings, practical settlements of investment disputes, and increased perception of the importance of fair treatment to the flow of private capital for development purposes. At the same time, a more formal global system has been difficult to achieve. The UN efforts have tended to look for a reshaping of the basic pre-existent pattern; efforts such as those of the OECD and private but important bodies, such as the International Chamber of Commerce, have at the same time looked toward crystallization and reinforcement of that same system.

One reason why the investment codes have made rather slower progress than trade agreements may stem from the fact that the concept of reciprocity plays a less visible role in investment codes. Trade negotiators make progress because market access is traded for market access. No similar symmetry exists in the investment area, at least not between countries that conceive of themselves mainly as host countries or mainly as home countries. However, as more countries come to see themselves simultaneously as host and home countries, reciprocity will become a stronger presence in investment code negotiations.

(c) The Importance of Consensus

The history of the effort to achieve international agreement on an illicit payments code illustrates the importance of consensus. The United States, roundly condemned in international forums as the major home of the major TNCs which had engaged in illicit practices, and caught up in the wake of the Watergate scandals, took the lead in proposing an international code on illicit payments. The United States position was reinforced by the fact that the Congress had (contrary to the recommendations of the Richardson Committee) "criminalized" actions by United States nationals which the Congress decided were illicit, even though the country in which these acts took place seemed tolerant, to say the least, of those same acts. Though the outcry abroad on disclosure of a few scandals was loud, few countries seemed enthusiastic about internationalizing such a standard of conduct. Whether this was because of a feeling that the United States was already "on the hook," or a result of drafts which referred to the evils of accepting or soliciting a bribe as well as offering one, the initial U.S. proposal was inaudibly applauded, and, though an "effort" was mounted by ECOSOC, and much effort went into it, little resulted. As pointed out elsewhere in this volume, and despite initial (mainly rhetorical) support and even pressure from the

LDCs (stimulated by the illicit payment episodes involving ITT and Lockheed), developing countries were never really enthusiastic about the project, and they came to see it as a way of diverting attention from other deficiencies in the *modus operandi* of multinational corporations. Eventually, the United States ceased to press the effort, and, probably with some sense of relief, it was allowed to become moribund. The United States is now concentrating on amending its own rules.

Curiously, the absence of consensus did not reflect formal disagreement as to the appropriate substantive rule. According to one story, the U.S. State Department sent out a circular letter to its foreign posts asking about anti-corruption laws. Almost all posts reported domestic laws against taking or giving bribes for official acts. In one of the few countries which did not have a law, the reporting officer noted that he recently passed two men hanging on a tree wearing placards which read: "They took bribes."

But international consensus on the substantive rule was more formal than real, and clearly did not translate into consensus on effective means of enforcing the rule, especially as against recipient officials, nor into consensus on the importance of the issue in the international scale of priorities.

Among the Codes examined, two must be reckoned as moribund: the UN Illicit Payments Code, and (despite desultory negotiations) the UN Transfer of Technology (TOT) Code. Another code is in precarious health: the UN TNC Code, on which an intensive effort to "update" the Code is scheduled for 1983. In all three cases, consensus proved elusive. For example, in the TOT Code, twelve "South" countries advocated a minority rule on the choice of forum for adjudicating disputes (the place of use of the technology) while the "North" countries advocated a majority rule (the choice of the parties). Neither group would legitimate the other group's rule. By contrast, the "successful" codes of the postwar period—successful in the sense that they have been enacted—have codified consensus rules.

2. Effectiveness of the Codes

Experience with the codes leads to an important generalization: the manner in which a code is to be interpreted, and the way in which it is to be made "effective," are not collateral matters, but importantly affect the principles of conduct stated in the code. Procedure thus becomes a matter of substance.

This was not always perceived to be so. The various multilateral agreements which form the Bretton Woods system generally relegated interpretation and implementation to the context of dispute resolution.

That was a context considered sufficiently tangential that it could be entrusted to the lawyers, a category of professionals whose qualifications to conduct substantive international negotiations were denigrated by such diplomatists as Sir Harold Nicholson, Walter Lippman, and George Kennan. What was considered to be of primary importance was the formulation of principles. How principles were to be either interpreted or carried into action was, it was thought, a matter that could be relegated to the realm of procedure. It was assumed that infrequent deviations from the accepted norms could be negotiated, and alleged violations outside of negotiated exceptions could be handled by a process of consultation. A few devices for dispute resolution, including such trade remedies as withdrawal of concessions, could be relied upon to achieve compliance.

These optimistic expectations have not been vindicated. Even in the basic Bretton Woods agreements, departures from established standards have become a major issue.[3] For example, the GATT has been held together largely because of the many exceptions which were permitted, and the many more which were intentionally overlooked. In the case of the IMF, departures from accepted standards were somewhat fewer—until the "Nixon shock" of 1971 led to wholesale revision and acceptance of floating rather than fixed rates of exchange. In the code system, interpretation has an ever larger dimension: the broad aims, the number and diversity of participants, and the highly suspect quality of real concurrence in the new generation of international economic agreements, have made the matter of how a code is to be interpreted, and how it is to be put into effective practice, integral to the principles themselves.

The importance of effective practice becomes all the more obvious when one looks honestly at the fuzzy language —the result both of hard bargaining and of stated or unstated reservations—which seems endemic to most of the newer international agreements. A principle desired and supported by all participants, agreed in a framework of mutual trust and confidence, does not demand much in the way of techniques of implementation or even of interpretation, just as an agreement to arbitrate is not essential to an understanding between friends. But where negotiation is difficult and surrounded by mutual suspicion, where the agreement is couched in ambiguities that conceal as much as they reveal, and when the body which will supervise the agreement is not likely to be a model of impartiality, the interpretation and implementation procedures become an integral aspect of the commitments themselves, and hence a substantive part of the negotiation of these commitments. Some of the important questions of interpretation and implementation may be briefly reviewed.

(a) "Mandatory" Codes.

The issue is often put whether the code shall be "mandatory"—that is, a legally binding agreement—or "non-mandatory" or "voluntary" or "legally non-enforceable" —that is, relying on the good faith and good will of the signatories. The older international economic agreements were generally framed as binding obligations: the GATT, the Articles of Agreement of the IMF and the World Bank, and, for example, the Treaty of Rome. However, some "binding" obligations in principle are not very binding in practice. For example, there may well be a binding obligation to "give sympathetic consideration" to the needs or aspirations or complaints of other signatories, or a binding obligation to consult or to give prior notice. Such obligations can usually be discharged with little inconvenience or consequence.

The newer codes, especially those involved in a new international economic order, tend to be of the non-mandatory sort. This is largely because codes which speak in broad terms—cover a wide area, are addressed to many participants of varying political and economic persuasions—and which have been negotiated against a backdrop of conflicting concepts of equity, are not phrased in terms of precisely formulated standards that can be cast in an obligatory mold. The reasons why many codes are couched as "recommendations" or "guidelines" are, however, largely identical with the reasons why participants are unwilling to grant large interpretive or executory authority to a secretariat or other international body. As a corollary to their non-mandatory flavor, most of the codes have been negotiated in the OECD and the UN, forums noted for a hortatory quality. By contrast, the codes with a mandatory flavor have been consigned to the GATT, with its greater emphasis on hard obligations.

The simple assumption that legally binding is in some sense superior to non-legally binding is questionable. Even a legally binding code is not likely to invoke penalties for infractions. The GATT very rarely authorizes compensatory measures, and the IMF tolerates assorted departures from the standards laid down in its Articles of Agreement. Even binding rules can be waived; this has happened to unconditional most-favored-nation treatment embodied in GATT Article I; to the GATT discipline of agricultural subsidies; and to the IMF Articles that called for fixed exchange rates. On the other hand, the more the code acquires a binding character, the less easy it will be to modify the substantive principles in response to changing circumstances. Moreover, the non-mandatory codes often deal with more important issues—in the sense that they affect a larger volume of commercial transactions.

A further advantage of non-mandatory codes is that they can usually be negotiated and implemented without the benefit of Parliamentary or

Congressional approval. As long as codes merely address executive branch "intentions" and create no binding obligations either on the executive or the private sector, then the achievement of international consensus can be greatly facilitated by keeping legislative involvement at a minimum. In fact, this means of achieving international agreement without formal legislative action can be used by executive departments to confer redistributive benefits on poor countries through code negotiations—benefits that might not pass muster either in European Parliaments or the U.S. Congress.

Problems that are perceived to derive from the "mandatory/non-mandatory" difference have generally been finessed, in the newer codes, by agreement that, whatever their nature, such codes should be "effective." This was the understanding reached by the UN Commission on Transnational Corporations, after a long and acrimonious debate on the "nature of the code." To concur that the code should be effective, of course, hardly settles matters. Problems remain: such codes are frequently couched in the ambiguous language of compromise; and somehow, if worst comes to worst, one must envisage the grim possibility that there will be an authoritative interpretation of the code, and some means of having that interpretation accepted by those whose actions it affects. However, as a practical matter, whether the code is mandatory or non-mandatory, the nature of remedial action among states is much the same, namely graded retaliation for transgressions thought to have been committed by another state.

Some codes have presented interesting lessons in the application of a nonbinding instrument. The highest exponent of this particular art form is the OECD Committee on Investment and Multinational Enterprise. In 1973–74, the trade unions, supported by the Swedish delegation, wanted a legally binding OECD code that would regulate MNC behavior. The United States, Switzerland and Germany said the *quid pro quo* was a legally binding investment protection code. Both ideas were dropped.

As negotiations on the OECD code progressed, negotiators became very sensitive to any suggestion of a forum before which companies would be brought. However, the instruction not to judge individual cases became a fig leaf for the procedure actually adopted—consideration of illustrative cases modeled in all important respects on live examples. Thus, the precedential function of case adjudication was retained, while the remedial function was abandoned. Note the difference, however, between the workings of the system in the Badger case and in the Canadian National Energy Policy case. The Badger case, which lay behind the sole revision of the OECD Guidelines in the 1979 Review of those Guidelines, concerned the closing of a Belgian subsidiary by a United States-based parent corporation, allegedly without adequate notice to the workers, and without provision for severance compensation satisfactory to workers or to the Belgian authorities. The OECD spent a great deal of time on the stylized facts of this case, and finally suggested, by illustrative examples, that parent firms should make financial provisions for severance pay when foreign subsidiaries are closed. The Canadian National Energy Policy Case involved assertions by the United States that Canada's policy violated the national treatment clause of the OECD Declaration. In this instance, involving government practices, there was never an illustrative example formulated nor did the case lead to a better description of permitted and proscribed practices.

Another example of the workings of a nonbinding instrument is provided by the succession of arrangements, under the auspices of the Berne Union and the OECD, to discipline official export credit practices. The voluntary nature of these agreements in part reflects negotiating history: the European Community has had to allow member states some latitude in crafting arrangements with the United States, first in respect of the Gentlemen's Agreement, later in respect of large commercial aircraft. In both instances, the European Economic Community had the negotiating mandate, but practical realities suggested that member states take the negotiating lead. This was best done within the framework of a voluntary code. In addition, voluntary codes entailed a convenient means of avoiding the rigors of national constitutional procedures required for binding commitments. Finally, in the supple world of finance, a voluntary code can be more easily amended to deal with new practices devised by the ever-ingenious financial mind. The weaknesses of this approach are obvious. Since no state is ever condemned, and only in the rarest circumstances are concessions withdrawn, the incentives to evade or avoid are strong. The strength of the approach is that successive generations of national policy officials must actively confront the precepts of the code in the process of continuing international negotiations and in designing their own policy initiatives.

The UN Restrictive Business Practices and Transfer of Technology Codes both preclude any measure to "sit in judgment" on individual companies. Just as the MNCs wanted to avoid public exposure, so LDCs were anxious not to have cases brought by trade unions, nor to have companies bring cases against governments. However, the "kangaroo court" fear was probably exaggerated: hearings before code committees are not necessarily preordained as to outcome, nor need they necessarily resort to arbitrary procedures.

The Treaty of Rome distinguished between regulations (binding) and directives (nonbinding). Even this distinction has been blurred with more precise drafting of directives (at one extreme, for example, the accounting directive), and the recent practice of the Community of moving away from binding regulations towards negotiating frameworks. The blurring of the distinction is also enhanced by the fact that a directive, when issued, does bind the states to which it is addressed.

In theory, the GATT Subsidy Code is legally binding with respect to states. Indeed, the Subsidies Code has many of the trappings of an international treaty, although it is not ratified as a treaty. The language has a binding quality in stating proscribed and permitted practices and in spelling out mechanisms for dispute settlement. But express remedies are limited to extensive consultations and panel findings.

Multilateral codes are not likely to be mandatory, or to give rise to "hard" international law, insofar as they deal with investment issues. Bilateral agreements are an exception, as perhaps is such an agreement as that establishing the World Bank's International Center for the Settlement of Investment Disputes, as to signatories. Conceivably, codes in the investment area may impose requirements on states which, in turn, are to impose those standards on entities within their jurisdiction. This would have been the case, had the international arrangements with respect to illicit payments come into effect as a mandatory code. The issue does not always affect the consequences of the code: The World Health Organization's work on the advertising and marketing of infant food formulas has probably directly affected the producers and sellers of that type of product as much as would the most directly applicable domestic law or international agreement.

(a) Who is the Addressee?

The addressee of the code substantially affects the implementing mechanisms. If the target is states, then the regular meetings of governments to discuss, criticize and perhaps embarrass one another may in fact have an impact. Criticism of Canadian discrimination against foreign oil firms has perhaps muted the nationalistic inclinations of the Trudeau government. European and Canadian criticism of the U.S. Domestic International Sales Corporation (DISC) muted the U.S. enthusiasm for expanding the scope of tax deferral to cover the export of services, paved the way for some scaling back of DISC benefits in the Tax Act of 1982, and prompted Administration proposals for a restructuring of DISC in 1983.

On the whole, the regulation of state practices has gone further than the regulation of MNCs. The Bretton Woods system was mainly designed to encourage rules that would allow private enterprise to flourish. By contrast, some of the latter day codes are designed to discipline private firms within the larger system. The effect on private sector targets works somewhat differently than the effect on states. Even though private corporations and trade unions are not invited to official meetings of the CIME (the OECD Committee on Investment and Multinational Enterprises), a thorough exchange of views takes place through the mechanisms of the Business and Industry Advisory Committee (BIAC) and the Trades Union Advisory Committee (TUAC) surrounding the OECD Guidelines. It is possible that a similar forum will arise around the Restrictive Business Practices Code.

(b) Customary International Law

Customary international law is created by the legitimization of precepts through their application to specific international problems. For example, a General Assembly resolution may be used as the guiding precept in an arbitration; or precepts on national treatment may be embodied in bilateral treaties. Voluntary codes may thus become part of customary international law by two avenues—indirectly through the writings of jurists, and more directly when governments choose to cite their propositions. An example of the latter application is Article 5 of the OECD Guidelines on disclosure of MNC financial operations. Other code propositions that seem to be passing into the realm of customary international law would include the precept that nations ought not to subsidize their exports, and the precept that multinational enterprises should not use their market power to damage the host country.

Even a non-mandatory code may come before a national tribunal, often in the context of an assertion that it represents a statement of customary international law. The debate on that point can be endless, particularly so if it is asserted that the code—or a General Assembly resolution—creates, as well as recapitulates, international law.

It may also be argued that a code may establish "state practice," and thereby eventually be regarded as customary international law. With respect to the declarations, resolutions, or codes related to "the new international economic order," most authorities reject this proposition. It seems unlikely that the majority of states would agree that, in adopting code provisions, they are making customary international law. Code provisions are characteristically both broad and vague; there are obvious dangers (some would say opportunities) if these provisions are thought to pass into the body of international law. But not everyone takes that rejection at face value. It has been suggested that the UN Transnational Corporation Code, for example, even though explicitly stated to be non-mandatory, might attain considerable international standing. A 1978 paper of the UN Center for TNCs on "Modalities for Implementation of a Code of Conduct in Relation to its Legal Nature" did state that

> A Code of Conduct on transnational corporations, whether in legally bind-
> ing or nonbinding form, represents an effort to formulate expectations
> which Governments collectively felt justified to hold . . . . It becomes
> thereby a "source" of law for national authorities as well as for the
> transnational corporations themselves.

The statement, as the careful choice of words emphasized, obviously
holds back from stating that a code would itself become a source of international law; it has nonetheless aroused worries—and possibly
hopes—on that score. Nor does the statement deal with the situation in
which a code might be adopted not by consensus but through General
Assembly resolution, against which a number of states have voted (as was
the case of the Charter of Economic Rights and Duties of States).

That a code provision might be regarded as a legitimate source of international law is a thought which, on reflection, could be equally
troubling to developing and developed nations. The argument has of
course been made, by developing nations, that the substantial majorities
which have been mustered for most of the resolutions related to the
"new international economic order" indicates that these indeed are legitimate sources. But the current codes—especially those having to do with
the conduct of TNCs—are expected to be reasonably "balanced" documents. That means that they will contain clauses establishing norms of
conduct for states, as well as for TNCs. Under these circumstances, the
argument that the code is a source of international law may well lose its
attractiveness for the developing nations.

Moreover, a step beyond the thesis that the UN resolutions establish a
source of international law is the argument that bilateral investment
treaties establish another legitimate "source." Such treaties are now in
force between some industrialized nations (mainly the UK, France, the
Federal Republic of Germany, and Switzerland) on the one side, and a
number of developing countries on the other. Treaties are a more traditional "source" than General Assembly resolutions, and it may be that
bilateral investment treaties are now numerous enough to establish a
general practice. That thought may lead to some hesitation in assertions
that codes are a source of international law, inasmuch as they represent
a general acceptance of particular standards. For if codes are a source,
then so may be investor protection treaties.

(c) Codes as National Law

A code can become part of a national law system. Even a mandatory
code is, however, not likely to be self-executing, and would therefore require a positive act of a national legislative or similar body before passing
into the body of national law. A more likely possibility is that code provi-

sions, mandatory or non-mandatory, will be taken as points of departure for national legislation.

In point of fact, it would seem that on many matters the more advanced of the developing nations are already ahead of proposed codes: Mexico, Brazil, and India, for example, have no need of instructions from proposed UNCTAD codes. Conversely, in the least developed of the developing nations, it is not likely that national laws tracking the codes will be enacted or enforced, mainly because of lack of skilled personnel and administrative capacities. Nonetheless, the code may seem useful to both groups: to the more advanced nations because it lends respectability and gives some international blessing to the prescriptions of national law; to the least developed, because the code may provide not only a substitute for the substantive provisions of what would otherwise be national law, but it can also make up—through the international secretariat—for a paucity of domestic administrative and enforcement capabilities.

(d) Applicable Law

Code-drafting exercises have often confronted the demand that the code be interpreted according to a given "applicable law," that is to say, in a given dispute covered by the code, the law of one of the signatories. In some codes the choice of applicable law has a very pointed impact: The proposed Transfer of Technology code, for example, would refer interpretation on technology transfer agreements to the law of the licensee (generally the developing country in a DC/LDC situation), whatever provision might have been made by the parties in the license agreement itself, or whatever might be their desires. In other codes there is a considerable insistence on the part of developing countries, especially those for whom the Calvo Doctrine is Holy Writ, that international obligations in the area of property rights must reflect, and be interpreted under, applicable national law. Disagreement among the prospective signatories as to the choice of applicable law can easily undermine the substantive commitment to which the parties are willing to subscribe.

3. International Cooperation

One way of dealing with issues of interpretation and implementation is to provide for cooperation among the signatories, and to establish some sort of central secretariat. In the context of any international agreement, it lies within the power of the parties to come together and consult, and thus seek both clarification and common understanding. The codes generally try to formalize this procedure, often in a way which makes it a mandatory obligation even within a non-mandatory code.

Two formal mechanisms have been particularly important: The secretariat can issue reports; and the signatories can "discuss their experience" under the code.

The difficulty lies in detailing the obligations supplementary to international cooperation. To what extent does the obligation of international cooperation compel the production of information; or require prior consultation before taking actions which might lie within the scope of the code; or allow an international secretariat to seek information from nationals of the signatories? Once more, the answers to these inquiries may affect the substantive commitments which a participant is willing to accept. An obligation to "take into account" the traditions and customs of a party may be viewed as relatively innocuous, but possibly not if it is coupled with a firm obligation to consult that party and to postpone action until its views have been heard and argued.

(a) Information and Reports

Most codes are entrusted for day-to-day administration to a secretariat of some sort, which is generally empowered to collect information and to draft and issue reports. These reports can be substantial instruments both of interpretation and of implementation. They are not typically subjected to the debate which takes place at meetings of the participants themselves; and they tend to have wider public impact than do the generally tedious reports of formal sessions of the international organization.

For this reason, the "Comprehensive Information System" of the UN Centre on TNCs was the subject of much attention. Information may have a powerful impact, as is testified by the attention given by many TNCs to their "corporate profiles" compiled by the Centre. When such information is broadened and made the basis of reports, it becomes a method of interpreting, and even of implementing, the code. Conduct is often influenced by the requirement that it be disclosed—a basic premise of U.S. securities legislation. The "Vredeling Initiative" in the European Economic Community is likewise based on the thesis that disclosure will affect action. Indeed, the Vredeling proposal can be read as a legally binding alternative to the OECD Guidelines. And the disclosure provisions of the OECD Guidelines are intended not merely to satisfy the curiosity of corporation scrutinizers, but also to deter conduct that corporations would be embarrassed to disclose and to strengthen the ability of labor unions, consumer organizations, and others to influence corporate decisions. Disclosure, in other words, may be both a method of implementing a code provision and a method of enacting a new standard. A report may also declare in fact, if not in theory, a new or amended standard of behavior: Reports on the deplorable effects of marketing of breast-milk substitutes in less developed nations gave powerful impetus both to the code adopted by the World Health Organization and to "voluntary" compliance by most manufacturers.

The information and reporting functions assigned to a secretariat may thus have more relation to the "effectiveness" of a code than does the mandatory or non-mandatory nature of the code. The role of the secretariat becomes even more obviously a determinant of the scope and meaning of the code if it is given the authority to "clarify" code provisions—as has sometimes been proposed.

(b) Review of the Codes

Most of the recent codes provide for a periodic review. This is intended both to shed light on the effects and the effectiveness of the code, and to enable participants to determine whether revision is needed.

"Review" does not explicitly require either interpretation or implementation. It can nonetheless influence conduct. Although most codes provide that the application of the code provisions to specific instances falls outside the purview of the reviewing group, identifiable cases may well underlie the discussion in a review meeting. The OECD Guidelines, when reviewed in accordance with the agreed schedule, were subjected to only one recommended change—in that part dealing with employment practices. It was hardly coincidental that there had been several, well-publicized disputes between labor unions and TNCs, and that the participants in the review sessions were clearly familiar with the stylized facts of those cases.

This type of review has some characteristics of a trial, which suggests that the interested corporation or union should perhaps have direct access to the proceedings. But this in turn would make review an instrument of implementation. Corporations dislike the idea of being "hauled" before a "tribunal"; thus they have mainly contented themselves with insisting on a code clause that no judgments on individual cases can be made or inferred, and with indirect procedural safeguards, such as participation by the Business and Industry Advisory Committee (BIAC) of the OECD, or, on the trade union side, on participation by the Trades Union Advisory Committee (TUAC). More indirect participation by individual firms would seem to carry with it the implication of submission to the authority of the panel, and something more of an obligation to comply than is indicated in the voluntary acceptance of voluntary guidelines.

How the review is to be carried out also has its difficulties. In a relatively homogeneous grouping such as the OECD, there are tolerable differences of view about possible "clarification" or revision. But if the reviewing body reflects the kind of fundamental divergences which characterize most United Nations economic bodies, there can be a justifiable fear that compromises carefully worked out will be upset by subsequent revision or "clarification."

Finally, while review and accompanying discussion are said to be useful in clearing the air, in promoting better understanding even of conflicting points of view, and to have other salubrious consequences, discussion in code forums carries with it at least the danger of exacerbating rather than mitigating disputes. Quite possibly defects or alleged defects in the provisions of the code will be given more attention than other matters, and suggestions for amendment or for implementation will lie in the direction of tightening up the standards contained in the code.

It is further possible that too many results are expected of the codes; code debates sometimes suggest that if new rules are established, giant steps will be made toward a new and better economic order. Whatever may be the benefits of a balanced and clear set of guidelines, they will not resolve major obstacles standing in the way of social and economic development. If expectations are high, and observable results are minimal, disappointment may take the path of proposals for still more new rules. Should this be so, one can anticipate a considerable amount of resistance to the process, seemingly so innocuous, of review itself. In any case, the signatories to the original code will try to ensure that the path to amendment has safeguards comparable or identical to those of the original code.

"Interpretation" by a review conference, adopted by a simple majority, while not an amendment, nevertheless can constitute the working instructions for the secretariat, and for a program of reports, special committees, and other implementing devices. Again, the tendency is likely to be in the direction of interpretations formed by the majority —in the U.N. context, the G-77. Open-ended review thus does not commend itself to at least some participants in the code drafting process.

4. How Effective are the Codes?

Codes are intended to be effective. Are they likely to be so? Are there criteria by which one can judge the extent of their effectiveness?

A first principle would seem to be that codes are not likely to reconcile deep and important differences. When there exists a considerable degree of consensus on the broad outlines of policy, codes can have a useful and indeed relatively important effect. Thus, such a "code" as the

Treaty of Rome, for all of the differences which have disappointed those with high expectations, does express a common point of view, establishes standards of both state and private conduct, and establishes a goal toward which important if sometimes hesitating progress can be made. Similarly, the "codes" in the trade field, most significantly the GATT itself, and the Tokyo Round codes, do represent an affirmation by the major trading nations of the desirability of a world in which trade barriers will be reduced. Again, when a subject of limited scope is involved, such as harmonization of policy related to export credits, or to "incentives and disincentives," they can often be reconciled. Even here there will be many instances in which that result is achieved more in nominal terms than in substance.

The point is that most codes seem to be effective at the fringes of policy, not at its core. Where there is a general agreement on fundamentals—as there is for trade policy among the industrialized nations, or investment policy in the OECD—the codes can yield beneficial results. But a code is not likely to be accepted or implemented when it runs counter to important and deeply felt national policies.

Even within codes in which there is a basis of broad agreement there are areas which, because they do touch on questions which are conceived to be vital, are avoided or treated in the most general and guarded of ways. Thus, even the GATT has never been able to deal meaningfully with agricultural trade, since each nation regards agriculture, for political as well as economic reasons, as being too sensitive a subject to concede its own freedom of action. Similarly, the Multilateral Trade Negotiation was not able to produce an acceptable "safeguards" code that would limit the ability of each nation to take action designed to restrain imports which it perceived as damaging to its own economy. Even in bilateral agreements, such as the US-Japanese FCN Treaty of 1953, exceptions were carved out not only for matters of "national security" but for situations in which the balance of payments was thought to require special protection.

These conflicts may well be handled on a bilateral basis, as when Japan and the United States agree to an accommodation on the number of automobiles to be exported; but the complications are compounded when the participants are many, and when the goals are diverse. In the multinational forums, when general principles suitable for inclusion in a code are being debated, the consequence may well be a provision so drafted as to give comfort to each of several essentially irreconcilable positions. The resulting ambiguity can be accepted only if each party has a considerable degree of faith in the reasonableness of the other (or confidence that the code will be substantially meaningless). A measure of ambiguity is usually acceptable only when the issues subject to the compromise are narrow, and when identifiable cases are in mind. But codes—certainly of the UN variety—generally seek to provide for a broad and unforeseeable range of issues. In those circumstances, the language of compromise does not inspire eagerness to entrust interpretive—and even less implementing—power to an untried and probably suspect international body. Illustrating the point is the reluctance shown by many nations to accept even the optional clauses of the International Court of Justice, or arbitration on such key issues as claims of territorial sovereignty or jurisdiction.

Broad principles of international economic conduct are less susceptible to acceptable codification today than was the case at an earlier date. To repeat: The actors are now more numerous than before; their perceived interests are more divergent; the new philosophic underpinnings are far from universally or even generally accepted (for example, the doctrine of "restitution" which partly underlies the "new international economic order"). Nor is the search for new and broad principles made easier by the heavy toll of violations of even such assertedly mutually beneficial codes as the GATT, where the "cornerstone of the GATT," most-favored-nation treatment, is today largely honored in the breach.

The strains even among the major industrialized nations themselves are heightened by the economic difficulties which characterize the post-GATT world. To list but a few:

- All GATT signatories are entitled to the concessions which were negotiated among only the few who participated in the early negotiating rounds, making for a sense of disequilibrium;
- Preferences, some possibly within GATT exceptions, many others not, have become endemic;
- Shifts in the factors of production require large and painful adjustments, as newly developed countries, and others following them, take over industrial sectors which were previously the province of the developed nations;
- Hidden trade restrictions give rise to calls for "reciprocity," used in this sense as a plea for sectoral protectionism and bilateralism;
- Performance requirements" imposed on investment are said to distort both such investment and trade patterns but are central to the policy of many nations.

Since none of these measures is likely in the end to alleviate the underlying problems of unemployment and inflation, the essential requirement—the belief that cooperation is in fact in the interest of all—is increasingly weakened in mutual recrimination. Between the generality of developed and developing nations, these strains are even greater. Such an atmosphere is hardly conducive to construction of a balanced and mutually beneficial framework for a new international economic order. When the perception is more of a competition for a limited quantum of benefits rather than the application of standards which will in the end benefit all, an attempt at drafting long-term rules may be futile.

5. A Future Look

This is not to say that the effort at creating a set of rules should be abandoned. The growth of interdependence among trading nations requires a concomitant growth of international law, mainly of the soft variety, to provide a stable framework of commercial expectations. The code efforts do have, moreover, an important educational consequence. In the field of transnational corporations, both multinational enterprises and governments have come to understand better the legitimate interests and limitations to which all are subject. Long before achievement of a code is a reality, conduct is in fact usefully improved.

The code experience has shown that U.S. enthusiasm or antagonism can be decisive. The central role of the United States was established in the negotiations that produced GATT, the IMF, and the World Bank, and it has continued—in attenuated form—to the present day. Thus, the codes on Transfer of Technology and Transnational Corporations have made limited progress, in part owing to U.S. antagonism; while the GATT Subsidies Code and the OECD Arrangements on Export Credits made headway because of U.S. enthusiasm. (But even U.S. enthusiasm was not enough to sell the Illicit Payment Code.)

The extent of U.S. enthusiasm or antagonism is not simply a matter of the disposition of the executive branch. On various occasions, U.S. negotiators have traded away "chips" that Congress and its constituents were not disposed to concede; and in many of those instances, Congress has refused to accept the result. The concessions on American Selling Price and Antidumping Duties in the Kennedy Round trade negotiations may be cited; so too may be the concessions on mining claims in the Law of the Sea negotiations. In the UN Transnational Corporation Code negotiations, the U.S. is being pressed to make concessions that are virtually unsaleable in Congress. In summary, executive branch enthusiasm is a necessary ingredient for the success of a code, but it is equally necessary that the results not create active opposition in Congress.

Another experience of the Codes is the importance of small groups. This of course is an old lesson. The basic Bretton Woods system was negotiated among a handful of major nations. So, in more recent years, the OECD Declarations, the GATT Subsidiaries Code, and the OECD Arrangements on Official Export Credits have been negotiated among a small group of countries before being generalized to a wider audience. Conversely, the UN Transnational Corporations Code has suffered from an excessive number of active participants.

Finally, what emerges from a review of the code experience, however, is an appreciation of the fact that multilateral codes are not likely to achieve either harmonization of fundamentally conflicting policies, or basic changes in essential national policies. Codes can reflect common aspirations, and set out some standards, some general principles, and some methodologies. Where their objectives are important but realistically limited—as in the reinforcement of the trading system—they can be a powerful force, subject though they will be to numerous stated and unstated exceptions or even violations. The identification of a common goal is important. "Man's reach should exceed his grasp" is relevant not only to art, as Browning reminds us, but even to international economic life. But the reach must take account of reality. In the case of the codes, looking toward either a new international economic order, or to reconstruction of the one which has experienced so many difficulties in the 1970's and 1980's, it would be wise to think of codes and guidelines as establishing common objectives, as providing a forum for regular discussion of issues, and for the preparation of specific agreements which could form a part of an integrated and coherent pattern for the desired order. More would be desirable. But the larger objectives may be attainable only as part of a gradual process of mutually beneficial cooperation.

Notes

1. It should be noted that though the terms "Bretton Woods system" and "post-Bretton Woods system" have been used, the "old" system continues to co-exist with the "post-Bretton Woods system." The GATT, the IMF, and the World Bank, all exemplars of the "Bretton Woods system," are still very much alive, even though modified in many ways. This does not affect the basic point sought to be made in using these terms to identify different attitudes and, to some extent, different institutional arrangements: that emphasis was, at one time, on achieving as liberal and open a system as possible; and that, while that objective continues to obtain real as well as merely verbal support, the recent period has put much emphasis on issues of redistribution of wealth—on equity as opposed to efficiency.

2. The phrase "code of conduct" was originally used, in the international agreement context, to denominate liner conferences which had the objective of dividing markets and fixing prices of international shipping, a very different sort of arrangement than the codes discussed here.

3. Such departures are neither inexplicable nor necessarily damaging, but may be rather a reflection of the reality of conflicting objectives held together within code language. For example, in the Subsidies Code, it seems clear that there is disagreement among the parties—or perhaps within the parties—as to the proper role of government in the national and, consequently, in the international economy. There is a general acceptance of state intervention in some aspects of all national economies, at the same time as there is

adherence to the traditional non-interventionist model which would reprehend subsidies. The problem thus is how to distinguish between acceptable and unacceptable forms of intervention. Putting it in other terms, a criterion such as that of Article 11 of the Subsidies Code (discussed in the chapter written for this volume by Professor Tarullo) suggests that subsidies are good because they stimulate growth and increase employment, and that they are bad because they can have deleterious effects on industries (presumably not subsidized) in other countries. Departures from stated standards can thus be merely a way of recognizing this kind of complexity, and of emphasizing that the main goal of many a standard is to reduce trade frictions, rather than establish a substantive common rule of conduct.

Index